✦ SHAKESPEARE
AND CHRISTIAN DOCTRINE

SHAKESPEARE AND CHRISTIAN DOCTRINE

BY ROLAND MUSHAT FRYE

PRINCETON, NEW JERSEY

PRINCETON UNIVERSITY PRESS

Roland M. Frye is professionally trained both in theology and literature, having pursued graduate studies at Princeton University and at Princeton Theological Seminary. He gave the L. P. Stone Foundation Lectures at the Seminary in 1959, and was visiting lecturer there in the spring of 1963. After teaching in the English department at Emory University from 1952 to 1961, Mr. Frye moved to the Folger Shakespeare Library in Washington, D.C., where he is permanent Research Professor. He is on the editorial board of *Theology Today*, has contributed numerous articles to leading literary and theological periodicals, and is the author of two books: *God, Man and Satan* and *Perspective on Man: Literature and the Christian Tradition*.

Printed in the United States of America

First PRINCETON PAPERBACK Edition 1965

TO

Gerald Eades Bentley

✦ ACKNOWLEDGMENTS

In the preparation of this book, I have been very greatly assisted by the encouragement, comments, and criticisms of Louis B. Wright, James G. McManaway, and Giles E. Dawson, my colleagues and friends on the staff of the Folger Shakespeare Library. Others who have been particularly helpful are Miss Virginia A. LaMar of the library and Professor Mark Curtis of the University of California at Los Angeles. As always, it is a pleasure to deal with the Princeton University Press and with its able and thoughtful managing editor, Miss R. Miriam Brokaw. Finally, there are my wife and my son, whose consideration and mere presence are a continued delight.

ROLAND MUSHAT FRYE

Folger Shakespeare Library
Washington, D.C.
April 9, 1963

✦ CONTENTS

✧ SHAKESPEARE

AND CHRISTIAN DOCTRINE

The purpose of this book is to consider the relations between Shakespearean drama and Christian theology. The subject is not only interesting and important in its own right, but has been much mooted in recent years. We will analyze the issues in the light of historical theology and as a result will, I trust, be able to arrive at a greater clarity of understanding.

In considering the relations between Shakespearean drama and Christian doctrine, I am purposely excluding any speculation as to Shakespeare's personal faith. Much has been written on that issue, most of it consisting of rationalization and special pleading. Were I able now to determine Shakespeare's personal beliefs or lack of beliefs, I would be eager to do so, but the present state of the evidence is simply inconclusive. All that we do know—and we know this on documentary evidence—is that he lived and died a conforming member of the Church of England, by which he and his children were baptized, and in which he was buried. There is no evidence that he ever violated the legal requirements of attendance upon Church of England services, and the lack of evidence to the contrary creates a strong probability that he was a regular attendant upon the established program of worship and sermons, for it is highly unlikely that a theatrical figure so well known as Shakespeare would have been able to violate the attendance requirements without attracting the notice of anti-theatrical London officials. Certainly Ben Jonson's recusancy can be fully documented.

Yet even when we recognize that the evidence both positive and negative indicates that Shakespeare was a conforming member of the Church of England, we are still not able to prove anything very definite about his own personal religious orientation and motivation. The Church of England was broad and inclusive; it encompassed such Lutheran views as those of Tyndale,[1] such "Catholicism" as that of Henry VIII, such Puritanism as that of the great popular preachers of London, such Calvinism as was influential in bishops and others as well as Puritans, and such developing "Anglican" theology as was represented by Hooker. It also included many persons of no particularly clear conviction, and surely some who conformed for the sake of convenience and personal safety while holding to heterodox, heretical, or even anti-Christian opinions.

To postulate Shakespeare's own personal position within so broad a range of possibilities would at worst be a task for rationalizing speculation and at best for personal surmise. At the present time there is simply no conclusive evidence upon which we may judge the issue. We will thus purposely ignore that presently insoluble question and concentrate instead upon a more accessible subject: the relation between Shakespearean drama and Christian doctrine.

The relevance of theology to Shakespeare's plays is open to considerable disagreement. Some, who may for convenience be epitomized in A. C. Bradley, hold that Christian theology is essentially irrelevant to Shakespeare's writing, while others, who may be conveniently placed in the train of G. Wilson Knight, hold that Shakespeare's plays are essentially and pervasively—even blatantly—Christian. Bradley held that even when Shakespeare's words refer directly and explicitly to God and the devil, heaven and hell, "these

[1] For a beautifully argued modification of the traditional view of Tyndale's Lutheranism, see Leonard Trinterud, "A Reappraisal of William Tyndale's Debt to Martin Luther," *Church History*, vol. 31, pp. 24-45.

ideas do not materially influence his representation of life, nor are they used to throw light on the mystery of its tragedy,"[2] whereas Knight and his followers find materially important and determinative references to the figure of Christ and to the Christian doctrines of redemption even where the words taken in themselves would seem to point to other meanings.

Two critical views could scarcely be in stronger contrast. "The constant presence of Christian beliefs," Bradley wrote, would "confuse or even destroy the tragic impression."[3] For Knight, on the other hand, the "unique act of the Christ sacrifice can . . . be seen as central" to Shakespeare's tragedies, while his "final plays celebrate the victory and glory, the resurrection and renewal, that in the Christian story and in its reflection in the Christian ritual succeed the sacrifice."[4] In the train of Knight's influence, we have had and continue to have a great wave of supposedly theological analyses of Shakespeare: again and again we are informed of the discovery of some new Christ-figure or Christ-allusion in the plays, or we are advised as to the eternal destiny in a future life of Shakespeare's stage characters, or we are introduced to some doctrine which serves as a theological structure upon which an entire play is built.

Now in my judgment Bradley often overlooks theological elements which are of considerable importance to a full

[2] A. C. Bradley, *Shakespearean Tragedy*, London: Macmillan and Co., 1937, p. 25.

[3] *Ibid.*, p. 325.

[4] G. Wilson Knight, *Principles of Shakespearian Production*, New York: Macmillan, 1937, p. 234. See also Paul N. Siegel, *Shakespearean Tragedy and the Elizabethan Compromise*, New York: New York University Press, 1957, p. 231, where he writes that "in terms of the Christ story, it is the analogy with the crucifixion which is the center of the tragedies and with the resurrection which is the center of the tragi-comedies."

understanding of Shakespeare's plays, but if I were forced to choose between Bradley and Knight, I would unhesitatingly choose Bradley, and I would do so for reasons which are equally theological and literary. Knight's approach offers almost limitless possibilities for distorting and even destroying a viable understanding of drama by applying to it a naïve, superficial, and often quite specious theological analysis. The more I have studied historical theology, especially in Shakespeare's age, the more convinced I have become that most of what passes for the theological analysis of Shakespeare is both literarily inept and theologically naïve. In this area as in any other, a little learning is a dangerous thing. When we find, as in one recent study, that Falstaff's selection of conscriptees "suggests more than anything else Gideon's selection of a band to serve the Lord," the time has surely come to call a halt.[5]

The analysis and appraisal of such theologizings of Shakespeare will be the function of Chapter One. Chapter Two will treat exaggerations of a diametrically opposite kind, namely, the contention that Shakespeare wrote with an anti-Christian intent. In my judgment, the anti-Christian contention is less dangerous in the current state of critical understanding than is the insistence upon a dominant theological meaning, but though it may be less dangerous it is equally false. Certain passages from the plays which have been taken as instances of Shakespeare's rejection of Christianity are discussed in the second chapter. An examination in each instance of the dramatic context and of sixteenth-century theological usage will show that these passages do not indicate such anti-Christian intent as is imputed to the drama-

[5] J. A. Bryant, Jr., *Hippolyta's View: Some Christian Aspects of Shakespeare's Plays,* n.p.: University of Kentucky Press, 1961, p. 66.

tist. At the same time, I will indicate the need for a sane and informed secularism in the interpretation of the plays, because the plays are themselves primarily concerned with the secular realm.

Secularism is a key concept here and throughout much of this book, so it will be well to say a bit about the senses in which I do and do not use the term. It should be understood from the outset that I do not use "secular" as a pejorative term and do not imply in my use of it any positive rejection of Christianity or antagonism to it. Such rejection and antagonism are sometimes associated with the word in other contexts, but should not be read into it here. My use should convey the meaning of temporal and "this worldly," somewhat after the fashion of the Latin *saeculum*, referring to an age or a generation, rather than to the domain of the eternal. Thus I use the word "secular" to direct attention primarily to Shakespeare's dramatic concern with the temporal order, without denying him a personal or other concern with the eternal. Such usage, in my judgment, is in keeping with Shakespeare's dramatic intent and practice.

The first two chapters will thus be devoted to clearing away irrelevant or excessive emphases (for and against Christian faith and theology) in the interpretation of Shakespearean drama. Throughout those chapters the underlying assumption is that Shakespeare's concerns are essentially secular, temporal, non-theological. Chapters Three and Four will attempt to demonstrate that such an emphasis is what the major theologians influencing England in the sixteenth century would have expected from literature.

In the third chapter we will see that literature as one of the liberal arts was understood by leading theologians as free from theological dominion and, indeed, as freed from theological infiltration. Literature was thus understood, if approached from this perspective of theology, as being independent of any specifically Christian theology and as being endowed with its own integrity—a major point which has escaped the attention of the theologizers.

Now it is a truism that literature was regarded as ethically instructive by almost everyone in the sixteenth century, including theologians. In the fourth chapter we will see how major sixteenth-century theologians contended that the ethics relevant to the concerns of the secular order were not exclusively Christian, but universally human. In other words, the ethics which were relevant to the area of Shakespeare's literary concern might be drawn with equal propriety from non-Christian as from Christian sources, according to the most representative and influential theologians of Shakespeare's religious milieu.

Chapters Three and Four thus show that literature, when judged by competent theological opinion, should be secular as regards theology and universal as regards ethics. In no sense was the function of literature regarded as indoctrination in revealed religion. The literary independence and integrity of such writers as Shakespeare is thus found to be in keeping with the major theological formulations of the sixteenth century.

The fact remains, however, that Shakespeare makes considerable use of theological material in his plays, and it is to the consideration of such uses that the final and longest section of the book will be devoted. Since Shakespeare's use of the Bible and the Book of Common Prayer has been comprehensively studied by Richmond Noble,[6] I have not

[6] Richmond Noble, *Shakespeare's Biblical Knowledge and Use of the Book of Common Prayer*, London: SPCK, 1935.

been concerned here with references to the liturgy or to the Scriptures, but have concentrated upon the doctrines of theology. My analysis will be selective rather than exhaustive, but the coverage is sufficiently ample to show how Shakespeare employed references to religious doctrine for his dramatic purposes. In my judgment, Shakespeare emerges from this analysis as a man who seems to have known Christian doctrine intimately, though not on any professional plane. His references to the commonplace topics of theology are never introduced into the drama for doctrinaire reasons, and the action of the plays is never subservient to the presentation of any systematic theology.

Our analysis of Shakespeare's theological usage is organized topically under such commonplace themes as Affliction, Atonement, Death, the Devil, God, Guilt, and the like. In each entry I attempt to clarify certain speeches of dramatic characters by considering these speeches in connection with the major and dominant theological currents of Shakespeare's age, as these may illumine the dramatic situation. The result is, in a restricted way, a handbook or guide to the theological allusions in the plays. While Shakespeare is patently not concerned with theology in any such way as are Spenser, Milton, and Bunyan, his plays do contain more theological allusions than have sometimes been recognized, and it behooves us to understand these as they occur. Their explication is a major concern of this study. Historical background is essential to this undertaking, for without reference to theology (and especially the theology of Shakespeare's age) we can scarcely do more than speculate subjectively on the relations between Shakespeare and Christian doctrine.

For a dozen years I have been attempting to understand the theological milieu of Shakespeare's age, so as to understand better the relations between his plays and theology. At one point I had hoped that it would be possible to trace Shakespeare's own theological reading, or at least his source materials for the theological references in the plays, if not the structure of his own doctrinal allegiances. After immersing myself in sixteenth-century theology, I must confess that I have not made even the most minimal of these discoveries. That Shakespeare was quite literate in Christian theology, and easily conversant in its categories, seems to me indisputably apparent, but beyond that statement I am unable to go, for the evidence leads no further. I have found nothing in connection with theology which even remotely parallels Shakespeare's use of North's Plutarch, for no theological document with which I am familiar was used by Shakespeare as such a basis for paraphrase and construction. This conclusion is based upon a fairly wide-ranging study of sixteenth-century theologians. Among sixteenth-century Church of England theologians, I have read with great care the complete works of Richard Hooker, John Jewell, Thomas Cranmer, Hugh Latimer, and William Tyndale, along with the official *Homilies Appointed to be Read in Churches*, and have read either most or all of the writings of the following: Bishop John Bale, Thomas Becon, John Bradford, James Calfhill, Bishop Thomas Cooper, Bishop Myles Coverdale, William Fulke, Archbishop Edmund Grindal, Bishop John Hooper, Roger Hutchinson, John Norden, Alexander Nowell, Archbishop Matthew Parker, John Philpot, Bishop James Pilkington, Bishop Nicholas Ridley, Thomas Rogers, Archbishop Edwin Sandys, William Whitaker, and Archbishop John Whitgift, as well as many contemporary theological letters, liturgies, and occasional or

special prayers.[7] I have also read virtually the complete works
of Martin Luther and John Calvin, both of whom wrote
voluminously, and the principal or most representative works
of Melanchthon, Bucer, Zwingli, Martyr, and Bullinger.
Among sixteenth-century Roman Catholic theologians, I
have read Parsons, Southwell, and Allen, as well as in and
about the Council of Trent. As for pre-sixteenth-century
theologians, I have in other connections read extensively in
the patristic and medieval writers, and have found no
demonstrable instances of Shakespeare's indebtedness, even
to Augustine or Aquinas. Concerning Augustine, Shakespeare would have had as easy access to his writings as to
those of any of the sixteenth-century writers, for Augustine
had immense prestige in Shakespeare's time and his works
were readily available in both Latin and English. For
Aquinas, the situation was markedly different. In the first
place, as Jacques Maritain reminds us, the baroque age was
not one in which Thomism was able to "manifest its poten-
tialities in the general movement of culture" even in Roman
Catholic countries,[8] and in the second place his works were
not in print in sixteenth-century England, under either the
Roman Catholic or Protestant establishments: A Short-Title
Catalogue of Books Printed in England, Scotland, and Ire-
land and of English Books Printed Abroad includes no Latin

[7] William Haller's authoritative studies of Puritanism and intimate
familiarity with the Puritan preachers give us assurance that, had there been
demonstrable relations between what they said and what Shakespeare wrote,
he would have found them. I have, therefore, not judged it necessary to
search extensively for Shakespearean affinities in the great Puritan preachers
of Shakespeare's London, though I am generally cognizant of their work
in other connections.

[8] Jacques Maritain, *Saint Thomas Aquinas*, New York: Meridian Books,
1958, p. 11.

or English versions of any of Aquinas' works for the hundred-and-sixty-six year period between 1475 and 1640. Though it is remotely conceivable that Shakespeare might have had access to Aquinas' writings in manuscript or other form, I have found no evidence to show that he did.

It is on the basis of such a study that I must report my inability to establish Shakespeare's theological affinities or to discover even a single unquestionable instance of indebtedness of the kind which can so frequently be found in the history plays, or of the kind which so unequivocally demonstrates Shakespeare's extensive use of the Geneva Bible, for example. Yet I do not claim to have exhausted the subject or to have eliminated all potential sources in the authors I have read, and it is possible that other scholars may yet succeed where I have failed in finding conclusive evidence of the specific theological works which influenced Shakespeare's mind. Though I would be delighted to see such conclusive evidence discovered, and hope that other scholars may yet succeed where I have failed, it is my judgment that the possibility of successfully demonstrating Shakespeare's theological reading must be placed today at a rather low order of probability.

Shakespeare's dramatic employment of theology, on the other hand, is readily accessible, and here we can draw some quite firm conclusions, both as to his intent in particular passages and as to his customary methods. When Shakespeare provides one of his characters with a theological allusion or comment, it is aptly and accurately subordinated to the characterization and the plot development within the context of which it appears. Always adjusted to the controlling interests of his drama, Shakespeare's theological usage seems to have been familiarly and almost instinctively drawn from intimate awareness. A knowledge of the sixteenth-century religious milieu should help us to understand both his particular references and his general practice in this regard, and it is the major purpose of this book to provide at least an introduction to such an understanding. After the first part of this book has analyzed the present state of criticism, and the second part has presented a background of theology relevant to art, the third section will provide a cross-sectional sampling of Shakespeare's references to theological matters along with comments on the same subjects by major sixteenth-century theologians. On the basis of this evidence, I hope to suggest that, although Shakespeare was certainly no Milton or Bunyan, he nonetheless emerges as an intelligent and maturely informed layman, whose citation of theological doctrines for purely dramatic purposes shows an easy and intimate familiarity with Christian theology. Always, however, the theology he knew and used is contributory to the drama, and not vice versa.

Had I been able to determine specific theological sources for a significant number of dramatic passages, the task of choosing theological authorities for citing in connection with the Shakespearean allusions might have been considerably simplified. Since Shakespeare's references seem to have been drawn from a general background of knowledge rather than from identifiable books, our task becomes one of choosing a manageably small and appropriately select number of theologians who between them will furnish a fair representation of the religious currents of the sixteenth century. The inclusion of material from all of the theologians I have mentioned would extend the limits of this book far beyond readable proportions, and also beyond immediate necessity. For my purposes here it seems wisest to select a few unquestionably eminent theologians and to cite primarily from them in developing a compact but authoritative sampling of doctrinal expression. With these needs in mind, I have chosen three eminent, representative, and influential theologians who in different ways epitomize the major religious attitudes of Shakespeare's culture. These three are Martin Luther, John Calvin, and Richard Hooker.

Other theologians are occasionally cited in this study, and it would have been possible to have chosen from my reading a different and much longer list of authorities. I do not believe that any short and manageable list would afford us such adequate and authoritative coverage, while a longer list would merely add to the bulk of this study without changing either its generally representative character or its conclusions. In terms of representing contemporary opinion and of influencing both sixteenth-century and future developments, Luther, Calvin, and Hooker stand out as the most obvious choices for our primary reference. Even though Shakespeare may not have read a single passage from any of their works, their teachings are centrally important to the development of the religious milieu of Shakespeare's time, and thus to the relations of his drama to that milieu. Furthermore, I bring from my saturation in sixteenth-century theology the decided impression that Luther, Calvin, and Hooker consistently furnish more cogent and immediately relevant parallels to Shakespeare's theological allusions than do any other religious writers I know.

The choice of these three theologians does not, however, imply—and I think the point is important enough to repeat—that the existing evidence demonstrates Shakespeare to have been a disciple or even a reader of any one of them.[9] It is simply that these three stand out as the most eminent theologians influencing and representing Shakespeare's religious milieu, and that between them they appear to furnish the most useful commentary upon Shakespeare's allusions.

Martin Luther should surely be included in any brief list, not only as furnishing the volatile and heuristic impetus to the Protestant Reformation, but also for the force, pertinency, and influence of his works. Calvin is included not so much because of his place as patron saint of a certain segment of English Protestantism as because he stands in relation to the sixteenth-century Reformation as Aquinas stood in relation to medieval scholasticism. As author of the protestant *summa*, Calvin not only exerted a wide influence both direct and indirect upon sixteenth-century religious developments, but he also included the full range of doctrine with such clarity and balance that virtually every theological development of the period can be charted by reference to agreement and disagreement with his expressions. In Hooker, we find at once an epitome of the Anglican past and a matrix of its future development.

It seems most appropriate, furthermore, to compare Shakespeare primarily with men whose eminence in their own field is most nearly commensurate with his, both as to magnitude of mind among their contemporaries and as to

---

[9] From this disavowal it will be clear that I disagree with Virgil K. Whitaker's contention that "Shakespeare demonstrably knew Hooker." This suggestion is not infrequently made, but I do not see that the evidence "demonstrates" more than the coincident use of popular ideas and common phrases. Neither can I find sufficiently convincing evidence to accept Whitaker's view that "Hooker was to a considerable extent responsible not only for the thought but also for the very structure of some of Shakespeare's greatest plays." (Virgil K. Whitaker, *Shakespeare's Use of Learning*, San Marino, California: The Huntington Library, 1953, p. 206.)

the respect which has been accorded them by competent critics in later generations. When judged by this criterion, the choice again falls on Luther, Calvin, and Hooker.

One further consideration should be mentioned, although it is admittedly less weighty than those already discussed; this has to do with power of style and pleasure of reading. Many theologians unfortunately make very dull reading, but Luther, Calvin, and Hooker as a general rule do not. In choosing a small number of writers for repeated and extensive quotation, I could find none who speak with equal authority and who could yet hold the reader's interest and attention as can these three. But the fact that quotations from them will be clearer, more readable, and more interesting is only a bonus to the primary advantage that they express the most influential, representative, and authoritative opinions of their time in Shakespeare's culture, and that their expressions often furnish us with significant comparisons to what Shakespeare wrote.

Other scholars will surely wish to add to what I have done here, and to correct it. The task which I have undertaken is far too broad for one man to cover in any final way. I do submit, however, that a responsible analysis of Shakespeare's theological usage can be made only by close reference to the theological materials available within the context of sixteenth-century culture and of the Christian tradition preceding it. I hope that what follows will serve to clarify certain aspects of the Christian tradition and of the manner in which Shakespeare on particular occasions employed that tradition in the service of his dramatic art.

PART ONE ✧ CRITICAL ANALYSES

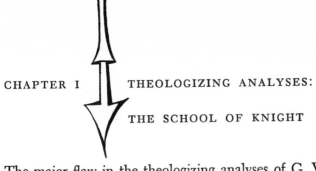

CHAPTER I   THEOLOGIZING ANALYSES:

THE SCHOOL OF KNIGHT

The major flaw in the theologizing analyses of G. Wilson Knight and his followers is the lack of evidence. What we repeatedly find in their work is the presentation of essentially subjective interpretations as though they represented the actual historical judgments of the Christian community in Shakespeare's time. We are repeatedly faced with assertions as to what sixteenth-century Christians would have thought of particular characters, actions, and speeches, but rarely—indeed, almost never—do we find evidence cited from the sixteenth century to buttress the assertions. In treating the type of literary interpretation which makes historical assertions without historical evidence, it is usually sufficient to note both what we are asked to believe and why, and then to allow such critical theories and interpretations to expose themselves. For the present chapter, nevertheless, a few citations of relevant evidence from sixteenth-century theology will be given to illustrate the vast distance separating actual Christian thinkers of Shakespeare's time from twentieth-century theologizing critics of Shakespeare. Basically, however, I will not draw heavily upon sixteenth-century theology until we begin the reconstruction of historical attitudes in Chapter Three and thereafter continue that reconstruction throughout the book. In the meanwhile, we will make an open examination of the methods followed by the School of Knight and of the conclusions reached by those who employ these methods, as they move further and further from the play itself and from its rootage in history, until the play eventually becomes not the controlling datum of their discussion but rather a mere point of departure for subjective reverie and reflection.

A case in point of theological assertion without theological evidence may be found in the often-cited essay of some sixteen years ago, in which Nevill Coghill expands the earlier suggestions of Sir Israel Gollancz, and analyzes the struggle between Portia and Shylock in *The Merchant of Venice* in terms of conflicting values of mercy and justice. Coghill concludes that "mercy has triumphed over justice" unilaterally, and finds no difficulty in the fact that Shylock was in fact "condemned" to forced baptism in a judgment which to us scarcely seems an act of mercy. Coghill declares, however, that this forced baptism was quite merciful, because "whether we dislike it or not, an unbaptized Jew had then no hope of entering into Christian eternity. . . . It would not have been his cruelty that excluded him (for cruelty can be repented) but his lack of baptism; he had no wedding garment."[1] Coghill completes the assertive argument when he assures us that contrary views would have been regarded as rubbish in Shakespeare's age.

Our confidence in Mr. Coghill's judgment may be somewhat shaken, however, when we find that contrary views were in fact held by Martin Luther, John Calvin, and Richard Hooker, whose agreement would scarcely have been dismissed as rubbish in Shakespeare's time. These three

[1] Nevill Coghill, "The Governing Idea: Essays in Stage Interpretation of Shakespeare," *Shakespeare Quarterly* (Vienna), vol. 1 (1947), 16, and Sir Israel Gollancz, *Allegory and Mysticism in Shakespeare*, London: printed for private circulation by Geo. W. Jones, 1931, p. 32.

agree that an unbaptized person was not excluded from salvation by the mere absence of baptism.[2] Nor was a person saved—or even made especially open to salvation—by enforced baptism, for as Luther put it, "even if a person is baptised but is without faith, he is lost."[3] Luther went further in developing the inner logic of this view: "No one should be forced to faith. One should only be called to it. If someone is to come, God will no doubt move him to do so by your calling. If he does not move him, what do you achieve by your compulsion?"[4] In these terms, the judicial sentence laid upon Shylock that he be baptized seems neither merciful nor sensible, and the applicability of Coghill's governing idea to the whole play is brought under

[2] Luther, Serm. on Mark 16.14-20, in *The Precious and Sacred Writings of Martin Luther*, ed. John N. Lenker, Minneapolis: The Luther Press, 1903-1910, vol. 12, p. 189 (hereafter, this edition will be referred to as Lenker ed.); Calvin, "Acts of the Council of Trent, with Antidote," in *Tracts and Treatises*, ed. Thomas F. Torrance, Grand Rapids: Wm. B. Eerdmans, 1958, vol. 3, p. 180 (hereafter, this edition will be referred to as *Tracts and Treatises*); Richard Hooker, *Of the Laws of Ecclesiastical Polity* 5.60.5; in *Works*, ed. John Keble, New York: D. Appleton and Co., 1849 (hereafter minor works in this edition will be referred to as Keble ed., and the *Ecclesiastical Polity* will be referred to merely as *Eccl. Pol.*). See also Thomas Aquinas, *Summa Theologica* 3.68.2.

[3] Luther, Sermons on the Catechism, in *Luther's Works*, American edition, St. Louis: Concordia Publishing House, and Philadelphia: Muhlenberg Press, 1955-   , vol. 51, p. 182. Hereafter, this edition will be referred to simply as Amer. ed.

[4] Luther, "On the Proscribed Books" in *What Luther Says: An Anthology*, ed. Ewald M. Plass, St. Louis: Concordia Publishing House, 1959, vol. 1, 1407. (Hereafter, references will be made simply to Plass anthol., with volume and entry number.) Similar statements may be found in Luther's Sermon for March 10, 1522, Amer. ed., vol. 51, p. 76, and in his treatise on secular authority in *Works*, Philadelphia: Muhlenberg Press, 1915-1932, vol. 3, pp. 259-60 (referred to hereafter simply as Phil. ed.). For a discussion of Luther's early tolerance, see William A. Mueller, *Church and State in Luther and Calvin*, Nashville: Broadman Press, 1954, pp. 17-18, 22, and 42, and for indications of his growing intolerance during his later years, pp. 62 and 65-66.

serious question.[5] We cannot extend the triumph of mercy over law beyond narrow and well-defined limits (i.e., Portia's appeal against exacting the pound of flesh), for immediately thereafter we find at work in the exaction of baptism a contrary movement, the triumph of legalism over mercy. No single theological formula covers these various actions, and to attempt to impose such a formula is at once indicative of bad literary criticism and of theological naïveté.

DAMNATION AND SALVATION

The theologizers of Shakespeare rarely go beyond proof by assertion. We are told what an Elizabethan's theological judgment would be, but we are not shown evidence for what we are told to accept. Thus Paul N. Siegel tells us that Gertrude is damned, but he gives us no evidence as to what Elizabethans might have thought of a case such as Gertrude's.[6] Now I doubt that many Elizabethans would have raised the issue at all, but—assuming for the sake of discussion that they did—it would be helpful to know what grounds there are for asserting her damnation. If one is to make a valid case for Gertrude's damnation it would be necessary to show by citation of evidence that Elizabethans would have regarded the signs of her late repentance as false or inadequate, and also by evidence that they would have interpreted her actions and words late in the play as similar to those characteristic of damned souls in the Elizabethan

[5] The Council of Trent, 7th Session, "Of Baptism: Canon 5" seems to have taken a somewhat different position on these issues: "If anyone says that baptism is optional, that is, not necessary for salvation, let him be anathema." See *Canons and Decrees of the Council of Trent*, H. J. Schroeder trans., London: B. Herder Book Co., 1941, p. 53.

[6] Siegel, *op.cit.*, pp. 114-15.

Romeo → Gertrude 22

view. Mr. Siegel makes no attempt to provide us with any such evidence. He merely makes an assertion.

But if we are told that Gertrude in *Hamlet* is damned, we are assured that Cassio in *Othello* is saved—and with equal lack of evidence. In Cassio, Siegel tells us, Shakespeare's audience "had a hopeful reminder of the possibility of the ordinary man . . . achieving salvation through faith and repentance,"[7] and we are assured in connection with Cassio's drunken remarks about forgiveness and salvation that he is saved. Nothing would be gained by attempting to reverse this contention as to Gertrude's damnation and Cassio's salvation, and I am not attempting to establish an hypothesis of their salvation or damnation which runs counter to the claims we have observed. Our purpose here is only to examine such claims, and the nature of the evidence (or lack of evidence) which is advanced in their support. Now even if we admit—which I do not—that Cassio's comic remarks made while drunk are to be taken seriously in connection with the state of his soul in the afterlife, still Siegel has offered no evidence to show that the Elizabethan audience to which he refers would have regarded Cassio's situation as Shakespeare presents it as being one of saving faith and repentance. If Mr. Siegel can show in a point-by-point analysis that Shakespeare's characterization of Cassio contains clear signs of what Elizabethans historically regarded as repentance and as a state of grace leading explicitly to a state of glory, then we would welcome that evidence. Until it appears, however, it is not theologically defensible to speak of the salvation of Cassio. Had a theological panel consisting of Richard Hooker, Martin Luther, and John

[7] *Ibid.*, pp. 134 and 136.

Calvin been asked as to the state of Cassio's soul before God, they would, I suspect, have replied that the question was not only irrelevant but that the evidence Shakespeare provided was not sufficient to allow a judgment even were the question an admissible one.

Attempts to apply theological categories consistently to the plays yield especially interesting results when the issue of suicide arises. The difficulties here are obvious: are Romeo and Juliet, for example, to be regarded as damned by suicide? If one is to be consistent in analyzing them by the established theological standards for judging actual rather than fictional suicides, then one can only say that they are damned. Here, then, is a significant test case: If we are unwilling to apply to Shakespeare's characters the universal condemnation of suicides (except for the deranged or those who explicitly repent), then we must abandon the entire process of theologizing Shakespeare's plays on any consistent basis.[8]

On no theological issue was there such universal agreement in Shakespeare's age as we find in the case of suicide. The Church of Rome has always regarded suicide as a damning sin, while the Protestant view was no less clear and the rejection of Purgatory precluded even the slightest hope for the future state of suicides.[9] Suicide was regarded

[8] As will become increasingly clear in the course of this study, I am not denying the relevance of theological material to the plays, but am only denying the consistent analysis of them by theological means.

[9] James Hastings, *Encyclopedia of Religion and Ethics*, New York: Charles Scribners Sons, 1908-1926, vol. 12, pp. 23-24, s.v. "Suicide." A recent book on the subject is S. E. Sprott, *The English Debate on Suicide from Donne to Hume*, La Salle, Indiana: Open Court Publishing Co., 1961. Sprott covers the subject fairly well, though some of the distinctions he draws (between Anglican and Puritan attitudes toward suicide, for example) are more specious than real.

as a far worse sin than murder,[10] it lowered man below the level of brute beasts;[11] it was an act of cowardice;[12] and it was thought to be a particular appropriate act which at once epitomized and provided retribution for a life of sin.[13] No one questioned that successful suicide, willfully committed,[14] led to hell.[15] Elizabethan theology saw lovers as

[10] John Downame, *The Christian Warfare*, London, 1634, pp. 78, 71; William Vaughan, *The Golden Grove*, London, 1600, sig. E1; Anthony Copley, *A Fig for Fortune*, Manchester: The Spenser Society, 1883, p. 29; Peter Barker, *Exposition upon the Ten Commandments*, London, 1633, pp. 317-18; George Strode, *The Anatomie of Mortalitie*, London, 1632, p. 267.

[11] George Strode, *op.cit.*, p. 267; Peter Barker, *op.cit.*, pp. 317-18; Edward Phillips, *New World of English Words*, London, 1658, sig. c2v.; John Downame, *op.cit.*, pp. 76-78.

[12] William Whitaker, *Disputation on Holy Scripture*, Cambridge: Parker Society, 1849, p. 95; William Vaughan, *op.cit.*, sig. E1v.; Peter Barker, *op.cit.*, pp. 317-18; Nathanael Carpenter, *Achitophel*, London, 1638, sig. H8; Andrew Willet, *Harmony upon I Samuel*, Cambridge, 1614, p. 172; John Downame, *op.cit.*, p. 72; Edmund Spenser, *The Faerie Queene*, I, ix, 41; Anthony Copley, *op.cit.*, p. 29.

[13] Andrew Willet, *op.cit.*, p. 173; *Homilies Appointed to be Read in the Churches in the Time of Queen Elizabeth*, Philadelphia: 1844, pp. 78, 379, 482, and 515; Thomas Becon, *Writings*, Philadelphia: British Reformers Series, n.d., p. 377; John Hooper, *Writings*, Philadelphia: British Reformers Series n.d., pp. 296, 369, 384-85, 390, 395, and *Later Writings*, Cambridge, Parker Society, 1852, p. 324; Henry Bullinger, *The Decades*, trans. H. I., Cambridge: The Parker Society, 1849-1852, *The Third Decade*, p. 79; George Strode, *op.cit.*, pp. 270-71; and Andrew Willet, *Harmony upon II Samuel*, Cambridge, 1614, p. 107.

[14] The insane, of course, were not responsible and so not damnable. The only other hope for a suicide was that, in God's mercy, time might have elapsed between the act and death, during which the sinner repented. See Andrew Willet, *Harmony upon I Samuel*, p. 174; George Strode, *op.cit.*, pp. 283-85; John Downame, *op.cit.*, p. 79; William Gouge, *Of Domesticall Duties*, London, 1634, p. 85. John Donne's *Biathanatos* is a highly technical treatise on suicide which concludes that it may be permitted in certain limited circumstances if it is in God's service, as with Samson. What Donne did not condone is of more importance to us here than what he excused. Of Achitophel's suicide, he wrote: "But if it were upon a mere dispute of his own disgrace, or fear of ill success, or upon any self respect, without proposing God's glory, and he repented not, he perished" (pp.

especially susceptible to the temptations of suicide, but suicide was regarded as being equally damning for them as for others.[16]

Here the theologizing critics face a basic problem. If theology is taken as a consistent guide for analyzing the plays, then Shakespeare's suicides (except for the mad Ophelia) must be regarded as damned. Yet to regard them as damned creates conflicts with other aspects of the plays, as in the case of Romeo and Juliet, who scarcely seem damnable to most critics and who do not seem so to Irving Ribner and Paul N. Siegel, though a consistent following of their

---

204-05). It is under this category that the suicides treated in this paper seem to fit. Indeed, as I read *Biathanatos*, it does not afford grounds for objection to anything which is said in this study. Even were this not so, however, Donne's work would be of little value to us here, for it is a highly learned, scholarly argument which admittedly challenged the established viewpoint of the time. Donne himself was unwilling to publish it, either during his lifetime or after his death, and left orders that it be committed neither to the press nor to the fire. John Donne, Jr., who first published the book, obviously regarded it as unique in its field. Writing to Sir Constantine Huygens on July 29, 1654, the younger Donne said that if his father's work had remained unprinted, then "those reasons, by which the Act (suicide), should be defended, or excused, would be also lost with it." This testimony is explicit enough as to the absolute uniqueness of any defense or excuse for suicide, even so limited a defense as that made by the Dean of St. Paul's. (The Donne-Huygens letter is found on the fly-leaf of the Grosart Collection first edition of *Biathanatos* in the Princeton Theological Seminary Library, and printed in full in *Notes and Queries*, vol. 197 [Nov. 8, 1952], pp. 495-96.)

[15] John Downame, *op.cit.*, pp. 71, 75, and 79; William Gouge, *op.cit.*, p. 85; William Fulke, *A Defense of the Translations of Holy Scriptures*, Cambridge: Parker Society, 1843, pp. 23-24; George Hakewill, *King David's Vow*, London, 1621, p. 310; Henry Bullinger, *op.cit.*, p. 415; Andrew Willet, *Harmony upon I Samuel*, p. 173; George Strode, *op.cit.*, pp. 281-82.

[16] John Bishop, *Beautiful Blossoms*, London, 1577, fol. 52v.; John Wing, *The Crown Conjugal*, Middelburgh, 1620, p. 76; Robert Crofts, *The Lover or Nuptial Love*, London, 1638, sigs. B1 and D7v.; Jacques Legrand, *The Book of Good Manners*, London, 1507, I, xii; Henry Smith, *A Preparative to Marriage*, London, T. Orwin for T. Man, 1591, p. 26.

own postulates would require such critics to declare the damnation of Romeo and Juliet as they declare the damnation of other characters.

Critics cannot legitimately escape from this dilemma by referring to a contrary Christian view, although this is precisely what Irving Ribner attempts to do. Boggling at the assignment of Romeo and Juliet to damnation, he interprets suicide as a mark of mature readiness for death, as "a recognition of the way of the world as the will of God, and by a calm, fearless acceptance of death as the necessary end of man which releases him from earthly evil and assures him of a true felicity in heaven"; Ribner ascribes this view to Christian humanism.[17] But he cites not a single example of any Christian in or before Shakespeare's time who held it.

If Ribner avoids damning Romeo and Juliet by suggesting the existence of a Christian condoning of suicide for which he cites no evidence and which in fact runs counter to the great mass of theological evidence we have, Siegel escapes by denying in this one instance the relevance of theological norms which elsewhere he insists upon as determinative. Here, he says, "Shakespeare relies upon his audience to free itself from conventional religious attitudes and regard the suicides of his heroes and heroines sympathetically as the noblest action that those guided by the attitudes and emotions of romantic love and by the philosophy of stoicism could take."[18] Thus these critics, while affirming the normative value of the theological tradition for interpreting Shakespeare, use it or abandon it as seems most needful, declaring damnation and salvation more by what

[17] Irving Ribner, *Patterns in Shakespearian Tragedy*, New York: Barnes and Noble, 1960, p. 33.
[18] Siegel, *op.cit.*, pp. 84-85.

appears to be modern whim than by reliance upon Elizabethan theology.

In the application of salvation and damnation to Shakespeare's plays, much attention has been devoted to the fate of Othello. Now if a theological question of this sort is to be raised at all—and many critics deny its relevance entirely—it can only be discussed in theologically relevant terms. But even among those who raise the question theologically, most neglect to discuss it in terms of a scholarly understanding of theology, or, when they do so, they often find the results so unsatisfactory that they do not wish to apply them to the drama. Thus in an essay of twenty years ago which did much to generate interest in the afterlife of Shakespeare's characters, K. O. Myrick finds in Othello "what the theologians would call repentance," although he recognizes that Othello expresses "no hope of pardon" and commits suicide.[19] Now if Mr. Myrick had said that Othello bitterly regretted the murder of Desdemona, he would have made a true, though rather dull and obvious, statement. When he refers, however, to "what the theologians would call repentance," he appears to be saying something both significant and exciting, whereas in point of fact what he is saying of a despairing suicide would have seemed utter nonsense to the consensus of theological opinion, whether Reformed or Roman, in Shakespeare's age. And, as is usual in this kind of criticism, Mr. Myrick has cited no evidence in support of his position. Thus a scholarly question is raised, but we do not find it treated in terms of a scholarly understanding of the theological tradition which the critic himself has invoked for answering the question.[20]

[19] K. O. Myrick, "The Theme of Damnation in Shakespearean Tragedy," *SP*, vol. 38, p. 244.

[20] Some critics have been more consistent, and, having once launched

The same issues arise for Irving Ribner's analysis of *Othello*, in which we find a near-allegorization of the entire play. Iago, Ribner tells us, "reveals himself to the audience as a personification of jealousy; he does so as thoroughly as any personification of a deadly sin had ever exposed himself in the medieval morality drama," while Desdemona "stands for . . . the cardinal virtue of love."[21] Torn between these two, Othello falls like Adam. Then a remarkable thing takes place: Othello acts for himself and by himself in such a way as to merit salvation. In Othello's last actions and words, Ribner writes, we see that "he undergoes remorse and penance. Finally by an act of will he executes true justice upon himself. He dies in reunion with Desdemona, and in his expiation for his sin, he merits divine mercy."[22] Here is one point (and there are others) at which the opinion of Richard Hooker, to whom Mr. Ribner refers as his major authority but from whom he never quotes, might have saved Ribner from misunderstanding the theological orientation with which he wishes to deal. Hooker describes the notion of merited salvation as follows:

"A strange and a strong delusion it is wherewith the man of sin hath bewitched the world; a forcible spirit of error it must needs be, which hath brought men to such a sense-less and unreasonable persuasion as this is, not only that men clothed with mortality and sin, as we ourselves are, can do God so much service, as shall be able to make a full and perfect satisfaction before the tribunal seat of God for their own sins. . . ."[23]

---

a theological analysis, have had the courage to assert Othello's damnation; of these, Paul N. Siegel is one.

[21] Ribner, *op.cit.*, pp. 94-95.

[22] *Ibid.*, pp. 95-96. See also p. 113.

[23] Hooker, Serm. vi, par. 21, Keble ed., vol. 2, p. 398.

To assume that anyone can by an act of will merit salvation is to pull up the doctrine of faith by the roots, as Hooker said, so that Hooker repudiated the position "which giveth unto any good work of ours the force of satisfying the wrath of God for sin, the power of meriting either earthly or heavenly rewards."[24] Elsewhere Hooker called down anathema upon anyone who denied this essential position of the Church of England.[25] As for Ribner's insistence that Othello's act merits divine mercy, one further quotation from Hooker (upon whom Ribner purports to base his analysis) should be sufficient: "We deny the grace of our Lord Jesus Christ; we imbase, disannul, annihilate the benefit of his bitter passion, if we rest in those proud imaginations, that life everlasting is deservedly ours, that we merit it, and that we are worthy of it."[26] Such opinions could be duplicated many times over in the writings of other Anglican divines of Shakespeare's time, as well as in the works of Luther and Calvin. Furthermore, as has already been suggested, there is no major element of either Roman or Reformed theology which would venture to assert with Mr. Ribner's confidence the salvation of anyone who committed suicide in the manner of Othello. If evidence exists to show that Elizabethans would have expected the salvation of a murderer who, in apparent despair, commits suicide, then it should be cited. If such evidence does not exist, then no claim should be made for responsible theological analysis in the assertion of Othello's salvation.

Surely one of the most ingenious of all interpretations of *Othello* is given to us by J. A. Bryant, Jr. Bryant advances

[24] Hooker, Serm. II, par. 32, *op.cit.*, vol. 2, pp. 320-21.

[25] Hooker, "Fragment of an Answer to a Letter of certain English Protestants," App. 1 to Bk. v of *Eccl. Pol.*, Keble ed., vol. 2, p. 28.

[26] Hooker, Serm. II, par. 34, *op.cit.*, p. 324.

the thesis that "Othello in this play reflects, if anything, the office of God and that Cassio, not Othello, stands for Shakespeare's figure of Adam."[27] Iago, in this interpretation, shares with Lucifer the experience of having been passed over for promotion, and as a result displays "wounded self-esteem" which in its turn leads him "to cause, first, a weaker creature (Cassio) to fall, and second, that weaker creature's creator (Othello) to slay a spotless victim in consequence."[28] And so we come to the invitable Christ-figure (in this instance Desdemona), though we may perhaps be pardoned for feeling some slight anxiety along the way as to the approaching suicide of God the Father. Such an analysis has the undeniable advantage of boldness, but whatever may be said for it, it simply cannot be qualified to the point where it avoids absurdity, both literary and theological.[29] Again, we do not attempt to disprove such assertions, but merely outline them and note that evidence has not been advanced to establish their validity.

ALLEGORIZING

There is much semi-allegorical treatment of Shakespeare throughout the work of these critics. Most of them, however, deny allegorization, and I believe that John Vyvyan is the only one who openly refers to the plays as allegories. He tells us that "the full sweep of Shakespeare's vision is not apparent until we have penetrated his allegories." We see what he intends when he informs us, in connection with

[27] Bryant, op.cit., p. 140.

[28] Ibid., p. 141.

[29] Bryant tries to qualify it by saying, among other things, that Othello "is a story at the literal level of a Moor who killed the dearest thing on earth to him. . . . We should see that first, and only that for a long time." Ibid., p. 141.

the romantic plays, that "the lady's eyes represent the baptismal font" and that in *Romeo and Juliet* "Juliet is, of course, love; and she is also represented as heaven. Allegorically there is no difference."[30]

Vyvyan's allegorizing technique may be fully illustrated by his analysis of *Hamlet*. According to Vyvyan, Ophelia is not only "the girl we all know" but also "an allegorical figure representing a quality in Hamlet's soul . . . that point of love in Hamlet which is the center of his true nobility."[31] Laertes is also of dual significance, for he "is not only the man we see on the stage; he is also an allegorical figure of the *new* content of Hamlet's soul (after the Ophelia-content has been expelled)—uninhibited vengeance."[32] In view of this analysis, Vyvyan declares that there is a sense in which Hamlet does not leave the stage, for "when Ophelia and Laertes are on stage, only Hamlet's body is missing, and we watch what is happening within him."[33] The degeneration of Hamlet's soul, according to Vyvyan, constitutes the central movement of the play, and it continues until "when the fifth act opens, we find him in a setting which is really a materialization of his new inner landscape—a graveyard."[34] Unlike other critics who follow similar methods of analysis, however, Vyvyan does not assert that a damned character is going to hell, for Vyvyan has discovered (without ever telling us how) that Shakespeare "does not accept the doctrine of eternal damnation."[35] What Shakespeare himself did and did not believe is of major interest to Vyvyan, for his purpose has been to lay bare not only Shakespeare's

[30] John Vyvyan, *Shakespeare and the Rose of Love*, London: Chatto and Windus, 1960, pp. 152, 49, and 176.

[31] John Vyvyan, *The Shakespearean Ethic*, London: Chatto and Windus, 1959, pp. 40-41.

[32] *Ibid.*, p. 50.   [33] *Ibid.*   [34] *Ibid.*, p. 55.   [35] *Ibid.*, p. 140.

intent for his public plays but also his private philosophy "fresh from the chalice of reason and love,"[36] and he finds that philosophy expressed in "ethical theorems of Euclidean logicality."[37]

Now we must acknowledge that Vyvyan's analysis of *Hamlet* is itself "a wonderfully adroit piece of allegorical construction,"[38] but Vyvyan has not demonstrated it to be either Shakespeare's interpretation or even a possible Elizabethan interpretation. He provides no evidence whatsoever that Elizabethans would have thought of the play in the terms he suggests, or even in any related terms. So far as I know, there is no evidence from any source contemporary with Shakespeare to support the notion that Elizabethan audiences customarily allegorized the plays they saw or that Elizabethan dramatists (save, possibly, in rare instances of clearly topical interest) allegorized the plays they wrote. Furthermore, anyone familiar with the public theater will doubt that any audience, faced with a fast-moving stage play, could follow so elaborate and consistent a structure of double-entendres. To be understood, allegory (if it is at all characterized by subtlety) requires the study, or at least the parlor; popular drama, once it has moved beyond the charming simplicities of the medieval morality play, is too fast-paced a vehicle to convey it. In the final analysis, all that can be said of Vyvyan's interpretation is that he has expounded his private understanding of the plays, for he has in no sense undergirded with evidence the contention that he is expounding either Shakespeare's philosophy or what Shakespeare could have expected his audience to find in his plays.

[36] *Ibid.*, p. 145.   [37] *Ibid.*, p. 53.   [38] *Ibid.*, p. 51.

CHRIST-FIGURES

Then there is the matter of the Christ-figures, who now appear in such weltering profusion as almost to crowd all other actors from the stage. In this late age of Shakespearean criticism, it often seems that everything which can be said about Shakespeare has already been said by someone, but surely no one prior to our time has seen Timon of Athens as a Christ-figure. Paul N. Siegel, however, assures us that "the perceptive theatergoer of Shakespeare's day" would have recognized in Shakespeare's "clear and distinct" allusions a "comparison between Timon's boundless generosity and Christ's overflowing love," while G. Wilson Knight has written of Timon that "Christlike, he suffers that their pain may cease, and leaves the Shakespearian universe redeemed that Cleopatra may win her Antony in death, and Thaisa be restored to Pericles."[39] Knight further writes of Timon's servants that "they meet, not as servants to the same lord, but rather as disciples to a loved and world-crucified master," and concludes that "when Timon's servants part to wander abroad separated, they are disciples of the Christ meeting after the crucifixion."[40] An even more recent critic, Irving Ribner, has gone so far as to invite us to see Flavius, Timon's steward, "as a Christ symbol offering salvation" and to assure us at the same time that Alcibiades is redeemed.[41]

It seems that Christ-figures are everywhere in Shakespeare's plays. Let us take the case of Antonio in The Merchant of Venice. J. A. Bryant, Jr., sees him as so clear a

---

[39] Siegel, op.cit., p. 90, and G. Wilson Knight, The Wheel of Fire, London: Methuen and Co., 1949, p. 236.

[40] Ibid., pp. 218 and 235.

[41] Ribner, op.cit., p. 149.

Christ-figure that it would be difficult to find anywhere in Renaissance literature a "neater parallel to Christ's voluntary assumption of the debt that was death to repay."[42] As Antonio prepares to yield up the pound of flesh to satisfy the bond made for Bassanio's benefit, he writes to Bassanio: "all debts are clear'd between you and I, if I might but see you at my death,"[43] words which Bryant interprets as "saying, in excusable contradiction to all acceptable codes for human behavior, 'I will excuse your debt if you will witness my execution. Come and be present at my death, if you love me.' And this is the invitation that only Christ properly extends."[44] What Bryant fails to demonstrate is that Elizabethans would have regarded any such suggestion as either sensible or reverent, that Shakespeare could have put it on the stage even if he had wished to, and that he wished to. The structure of this interpretation is marvelously ingenious but equally fragile.

Or take the disguised Duke in *Measure for Measure.* G. Wilson Knight tells us that "the Duke's ethical attitude is exactly correspondent with Jesus'. . . . So he, like Jesus, moves among men suffering grief at their sins and deriving joy from an unexpected flower of simple goodness in the deserts of impurity and hardness."[45] This interpretation translates Shakespeare out of dramatic and into theological terms—though not even into good theology, but rather into sentimentalized and maudlin ethical emotionalism.

Roy W. Battenhouse is an exception to the general rule

[42] Bryant, *op.cit.*, p. 38.
[43] *Merch.* 3.2.318-20. All references to Shakespeare are to the text of the G. L. Kittredge edition, *The Complete Works of Shakespeare*, New York and Boston: Ginn and Company, 1936.
[44] Bryant, *op.cit.*, p. 39.
[45] Knight, *The Wheel of Fire*, p. 82.

of theological ignorance, but unfortunately his knowledge does not directly support his contentions. When he comes to interpreting *Measure for Measure*, which he assures us Shakespeare formed after the pattern of the Christian doctrine of the atonement, he refers to the Elizabethan familiarity with theology, but in buttressing his semi-allegorical interpretation of the play he quotes from patristic and scholastic writers and largely ignores the sixteenth-century theology which Elizabethan and Jacobean Englishmen primarily knew, so that his use of theology as such remains less than immediately relevant. As a result he can invoke medieval responses which would scarcely have occurred to Elizabethans, as for example when he treats Mariana as representing the atonement in the sinless laying down of her body for the satisfaction of another's sin, thus making her perhaps the most droll of all the Christ-analogues.[46] One schooled in scholastic methods of analysis might have seen such an analogy; but I know of no reason to think it would have seemed appreciably less far-fetched to Elizabethans than it does to us.

To say that Desdemona dies with Christian patience and forgiveness would be to state the obvious, but we are urged to go further and to see her as a saving symbol of Christ. "Desdemona raises and redeems such earthly souls as Emilia," Siegel declares. "Belief in her, the symbolic equivalent in the play of belief in Christ, is a means of salvation for Cassio as well as for Emilia."[47]

According to Siegel, Cordelia also operates analogously to Christ and through her Lear is provided Christian sal-

[46] Roy W. Battenhouse, "*Measure for Measure* and Christian Doctrine of the Atonement," *PMLA*, vol. 61, p. 1,038.

[47] Siegel, *op.cit.*, p. 134.

vation: "the redemption of Lear for heaven, a redemption analogous to the redemption of mankind, for which the Son of God had come down to earth," sums up his view, and he assures us that "the analogy between Cordelia and Christ, who redeemed human nature from the curse brought on it by Adam and Eve, is made unmistakable, although not crudely explicit, by the choric comment of her gentleman."[48] But to whom is the analogy unmistakable? I know of no evidence that Elizabethans would have regarded Cordelia as a Christ-figure, and Siegel gives none, though surely evidence is needed if we are to convert a secular drama set in a pre-Christian and explicitly pagan world into a Christian parable.

The whole Christian drama of redemption is spelled out in *The Winter's Tale*, as Professor Bryant tells us that this play "with its suggestion of analogies for Jew, Gentile, Christ, Paul, and the Christian Church comes closest to incorporating the whole view"—that is, "the Christian view of the historical redemption of the human race."[49] Now that statement, if true, is immensely significant, and deserves to be demonstrated by the citation of relevant evidence, but aside from one or two scriptural passages which have no necessary bearing upon the play or upon his contention about the play, Mr. Bryant does not support his contention with any evidence of Elizabethan-Jacobean attitudes which would be convincing to the theologically literate. He does, however, assert much, telling us that "the appropriate analogy for Leontes is the Jew whom St. Paul declared it was his heart's desire to see saved,"[50] adding that "fortu-

[48] *Ibid.*, p. 186. The reference is to *Lear* 4.6.210-11.
[49] Bryant, *op.cit.*, p. 222.
[50] *Ibid.*, p. 212.

nately Leontes has a St. Paul to help him . . . for this is precisely the function of Shakespeare's Paulina,"[51] while "Mamillus, who dies, suggests the Jewish Church" and finally "Perdita, who is consistently referred to as the *heir* in the play, suggests the true Church."[52] It seems, then, that we are to accept *The Winter's Tale* as Shakespeare's dramatic version of *The Faerie Queene* and *The Pilgrim's Progress* combined, and perhaps bettered. Particularly striking are Bryant's references to Hermione's "correspondence to the incarnation of divine grace, Jesus Christ," and though Bryant denies that correspondence to be direct and allegorical,[53] he feels that a reading of Hermione's defense of herself[54] "makes it hard to avoid the notion that Shakespeare himself . . . saw emerging from it the central analogy of the play," which Bryant identifies with "the familiar career of Jesus from Gethsemane to Golgotha."[55]

Although one might quite properly question whether distinguishing between such an interpretation and an allegorical one is not in fact to put more emphasis upon distinctions than differences, let us accept Bryant's choice of terms and move on to a more crucial point. A basic fallacy of Bryant's approach is exhibited in his assertion about Hermione and divine grace: "We can be confident that only a very dubious dialectician would ever attempt to disprove the connection between Hermione and that Christian grace which comes not so much as the result of man's deserving it as of man's contrition and willingness to receive."[56] This statement assumes in the first place that the analogic interpretation of Hermione has been proved, whereas it

[51] *Ibid.*, p. 216.   [52] *Ibid.*, pp. 212-13.   [53] *Ibid.*, p. 210.
[54] W.T. 3.2.92-117.   [55] Bryant, *op.cit.*, p. 211.
[56] *Ibid.*, p. 209-10.

has been stated only, and the reference to the dialectician (however dubious) indicates a basic misunderstanding which underlies Mr. Bryant's analyses. Literary interpretations are not matters for "dialectic" either to prove or disprove, for dialectic is not the basic means for ascertaining the meaning of an historical literary text, as the Renaissance humanists successfully demonstrated several centuries ago. In attempting to provide a radically new interpretation of literary texts, Mr. Bryant has ignored the basic canon of literary scholarship: the provision of relevant evidence. Dialectics and assertion, however persuasive, are not enough.

It should be unnecessary to go beyond this point in illustrating the effort to find Christ-figures in Shakespeare. So far as I know, we have no objective evidence that an audience which found types of Christ in the Old Testament would for that reason have sought them in Shakespeare. Everyone admits that Elizabethans found such typology in Scripture under the old convenant, but I know of no reason to believe that Elizabethan drama was so confused with Holy Writ as to require the same methods to be applied in both cases. Nor has anyone yet made a convincing case, in terms of historical theology, for such identification.

FALSE CLAIMS FOR CHRISTIANITY

In addition to the Christ-figure mania, we find a related tendency to restrict the general applicability and relevance of Shakespeare's themes in specifically Christian ways. "Shakespeare's villains," Paul N. Siegel informs us, "embody values destructive to the ideal of Christian humanism,"[57] to which we can only reply: of course they do! But why restrict the humanism they destroy so as to make it explicitly

[57] Siegel, *op.cit.*, p. 87.

Christian? Don't these villains embody values destructive of all humanity and of all humanism?

J. A. Bryant, writing of Antony and Cleopatra, holds that "the Christian perspective" enables us "to see the main thing about them,"[58] but again I wonder why one needs the distinctively Christian perspective to be able to understand "the main thing" about these characters. That the Christian faith is at once unique and divine in its origin, I for one have no desire to deny and every desire to affirm, but I am utterly unable to see how it enables me to understand the major aspects of this play in a way in which I could not were I a non-Christian. Bryant's assertion that the treatment of human greatness in the play "makes complete sense only when viewed from the Christian perspective that Antony's allusion to the messianic psalms explicitly invites"[59] seems at once unfounded, pretentious, and false. Bryant repeatedly finds unique advantages to being a Christian which I must confess that I fail to discover. Somehow, Mr. Bryant feels, the Christian poet has a poetic advantage over the non-Christian poet, though I cannot imagine what theological grounds could justify such an assumption. In the beautifully drawn pagan atmosphere of Antony and Cleopatra, one feels as far removed as might be from the Christian gospels and Christian theology, but even here Bryant finds "redemptions such as only a Christian poet can understand."[60] But could not—indeed did not—the Greek and Latin poets understand "redemptions" of the order which occur in the play? Surely the great theologians have always recognized great areas of knowledge apart from Christian revelation where the Christian has no advantage whatsoever over the

[58] Bryant, op.cit., p. 191. [59] Ibid.
[60] Ibid., p. 183.

non-Christian, and it is a mark of considerable theological naïveté to overlook or deny this fact. Of *Hamlet*, Bryant writes that "from beginning to end Shakespeare's transformation of his material was creative and revelatory in the way in which the act of a Christian poet is always creative and revelatory."[61] But why must the act of a Christian poet *always* be creative and revelatory? Most Christian poets (like most other poets) are rarely either creative or revelatory, and the implicit assumption that Christianity provides some sort of aesthetic advantage is at once theologically unsophisticated and pragmatically false.

CONCLUSION

The history of criticism should have taught us that there are no shortcuts to productive criticism, but in our time we again need to learn that lesson, and nowhere can we find more blatant abuses of criticism than in the theological analyses of Shakespeare. The union of the subjective methods of the New Criticism with a naïve understanding of theology has produced a peculiarly facile device, by means of which people can write too much without having read enough.

From the appearance of *The Wheel of Fire* some thirty years ago to the present, those who have followed Knight's type of analysis have proliferated in number and in productivity, but they have contributed very little of any real worth to the understanding of Shakespeare. Their efforts have by and large been subjective, and although they have appealed to the presence of an objective tradition, they have all too rarely given scholarly attention to that tradition. They have not cited evidence for their contentions, and their assertions

[61] *Ibid.*, p. 138.

have generally shown them to be at best theologically un-sophisticated and at worst theologically illiterate. Assertion—at times an almost pontifical assertion—replaces scholarship, and the result is a confusion of issues.

The same method which Knight's disciples have applied to Shakespeare has been applied to Greek literature by Simone Weil. Miss Weil has written of Sophocles that "he is to my knowledge much more Christian than any tragic poet of the last twenty centuries"—so much so, indeed, that we can find Christ-figures in Sophocles as well as in Shake-speare. We are told: "If one accepts that Electra is the human soul exiled upon earth, fallen into affliction and that Orestes is the Christ, how poignant then do the words of Orestes become." So interpreted, the words may indeed be poignant, but they are no longer the words of Sophocles.[62] The reductio ad absurdum of criticism, clearly seen in this analysis of Sophocles, is no less distorting when applied to Shakespeare.

[62] Simone Weil, *Intimations of Christianity among the Ancient Greeks*, London: Routledge and Kegan Paul, 1957, p. 8.

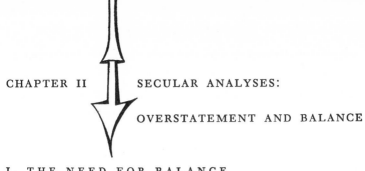

CHAPTER II SECULAR ANALYSES:

OVERSTATEMENT AND BALANCE

I. THE NEED FOR BALANCE

If the "theologizing" analyses which we have just examined are almost totally inadequate, certain secular analyses are occasionally so. Even when the secular reading errs, however, it rarely errs so dangerously as do the readings of Knight and his followers, for the secular analyses do not violate the dramatic texture of the plays themselves and are in accord with their theological milieu, as I will show in two later chapters.

Though the secular analysis provides the most useful approach, both literarily and theologically, to Shakespeare's works, it is patently not immune to error, and in our study of the relations between Shakespeare and theology it is incumbent upon us to note, at least by example, certain types of error into which secular criticism has at times fallen when it has ignored theological evidence at points where that evidence is relevant. The matter may be stated in this fashion: Shakespeare's works are pervasively secular, in that they make no encompassing appeal to theological categories and in that they are concerned with the dramatization (apart from distinctively Christian doctrines) of universally human situations within a temporal and this-worldly arena. Shakespeare is thus not to be interpreted as though he were a Milton or a Bunyan, but though the overt evidence indicates that he was writing within the overall restrictions of secular concerns, the evidence also indicates that within this secular sphere he at times introduced such theological material as might contribute to his presentation of particular characters and situations. To ignore such instances, or to treat them without reference to their theological meanings, would be to foreshorten our understanding of Shakespeare.

A secular analysis of Shakespeare will thus fall into error *if* it ignores theological references placed within the plays for purposes of characterization and situation. When such errors are compared with the errors produced by G. Wilson Knight and his followers, however, they pale into relative insignificance, for they are more restricted and thus less damaging, whereas the theologizing method of Knight's school not only makes possible the warping of the entire framework of Shakespearean drama but even encourages that warping. To apply a distinction drawn from theology, we might say that the "sins" of secular analysis are venial, while those of the theologizing analysis are mortal, and we might well apply to the type of theologizing we have already examined Shakespeare's own words:

> Thy sin's not accidental, but a trade.
> Mercy to thee would prove itself a bawd.
> 'Tis best that thou diest quickly.[1]

Though Shakespeare's plays cannot be properly read as pervasively theological, there are numerous points within the plays where the words and actions may be illuminated by reference to historical theology. To say this is to claim for theology what is claimed for such fields of inquiry as history, social customs, political ideologies, and sports, to name but a few. We readily admit the proper relevance of such areas to the full interpretation of Shakespeare, but the

[1] *M. for M.* 3.1.149ff.

field of religion (though in itself at least as significant as any of these others) offers its own particular perils, for few of us react negatively to religious subjects. We tend, indeed, to react vigorously in favor or vigorously in opposition, and even when we decide to ignore religious concerns, we often ignore them in a peculiarly passionate manner. Religion is too important to be shunted aside entirely, but in view of the peculiar problems just cited we must be especially careful not to speak in this area unless we speak on the basis of concrete evidence, and this procedure is necessary regardless of whether we are Christian, non-Christian, or anti-Christian.

In this chapter, we will examine two types of error into which secular analyses have at times tended to fall, when such analyses were not supplemented at relevant points by theological knowledge. Our examination is not intended to be complete, but is illustrative and suggestive. We will first note the dangers inherent in the application of certain popular misunderstandings of the Christian tradition, and the manner in which the application of two such misunderstandings to Shakespeare has produced distorted interpretations. Next we will examine the misconstruction of certain conventional phrases used by Shakespeare, so as to read into those phrases agnostic meanings quite in keeping with the twentieth-century vocabulary but out of accord with accepted sixteenth-century usage. Finally, the chapter will return to an appraisal of the essential correctness of a secular analysis of Shakespeare.

II. POPULAR MISUNDERSTANDINGS

It is not the purpose of this book to correct popular misconceptions of Christian doctrine as such, but when such misconceptions become the tools of criticism they should be noted. We have already cited instances of the dangers of such misunderstandings when applied by the theologizing school, and we will now turn to two examples of the application of misunderstanding for an opposite purpose, that is, the repudiation of Christian meanings in Shakespeare.

A book too little known today, though it was published over thirty-five years ago, is George Seibel's *The Religion of Shakespeare*.[2] This delightful and militantly "un-Christian" book is significant not so much for what it proves as for what it represents, for it brings together many of the arguments against assuming Christian meanings in Shakespeare's plays and exemplifies many of the misunderstandings of Christianity which are current in the twentieth century. The book is at once a witty attempt to prove that Shakespeare himself accepted no religious dogmas, and a sharp, salutary, and amusing castigation of those who attempted to prove on the basis of his writings that Shakespeare was a pious believer. Though Seibel's work was published several years before G. Wilson Knight entered the field, it can be read as a splendid palliative against the work of the theologizers. Seibel is as outrageously unhistorical as the school of Knight, and plays just as fast and loose with evidence, but he is far more amusing, and intentionally so. Though Seibel proves little or nothing, he does provide a rich mine of quotations from those who deny Shakespeare to have been within the Christian tradition, and he produces a book at once almost as delightful and almost as unscholarly as Mark Twain's *Is Shakespeare Dead?*

Many misunderstandings of Christian doctrine can be found in Seibel, but the one upon which I wish to focus

[2] George Seibel, *The Religion of Shakespeare*, London: Watts and Co., 1924.

at the moment concerns conscience, the law, and love, for this is an area in which confusion often arises. "The assertion in Sonnet CLI that 'Conscience is born of love,' " Seibel writes, "plays havoc with orthodox ethics and ignores Sinai's thunder."[3] Actually, the passage to which Seibel refers represents the kind of easy paraphrase of Biblical and theological commonplaces at which Shakespeare was a master, when he chose to be. The juncture of the relevant Biblical and theological traditions may be seen in the following passage in which Luther quotes and comments upon two New Testament verses: " 'This is my commandment: that ye love one another' (John 15.12). 'Love is the fulfilling of the Law,' says the apostle (Rom. 13.10). When a person has love, no law is necessary; without love no law is adequate."[4] Or again: "All the commandments of the law depend on love" and "all works must issue from love; otherwise they are nothing."[5] William Tyndale wrote to the same effect that "lack of love is the breaking of the commandments and cause of sin" and that "whatsoever proceedeth not of love is damnable."[6] Scriptural teaching on this point is quite clear, and though that teaching has often been flagrantly violated by Christians, the Christian doctrine

[3] *Ibid.*, p. 22.

[4] Luther, Exp. Decalogue, W*erke*, Weimar: Böhlau, 1883-   , vol. 1, p. 436. Hereafter, this edition will be referred to as Weimar ed. This is the authoritative edition of Luther's Latin and German works, and I have made frequent collations between the major translations I have used and this edition to be sure of their accuracy for our purposes at critical points. Where a translator has seemed ineffective, when judged on this basis, I have sometimes altered his translation, as with Lenker ed., on occasions.

[5] Luther, Serm. on Matthew 22.37-39, Amer. ed., vol. 51, p. 106. See also Phil. ed., vol. 5, p. 244, for similar statement.

[6] William Tyndale, *Expositions of Scripture*, Cambridge: Cambridge University Press, 1849, pp. 203 and 56.

of the relation between love, law, and conscience could scarcely be better summarized than in Shakespeare's words:

Love is too young to know what conscience is;
Yet who knows not conscience is born of love?

But it is only out of context that we may take these lines as a reference to Christian charity, for within the sonnet itself Shakespeare is using an apt theological allusion to point up his treatment of his physical relations with the Dark Lady. The force of the allusion here depends on the fact that the distinction between the Greek words *agape* (Christian love) and *eros* (sensual love) is blotted out in English, where both meanings are included under the single word "love." We thus see that whereas Seibel was wrong in assuming that Shakespeare here defined love and conscience in an un-Christian way, it would be equally wrong to assert that simply because Shakespeare here demonstrated an apt and accurate knowledge of an elementary point in theology, he was therefore talking in theological terms. The reference was from the theological to the secular, and in my judgment the pattern illustrated here was the one which Shakespeare primarily employed: the use of theological material (when such material was used) in an allusive way to support an essentially secular analysis of character or situation.

Seibel's treatment of the sonnet is one of two examples of the way in which a misunderstanding of the Christian tradition may lead to an interpretation of a Shakespearean work as essentially non-Christian. The second instance of such erroneous analyses may be found in Clifford Leech's study of Shakespearean tragedy. Leech discusses Rymer's famous objection to *Othello*, and suggests that Rymer's reaction against the play is not to be found in his "merely abusive description of the play as a 'Bloody Farce'" but rather in the fact that he does not find virtue rewarded in the play. In support of his contention, Leech cites Rymer's question about Othello's fate: "If this be our end, what boots it to be Vertuous?" Now Leech may be correct in his analysis of Rymer, and he is surely correct in holding that Shakespearean tragedy is not concerned with passing out rewards to virtuous characters, but he goes far afield when he concludes that Shakespeare's great tragedies are therefore irreconcilable with Christianity. Leech states his position as follows, beginning with Rymer's distaste for the absence of prudential morality in *Othello*: "Rymer realized far more clearly than most critics that *Othello* and Shakespeare's other great tragedies present a view of the world that cannot be reconciled with Christianity."[7] Leech's position here seems to be that since *Othello* and the other tragedies do not present a world in which men may be good with assurance of reward, then those tragedies are irreconcilable with Christianity: such a view ignores not only the Pauline-Augustinian tradition throughout Christianity, but especially the powerful restatement of that tradition in the Protestant Reformation of Shakespeare's own century.

The renascence of the Christian repudiation of prudential morality may be illustrated by Luther's words: "we ought not to be devout [or righteous] in order to earn or to avoid something. All of that character are hirelings, servants, and paid workers; not willing children and heirs. These latter are devout and pure for the sake of godliness itself, for God's own sake. . . . But the man who seeks gain, or flees pain,

[7] Clifford Leech, *Shakespeare's Tragedies and Other Studies in Seventeenth-Century Drama*, London: Chatto and Windus, 1950, p. 103.

never finds God. He makes a God out of his gains. For the very aim or ground of a man's actions is, in itself, his god."[8] What Leech, and perhaps Rymer too, failed to find in the tragedies was an exchange market between works and rewards, but it was exactly that conception of religion which the Reformers repudiated as un-Christian. "God will not tolerate a cheap exchange market,"[9] Luther declared, and in view of such an understanding of Christianity it is difficult to accept Leech's argument that the absence of prudential ethics in Shakespeare's plays renders them un-Christian. John Calvin reinforced Luther's point: "For if it is only a matter of men looking for reward when they serve God, and hiring and selling their labor to him, it is of little profit," and he continues to point out that the man God approves of is the man who continues in righteousness when all hope of reward has been cut off.[10] Like Luther and Calvin, Richard Hooker denied that man was able to be so disinterestedly virtuous as to deserve reward, and like his predecessors he too undercut the very grounds of a prudential morality: "We see how far we are from the perfect righteousness of the law; the little fruit which we have in holiness, it is, God knoweth, corrupt and unsound: we put no confidence at all in it, we challenge nothing in the world for it, we dare not call God to a reckoning, as if we had him in our

[8] Luther, "Three Sides of the Good Life," in *Reformation Writings of Martin Luther*, ed. Bertram Lee Woolf, London: Lutterworth Press, 1956, vol. 2, p. 123. Hereafter this edition is referred to as Woolf ed.

[9] Luther, Serm. on John 6.30-32, Plass anthol., vol. 2, 1894. See also Amer. ed., vol. 23, p. 36.

[10] Calvin, *Institutes* 3.16.2, hereafter referred to as *Inst.* Unless otherwise stated, all such references are to the two-volume *Institutes*, ed. John T. McNeill and trans. Ford Lewis Battles, Philadelphia: The Westminster Press, 1960.

debt-books."[11] Such typically Reformation judgments suffice to demonstrate the fallacy of Leech's particular argument for the incompatibility of Shakespearean tragedy with Christianity. Indeed, the very absence of prudential morality and the repudiation of an ethic based upon a balance between works and rewards may constitute one of the greatest contributions made by the Christian tradition to Shakespearean drama. Even as we deny that Shakespeare was writing theological dramas, we must be careful not to deny the correspondences between Shakespeare's writings and the Christian tradition, when those correspondences may be demonstrated by the citation of relevant evidence.

III. ANACHRONISTIC READINGS

One of the most basic and patent facts of Shakespeare's dramatic writing is that he does not seem much concerned with placing his characters in heaven or hell. Though there are a few suggestions of contrary practice in the plays (and these should not be overemphasized), it remains true that in the overwhelming number of cases Shakespeare is simply and totally unconcerned with extrapolating the lives of his creations beyond the stage and into a future estate of blessedness or damnation. In a later chapter, I will outline the theological presuppositions of Shakespeare's time which accord with his customary dramatic practice in this regard, but in the meanwhile we must look to his general and to certain of his specific uses.

The best summary of Shakespeare's dramatization of death is found in the words of Robert Stevenson: "In his

[11] Hooker, Serm. II, par. 7, in Keble ed., vol. 2, p. 302. See also Serm. VI, par. 21, *ibid.*, p. 398.

histories and tragedies set in Christian times and countries, 31 persons die on stage (this count includes only those who actually expire before the eyes of the audience). None, however, dies with so much as the name of Christ on his lips. Only one mentions the name of God at the hour of death—King Henry VI. If all Shakespeare's Christians die as did Hamlet with no other last comment than 'The rest is silence,' a priest's omission of any appropriate words expressing Christian faith when officiating at Ophelia's burial service merely conforms with an observable pattern in his plays."[12] Stevenson has cogently expressed the "observable pattern" of Shakespeare's plays, and in the present state of Shakespearean criticism it is imperative that we do not allow that pattern to be obscured. That much is primary. At the same time it must be said that in his generally impeccable statement Stevenson carries on one misinterpretation which has received a kind of currency, when he treats Hamlet's "the rest is silence" as an essential denial of the Christian hope for life after death. H. B. Charlton interprets the phrase in a similar fashion as an implicit denial of immortality, while George Seibel suggests that it represents "the epitaph of an agnostic," and Harry Levin writes that "for Hamlet, welcoming death when it comes unsought, felicity seems to loom ahead in the prospect of nonexistence rather than the relish of salvation."[13]

Now I do not believe, any more than these critics do, that Shakespeare was trying to determine what would happen to Hamlet after the play ended (he knew, after all, that

[12] Robert Stevenson, *Shakespeare's Religious Frontier*, The Hague: Martinus Nijhoff, 1958, p. 30.

[13] H. B. Charlton, *Shakespearian Tragedy*, Cambridge: Cambridge University Press, 1952, p. 11; George Seibel, *op.cit.*, pp. 29 and 43-44; Harry Levin, *The Question of Hamlet*, New York: The Viking Press, 1959, p. 99.

he would doff his costume and go home as that respectable citizen, Richard Burbage), but the words spoken by the dying Hamlet were interpreted in sixteenth-century theology as being at once words of faith in an afterlife and of regret for the cessation of work in the present life. To ignore this fact is in some measure to distort Shakespeare's characterization of Hamlet. The reference to death as silence is common in Scripture[14] and was interpreted by orthodox commentators as referring to the faithful man's inability to continue his vocation in this world after his death.[15] In terms of the twentieth-century connotation of words, it is natural to interpret "the rest is silence" agnostically, but to read such an interpretation back into the period of Shakespeare is to apply a foreign meaning to the characterization of Hamlet. The prince who came to rely on the "special providence in the fall of a sparrow"[16] did not repudiate that faith in his death, and the last words he speaks would have indicated to Shakespeare's contemporaries a continuing reliance upon providence and at the same time an equally appropriate regret that he could not continue his work and justify in words his own actions. Shakespeare was not in the least interested, in my judgment, in inspiring his audience to leave the theater contemplating Hamlet in the state of glory, but he was clearly interested in having the audience form an image of Hamlet as he lived and died on the Globe stage. To read

[14] See Ps. 115.17; Ps. 6.5; Ps. 30.9; Ps. 94.17; and Isa. 38.18.

[15] See Calvin's commentaries on Ps. 30.9, on Ps. 94.17, and on Isa. 38.18. Unless explicitly stated to the contrary, all references to Calvin's Biblical commentaries and expositions refer to the monumental Calvin Translation Society (or Edinburgh) translation, republished at Grand Rapids by Wm. B. Eerdmans in 1948. For a Roman Catholic analysis, see Maurice J. Quinlan's "Shakespeare and the Catholic Burial Services," *Shakespeare Quarterly*, vol. 5, p. 306.

[16] *Ham.* 5.2.230.

the prince's dying words as agnostic is in greater or less degree to miss the utter appropriateness of those words, encompassing as they do both faith and regret.

Shakespeare's repeated references to death as sleep have been interpreted as agnostic on the same basis as his treatment of death in terms of silence.[17] Father Herbert Thurston seems particularly concerned at this point, for he feels that "the number of Shakespearean utterances expressive of a fundamental doubt in the divine economy of the world seems to go beyond the requirements of his dramatic purpose and these are constantly put into the mouths of characters with whom the poet is evidently in sympathy."[18] Father Thurston then proceeds to cite as "a conspicuous example" Prospero's speech ending:

> We are such stuff
> As dreams are made on, and our little life
> Is rounded with a sleep.[19]

The image of death as sleep is Biblical, and was interpreted in the sixteenth century as implying a rest which looks forward to the raising of the dead. It was a favorite image with Martin Luther, who repeatedly dwelled on the fact that for the righteous "death is a sweet slumber" which, though deeper than that of this life, gives the body rest while the soul communes with God.[20] On another occasion Luther declared that "by these lovely similes, God in his mercy reveals beforehand to us in our infirmity that, al-

[17] Seibel, op.cit., pp. 29 and 43-44.

[18] Herbert Thurston, "The Religion of Shakespeare," The Catholic Encyclopedia, New York: Robert Appleton Co., 1907-1912, vol. 13, p. 750.

[19] Temp. 4.1.156ff.

[20] Luther, Lectures on Gen. 25.7-11, in Commentary on Genesis, trans. J. T. Mueller, Grand Rapids: Zondervan, 1958, vol. 2, pp. 54f.

though death cannot be taken away, He has drained its power until it remains only in appearance. Wherefore, the Scriptures call it sleep rather than death"[21] and he taught that "we must accustom and discipline ourselves to despise death in faith and to regard it as a deep, strong sleep."[22] The joyous connotations of this image of death as sleep become especially clear when Luther says that "we must sleep until He comes and knocks at our little grave and exclaims: 'Dr. Martin, get up!' Then in the twinkling of an eye I shall rise again and will rejoice with Him eternally."[23]

Calvin's treatment is essentially the same. In his commentaries he notes that Paul "speaks of death as a *sleep*, agreeably to the common practice of Scripture—a term by which the bitterness of death is mitigated, for there is a great difference between *sleep* and *destruction*,"[24] and in the *Institutes* he explains the aptness of sleep as a symbol when he writes that "our sleep itself, which astonieth a man, and seemeth to take life away from him, is a plain witness of immortality, forasmuch as it doth not only minister unto us thoughts of those things that never were done, but also foreknowings of things for time to come."[25]

So we see that the sleep image no more indicates an agnostic view of death than does the image of silence, but

[21] Luther, "Comfort for the Weary and Heavy Laden," in Woolf ed., vol. 2, p. 52.

[22] Quoted in Heinrich Quistorp, *Calvin's Doctrine of the Last Things*, Richmond, Va.: John Knox Press, 1955, pp. 99-100.

[23] *Ibid.*, p. 99n.

[24] Calvin, Comm. I Thess. 4.4, p. 279. For a detailed treatment of the orthodox interpretation of death as "sleep" and "silence" and the heretical interpretation of the same Biblical passages by the mortalists, see Calvin's *Psychopannychia*. I am not entering into these discussions, for they are quite irrelevant to our concerns here.

[25] Calvin, *Inst.*, 1.15.2, Norton trans.

we should be careful to note that the use of sleep as a symbol for life after death is not exclusively Christian. Shakespeare could have found it in the writers of classical antiquity as well as in the Christian tradition and Scriptures, and Calvin notes that heathen writers "grandly extol and depict" the idea in even more brilliant language.[26] We are thus in a position to see that the disguised duke in *Measure for Measure* is to some extent at least encouraging Claudio with a time-worn hope when he says:

> Thy best of rest is sleep,
> And that thou oft provok'st; yet grossly fear'st
> Thy death, which is no more.[27]

But we should also note that this hope of immortality is expressed in no more explicitly Christian form than is any other part of the Duke's famous counsel on death. And I would point out again that even though Shakespeare makes use of such images as they suit his poetic and dramatic purposes, I see no evidence that he makes any serious attempt to interest his audience in postulating the after-life of his characters. Helen Gardner's delightful remark is quite appropriate here: "It is a little curious that members of a generation which has been so harsh to Bradley for inquiring about Lady Macbeth's children, and has rebuked Ellen Terry for speculating on how Sir Toby will get on with Maria as a wife, should pronounce so confidently on the eternal destiny of fictitious characters."[28]

[26] *Ibid.*

[27] *M. for M.* 3.1.17-19.

[28] Helen Gardner, "The Noble Moor," *Proceedings of the British Academy*, vol. 41 (1955), 191n.

IV. THE SECULAR FOCUS

The hazards of ignoring the theological meaning of theological references where they occur within the plays are quite clear, and the examples which I have cited give at least some indication of the extent and limits of those hazards. The fact remains, however, as the mainstream of Shakespearean critics has always recognized, that these theological references were enclosed by Shakespeare within clearly secular and this-worldly bounds. Shakespeare's concern as an artist was for the life of man as he exists in the world of human society, and when his theological references point beyond the realm of time and death, they do so to illumine the state of mind or course of action of a dramatic character who is both presented within, and to be judged in terms of, a purely human situation. "Shakspere," Kittredge tells us, "sets forth life and character in action. It is not his office to reconcile the everlasting antinomies. As for you and me, we may do so if we can; but"—and the caveat is an urgent one—"we must not distort the drama."[29] The limits of that drama are appropriately traced in the following remarks from A. C. Bradley:

"The Elizabethan drama was almost wholly secular; and while Shakespeare was writing he practically confined his view to the world of non-theological observation and thought. . . . He looked at this 'secular' world most intently and seriously; and he painted it, we can not but conclude, with entire fidelity, without the wish to enforce an opinion of his own, and, in essentials, without regard to anyone's

[29] G. L. Kittredge, *Shakspere: An Address*, Cambridge: Harvard University Press, 1916, p. 23.

hopes, fears, or beliefs. His greatness is largely due to this fidelity in a mind of extraordinary power."[30]

If such views are essentially correct—as I believe them to be—then we must not deal with the text of the plays so as to insert or derive a theology which Shakespeare has not himself made patent. "Nothing that is omitted is of any significance," Kittredge writes. "We are not at liberty, therefore, to enrich the plot with our own inventions, or to substitute anything whatever for the plain statement of an expository passage."[31] Since the time Kittredge made these remarks, the course of Shakespearean criticism has made his advice even more urgently pertinent.

Kittredge's caveat has been echoed in recent years by Sylvan Barnet in a brilliant essay entitled "Some Limitations of a Christian Approach to Shakespeare," in which he marshals exceptionally telling objections to the theologizing efforts. Citing the attempts of Bethell, Siegel, Myrick, and others to interpret the tragedies as extending beyond the deaths of protagonists even till the day of judgment, Barnet concludes that "the rigidly Christian interpretation forces a tragedy to fit ideas which Shakespeare doubtless held but did not dramatize." Shakespeare's dramas are not a canvass reaching from hell to heaven, he reminds us, "but a picture of man's achievements and failures, hopes and fears, life and death" within the present order. Barnet of course admits

[30] Bradley, op.cit., p. 25. Bradley also declared that there was no substantial difference between Shakespeare's treatment of Christian and pre-Christian stories, a position which I regard as requiring modification. Like Bradley, Santayana sees that Shakespeare's dramatic world "is only the world of human society," but it is not the least of Santayana's failures as a critic of Shakespeare that he sees this fact as constituting a dramatic "vice." See George Santayana, *Essays in Literary Criticism*, ed. Irving Singer, New York: Charles Scribner's Sons, 1956, p. 141.

[31] Kittredge, op.cit., p. 22.

that "Shakespeare presents such full worlds that it is possible, with a little ingenuity and effort, to find in him almost
any theory which the researcher wishes to discover," but the
result of the theologizing efforts is to fit the drama to a
Procrustean bed, "reconstructing the play and shaping it
into something with which Shakespeare probably would
have agreed but [which he] did not himself write."[32]

Even more recently than Sylvan Barnet, Helen Gardner
has reasserted the primacy of the conventional criticism as
against the approach of Knight and his followers. Her
critique, though moving along different lines, is as brilliant
as that of Barnet, and her major arguments have been as
carefully evaded by the theologizing critics. "Patterns have
been found in plenty and meanings are being pointed to
everywhere," she writes; "but the true meaning of the
work—its supreme value when we re-read it, or when we go
to see it acted, or when the memory of it comes back to us—
seems less illuminated than obscured by the interpreter's
efforts."[33] Apropos of Janet Spens' 1934 dictum that we
should not read Spenser as though he were Shakespeare,
Miss Gardner suggests the modern corollary that we should
not read Shakespeare as though he were Spenser.[34] As
against the analogical and allegorical methods, Miss Gardner
declares that "the insistence of Protestantism on the reading of the whole Bible and on the primacy of the literal
sense of Scriptures is not unconnected with the flowering
of our literature in the reign of Elizabeth," and although
she refrains from opposing one partial truth with another,

[32] Sylvan Barnet, "Some Limitations of a Christian Approach to Shakespeare," ELH, vol. 22, pp. 92 and 87.

[33] Helen Gardner, The Business of Criticism, Oxford: Clarendon Press,
1959, p. 132.

[34] Ibid., p. 134.

she provides clear evidence of the post-Reformation repugnance to "that spiritual wantonness of finding more than necessary senses" in a passage, as John Donne put it.[35]

Barnet and Gardner have so effectively stated the hermeneutic and exegetical objections to a theologizing of Shakespeare that I need say no more in that regard. In literary terms, the weight of evidence and of critical opinion is in favor of the secular analysis of Shakespeare. What I will now attempt to show, in the next two chapters, is that those theological positions which were most influential in Shakespeare's England, and most representative of its religious currents, furnish a theological validation of the primarily secular approach to literature. We will thus turn away from the essentially medieval analysis followed by the school of Knight, and look instead to those theological influences which were most active in Shakespeare's time and culture. "Christianity," as Paul Oskar Kristeller reminds us, "is not only medieval, but also ancient and modern, and thus it was possible for Christian thought during the Renaissance to cease being medieval in many respects, and yet to remain Christian."[36] Our next concern will be to see the relevance of sixteenth-century theology to our primary interests in Shakespeare.

[35] *Ibid.*, pp. 136 and 139. She also cites Roman Catholic opinion to the same effect.

[36] Paul Oskar Kristeller, *Renaissance Thought*, New York: Harper and Brothers, 1961, p. 74.

PART TWO  HISTORICAL BACKGROUND

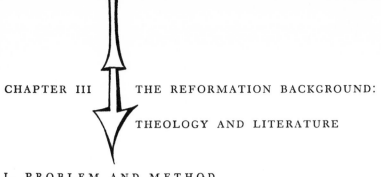

CHAPTER III   THE REFORMATION BACKGROUND:

THEOLOGY AND LITERATURE

I. PROBLEM AND METHOD

The role of theology in Shakespeare's age may be misunderstood or distorted, but its importance can scarcely be overestimated. Theology was everywhere discussed, and the level of theological literacy among educated people was considerably higher than in our own time. Approximately half of the books published in England between the inception of printing and the parliamentary revolution bore explicitly religious titles, and religious ideas figured prominently or pervasively in many if not most of the others. An intelligent Christian of the Elizabethan age would have had a rather sophisticated grasp of theology, when judged by our standards. That much seems to me basic to any discussion of theological matters in Shakespeare's age, but we must not leap from this premise to a hasty conclusion about how theology would have been applied in specific cases. What we must do now is to find evidence as to how the widespread interest in theology was in fact related to the field of literature as one of the liberal arts.

Our concern here is not with those who took no interest in theology, or who had an active antagonism toward it, for we may assume that they would have made no effort to relate religious and literary materials. Nor are we concerned with those Christians—representing theological positions so varied as to include dissenters, bishops of the established church, and Roman Catholic authorities—who reprobated stage plays as such. We recognize the presence of both groups, and recognize at the same time the need for more study of their particular views, but such study is not our task here. Our purpose is to reconstruct the attitudes toward literary work which were held by the dominant theologians of the sixteenth century—the attitudes, in short, of men who did most to shape and who best represented the theological consciousness of Shakespeare's culture.

We will, therefore, marshal evidence of the attitudes towards literature and related liberal arts which were held and inculcated, whether implicitly or explicitly, by representative leaders of the major forces in the sixteenth-century Protestant Reformation. So far as I know, there has been no previous attempt to provide so full an account of this subject. As the evidence accumulates we will be able to draw conclusions at least as to the major currents of ideas about this subject in the Protestant milieu of Shakespeare's age, and we can consider the relevance of these general conclusions to our particular interest in the relations between Christian theology and Shakespearean drama.

It will be apparent at the outset to all who are familiar with the Renaissance-Reformation period that "literature" or "bonnes lettres" at this time meant the Greek and Roman classics, and it goes without saying that these were non-Christian. It was thus almost entirely to the pagan authors that the leading Reformed theologians referred when they spoke of great writing. When they thought of literature they did not think of the medieval and "scholastic" poets Dante and Langland, nor of the later integration of Protestant theology with literary form in Spenser, Milton, and Bunyan; they thought rather of the great writers of classical antiquity.

We must, therefore, seek to discover the major attitudes towards classical literature in particular and towards classical culture in general if we are to arrive at the theological understanding of literature which we seek. When the entire analysis is completed, it will be clear that the most influential Reformation theologians viewed literature and the liberal arts as having an integrity quite independent of Christian revelation, or of Christian theology, or of any theological reference to the patterns of Christian salvation. The Reformation resulted in effect in what we may call the theological "laicization of art," to borrow a famous phrase from Emile Doumergue.

II. THE EVIDENCE OF MERES

Before we turn to the task of reconstructing the attitudes towards literature which were expressed by major sixteenth-century Protestant theologians, we should first consider the only direct and significant treatment of Shakespeare written during his own lifetime by a clergyman. When the Reverend Francis Meres wrote admiringly of Shakespeare in 1598, he gave not even the slightest hint of finding Christ-figures and the like, but rather made a solid linking of Shakespeare with the non-Christian classics. "So," Meres wrote, "the witty soul of Ovid lives in mellifluous and honey-tongued Shakespeare" while he went on to say that "as Plautus and Seneca were accounted the best for Comedy and Tragedy among the Latins: so among the English Shakespeare is the most excellent in both kinds for the stage."[1]

In this appraisal we see that Shakespeare was linked by

---

[1] Francis Meres, *Palladis Tamia*, quoted by E. K. Chambers, *William Shakespeare: A Study of Facts and Problems*, Oxford: The Clarendon Press, 1930, vol. 2, p. 194.

an Elizabethan clergyman with Ovid, Plautus, and Seneca, and not with the Christian theologians, nor with the Christian drama, nor with the Christian tradition of epic and allegory in Dante, Langland, and Spenser. Furthermore, the evidence of sixteenth-century Reformation attitudes towards the three classic writers cited by Meres indicates that they were highly regarded literarily, but there is not the slightest trace of allegorizing them in terms of Christian redemption, at least among the major theologians. Calvin's first work was a learned humanist commentary on Seneca, and he remained a sympathetic and admiring reader of Seneca throughout his life, but, though there are many citations of Seneca in his writings, there is no search for Christ-figures and analogues to the Christian drama. As for Plautus, Martin Luther felt that there was some objectionable matter in his comedies but nonetheless refused to omit his works from the school curriculum—and Luther's judgment was not based upon allegorizing and analogizing Plautus, but upon the fact that in his plays "real life and real people are so excellently portrayed."[2]

As for Ovid, we have the words of Arthur Golding in the prefatory letters to his edition of the *Metamorphoses*. One of the greatest of the Elizabethan translators, Golding was known in his own lifetime not only for his superb English version of Ovid but also as the most prolific of the translators of Calvin's commentaries. Here, then, was a literary critic steeped in Reformation methods of Scriptural analysis, and it is certainly significant that he never once cites a Christ-figure or redemption analogy in the *Metamorphoses*. He does indeed hold to the erroneous notion so common

[2] Karl Holl, *The Cultural Significance of the Reformation*, New York: Living Age Books, 1959, p. 116.

in the Renaissance that "the books of Moses" had exerted some influence upon classical thought, but he never goes beyond the moral law, which, like the Reformers, he thought was universal to all men, in his treatment of the positive didactic values of Ovid. On the negative side, Golding denied that Ovid's accounts contradicted the Pentateuch, and he accounted for this fact by referring to the same widespread Renaissance notion we have just cited. But Golding's view of the "teaching" of Ovid was purely ethical, without admixture of Christian theology. Golding praised Ovid highly for his representation of the course of human evil and folly, and he pointedly ridiculed those who could read nothing but theological material, for "nothing can digest with them unless it be divine."[3] He points to many admirable and fruitful moral examples in Ovid—warnings against ambition, weak rule, jealousy, idleness, envy, intemperance—as he declares that Ovid "as in a glass":

> giveth us instruction to address
> Ourselves to know our own estate. . . .[4]

When he refers to classical writings as "gifts of grace" which we should not marvel to find among the heathen,[5] Golding is merely applying the doctrine of common grace as God's operation among the heathen, a doctrine which he came to know intimately from his studies of Calvin. Indeed, Golding's commentaries upon Ovid are merely applications of

[3] Arthur Golding, "The Preface to the Reader," line 172, *The Metamorphosis*, in *Shakespeare's Ovid, being Arthur Golding's translation of the Metamorphoses*, ed. W. H. D. Rouse, London: The King's Library, 1904, p. 18.

[4] Arthur Golding, "The Epistle to the Earl of Leicester," lines 460f., *op.cit.*, p. 10.

[5] *Ibid.*, lines 308 and 310-51, pp. 7-8.

Calvin's theology to the exegesis of classical literature, and Calvin's theology at this point (as we will soon see) was consistent with the views of Luther and of Hooker. The classics, then, gave valuable and delightful moral instruction for the wise conduct of this life, but Golding does not at any point confuse such instruction by "reading in" analogues of Christian redemption. Golding sums up one aspect of his praise of Ovid as follows:

> The use of this same book therefore is this: that every man
> (Endeavoring for to know himself as nearly as he can
> As though he in a chariot sat well ordered) should direct
> His mind by reason in the way of virtue, and correct
> His fierce affections with the bit of temperance, lest perchance
> They taking bridle in the teeth like wilful jades do prance
> Away, and headlong carry him to every filthy pit
> Of vice, and drinking of the same defile his soul with it.[6]

Parallel to such warnings against sin and folly, there are incitements to virtue, so that Golding also praises the *Metamorphoses* as

> This worthy work in which of good examples are so many,
> This orchard of Alcinous in which there wants not any
> Herb, tree, or fruit that may man's use for health or pleasure serve,

[6] *Ibid.*, lines 569ff., p. 12.

This plenteous horn of Alchelory which justly doth
    deserve
To bear the name of treasury of knowledge. . . .[7]

The treasury, then, is a treasury of natural knowledge viewed
as having its own integrity and its own indispensable value.
When Francis Meres lauded Shakespeare as possessing the
soul of Ovid, he may or may not have been willing to go so
far in finding didactic elements in Shakespeare as Golding
did in finding such values in Ovid, but I know no reason
to believe that he would have gone further.

III. THE REFORMATION AND LITERARY EDUCATION

We have now seen that the only extant sixteenth-century
commentary upon Shakespeare made by a theologian connected him with the three Latin authors Seneca, Plautus,
and Ovid, and we have given some indication of the extent
and limits of the "spiritual values" found in these writers
by representative Protestant thinkers. This linking of Shakespeare with the classics is significant and indeed inevitable,
for sixteenth-century Christian attitudes towards literature
were the products of classical learning.

For all major Christian groups in the sixteenth-century,
liberal education was almost entirely classical.[8] In this connection it is of primary importance for us to recall that the
sixteenth-century Reformation was accustomed to thinking
of the liberal arts as quite clearly differentiated from Christian revelation. The liberal arts were understood as dealing

[7] *Ibid.*, lines 581ff., p. 12.
[8] The only groups to whom this statement does not apply would be the
Anabaptists and similar sects. Both Protestant and Roman Catholic schools
followed the classical curriculum.

in the province of natural truth, while theology concerned special revelation and the gift of salvation. Both provinces were established by God, and each was thought to supplement the other (Luther held that there could have been no Reformation without a preceding Renaissance),[9] but the two were not to be confused or equated. The literature which young Protestants were taught was almost entirely non-Christian, and was clearly recognized as such, yet the great Reformers fought for the establishment or the strengthening of schools, academies, and universities to perpetuate the pagan classics and to provide Christian students with an education in those classics.

The reasons for this insistence upon classical education were the traditional and perennial ones. In the first place there was the conviction that without a firm base in the liberal arts, professionals in any field (including professional theologians) would be gravely handicapped. "That religion be rightly taught," Philip Melanchthon held, "implies as a necessary condition sound instruction in Letters,"[10] and in those words he exemplified the typical Reformation attitude. In short, the Reformers held to the perennial view of the liberal arts as an independent body of studies which, without being in any sense professional, nonetheless provided the best possible basis for future professional endeavor. The arts were to be studied for their "liberalizing" value, and not as saving graces.

In this connection we cannot forget that the Reformation

[9] Luther, "Letter to Eoban Hess, March 29, 1523," in *Luther's Correspondence*, trans. and ed. Preserved Smith and Charles M. Jacobs, Philadelphia: United Lutheran Publishing House, 1918, vol. 2, pp. 176-77.

[10] William H. Woodward, *Studies in Education during the Age of the Renaissance: 1400-1600*, Cambridge: Cambridge University Press, 1906, p. 224.

was born in a university. As E. H. Harbison has put it, "In its origins the Reformation was a learned movement, an academic affair, a scandal in the university, begun by a professor and spread by his colleagues and students."[11] Indeed, Martin Luther at first was regarded as but another disciple of Erasmus. "The first fruit of his [Luther's] attack on scholasticism," to quote again from Harbison, "was a curricular revision in the spring of 1518 which provided for adequate instruction in Greek and Hebrew and led to calling Melanchthon to join the faculty."[12] Martin Bucer lauded the abandonment of the old scholastic textbooks, as Wittenberg adopted a program of studies in keeping with the renascence of humane learning,[13] and under Melanchthon's influence Wittenberg was "reorganized on humanist principles with a thoroughness that would have satisfied Lorenzo Valla himself."[14]

Now it is true that Luther would attack any human endeavor which offered eternal salvation by purely human effort, and his assaults upon presumptuous reason in this regard are well known. Were we to stop only with that side of Luther's opinion, however, we would as scholars be guilty either of unpardonable ignorance or of suppressing evidence. Luther had the highest respect for classical education of the kind we have been discussing. Devoted as he was to the ministry, he found in the teaching of classics a vocation which was almost equally attractive to him personally, and

[11] E. Harris Harbison, *The Christian Scholar in the Age of Reformation*, New York: Charles Scribner's Sons, 1956, p. 112.

[12] *Ibid.*, p. 113.

[13] Bucer, in *Luther's Correspondence*, vol. 1, Ep. 57.

[14] Woodward, *op.cit.*, p. 230. The Scottish universities were similarly reorganized under Buchanan and the Melvilles. See M. L. Clarke, *Classical Education in Britain: 1500-1900*, Cambridge: Cambridge University Press, 1959, pp. 140-42.

he even said, comparing the ministry and teaching, "I am not sure which of the two is to be preferred."[15]

In 1523 Luther addressed to the mayors and aldermen of Germany a famous letter in which he urged the establishment of universal compulsory education.[16] While it is probably true, as Robert R. Rusk has said, that "it was only on religious grounds that such a faith in the universal education of the people could at that time be based,"[17] we must be careful to recall that Luther's insistence on universal literacy was based not only on the desideratum that all could read the Scriptures, but also on a very pragmatic concern for the temporal well-being of the people. In 1530 Luther commended "the wise council" of Nuremberg, which, in establishing an effective educational program, "showed a Christian regard for their subjects." Luther called this a "Christian" action in two regards: it "provided *not only* for their [i.e., the citizens'] eternal weal but *also* for their temporal needs and honor."[18] Luther repeatedly used such double praises, underscoring his point by referring to "both the spiritual and the secular sphere" as benefiting from liberal learning.[19] In his sermon "On the Duty of Sending Children to School," Luther met head-on the objection that a child may, through the exposure of education, become a heretic,

[15] *Luther on Education*, St. Louis: Concordia Publishing Co., n.d., p. 264.

[16] *Ibid.*, pp. 169-209. For other evidences of the Protestant appeal for universal education, see John T. McNeill, *The History and Character of Calvinism*, New York: Oxford University Press, 1954, p. 135; M. M. Knappen, *Tudor Puritanism*, Chicago: University of Chicago Press, 1939, p. 468; Robert R. Rusk, *The Doctrines of the Great Educators*, London: Macmillan and Co., 1918, p. 92; John Edgar, *History of Early Scottish Education*, Edinburgh: J. Thin, 1893, pp. 262-63.

[17] Rusk, *op.cit.*, pp. 89-90.

[18] *Luther on Education*, p. 212. Italics mine.

[19] *Ibid.*, pp. 213 and 218.

and responded forthrightly: "Well, you must run that risk."[20] The risks which concerned him far more were that, without learning, the Reformation would fail in the sphere of religion while the secular order, deprived of learning, would degenerate till men became "Tartars or wild beasts."[21] Liberal learning not only formed a necessary substratum for theology, but raised the individual and society above the level of barbarism. Thus, as Melanchthon put it, "the ultimate end which confronts us is not private virtue alone but the interest of the public weal."[22]

Luther insisted on the importance of liberal learning, then, as much for the benefit of the state as for the benefit of the church. In urging the German mayors and aldermen to establish free and compulsory public schools, Luther wrote that "though there were no soul, nor heaven, nor hell, but only the civil government," and again "even if there were no soul," still "this consideration is of itself sufficient, namely, that society, for the maintenance of the civil order and the proper regulation of the household, needs accomplished and well-trained men and women."[23] He declared that students would benefit in that "they would be able to comprehend, as in a mirror, the character, life, counsels, undertakings, successes, and failures of the whole world from the beginning," and pointed out that it was due to liberal education that the Greeks "became wonderfully skillful people, capable for every undertaking."[24]

In the support of liberal education by the major Reformers there is not the slightest hint of a narrow Biblicism. Of those who suggested that a knowledge of Scripture alone was

[20] *Ibid.*, p. 236.   [21] *Ibid.*, p. 217.
[22] Woodward, *op.cit.*, p. 224.
[23] *Luther on Education*, pp. 194-95 and 196.
[24] *Ibid.*, pp. 197 and 199.

sufficient apart from the classics, Luther declared that they "must always remain irrational brutes," and deserve to be so called.[25] Of the New Testament injunctions that the follower of Christ must be as a little child, Calvin commented that "The Christian profession requireth us to be children, not in understanding, but in malice."[26]

Though Luther was a strong advocate of the liberal arts, he had himself received an education more largely monastic than liberal, and in later life he regretted having been so immersed in scholasticism by his superiors "that I did not read more poetry and history, and that no one taught me in these branches."[27] With John Calvin it was far otherwise, for he was steeped in the Renaissance, and wanted for himself nothing more than a life of study. It was only at his father's insistence that he abandoned humanistic studies in order to take a doctorate in law. As soon as his father died and the degree was earned, he returned to the study of the classics and brought out his elegant commentary on Seneca. When he was called to lead the Reformed Church in Geneva, Calvin threw himself into theology without ever really abandoning his humanistic studies. Throughout the later editions of the *Institutes*, classical references of all types increase in number, indicating his continued saturation in the Greek and Roman masters.[28] Quirinus Breen is surely correct in holding that though all the sixteenth-century Reformers "had diligently studied the humanists," Calvin

[25] *Ibid.*, p. 183.

[26] Calvin, *Concerning Offenses* (Golding trans.), London, 1567, sig. B3v.

[27] *Luther on Education*, p. 199.

[28] Harbison, *op.cit.*, pp. 145-46, and Quirinus Breen, *John Calvin: A Study in French Humanism*, Grand Rapids: Wm. B. Eerdmans, 1931. p. 162n.

was the most sophisticated of them all.[29] E. H. Harbison's judgment reinforces and goes beyond Breen's, for in his study of the succession of Christian scholars, including Jerome, Augustine, Abelard, Aquinas, Petrarch, Valla, Pico, Colet, Erasmus, Luther, and Calvin, he concludes that Calvin "had read more widely and was sensitive to more opposing points of view both within and outside the Christian tradition than any of those whom we have considered except Pico."[30] Only those whose knowledge of Luther and Calvin is grounded in ignorance can assume that either of them was hostile to liberal learning.

As at Wittenberg, so at Geneva, there was a striving for excellence in the liberal arts. The University of Geneva, founded in 1559, was rooted not in theology (which was a separate professional program) but in the classics.[31] The course in "la vraie religion" was begun only after the completion of that in "bonnes lettres,"[32] and when the Rector Theodore de Beza arrived to inaugurate Calvin's new university, he seems at first to have devoted more attention to teaching Demosthenes and Aristotle than to expounding the Holy Scriptures. Similarly, the courses assigned to François Berauld called for concentration upon Aristotle, Plato, the poets, orators, and historians, and either Plutarch or (almost as an addendum) some Christian author. Now, no one will suppose that Calvin, Beza, and Berauld expected men to gain admission to heaven by dint of studying the classics, and yet they primarily emphasized the traditional liberal arts curriculum in Greek and Latin—a fact which under-

[29] *Ibid.*, pp. vii and 155-56.

[30] Harbison, *op.cit.*, p. 240.

[31] Charles Borgeaud, *Histoire de l'Université de Genève: L'Académie de Calvin*, Genève: Georg et Co., Libraires de L'Université, 1900, pp. 43-44.

[32] *Ibid.*, pp. 48-49.

scores the sixteenth-century Protestant affirmation of the independent (i.e., non-theological) values of literature and of a classical education. Education, as established within Protestantism, was primarily literary—but so far as I have been able to determine from a rather wide-ranging analysis of the Reformers' own practices and ideas, none of them ever expected to find theological typologies or allegories in literature. The major literature they knew was non-Christian, and the minds of Protestant children from childhood onward would have been accustomed to think of literature within a non-theological and non-redemptive context. By analogy, they may be expected to have thought of Shakespeare's art in the same way.

Surely there was little if anything in the programs of the schools and universities which would lead a student to expect to find theological concerns treated in creative literature. According to Christian Pedersen, the Protestant educator of Denmark, secular writings were not only youth's profit, but also its pleasure and delight, "studies which the Greeks in olden time taught their children."[33] The Reformation brought little if any departure from the educational programs of the Renaissance. The primary schools, devoted to providing a basic vernacular literacy for the youngest school children, did involve the study of basic religious materials and catechisms. "The primary objective of the petty school was religious and moral," T. W. Baldwin tells us, and the texts were "mostly religious," but the petty school covered only the very first years of instruction. The curriculum devised for the petty school student, to quote again from Baldwin, "was chiefly aimed at preparing [him]

[33] E. H. Dunkley, *The Reformation in Denmark,* London: SPCK, 1948, p. 108.

to read and write sufficiently well to read and memorize the accidence and rules of the authorized Latin grammar in English during [his] first year in grammar school."[34]

The grammar school was, of course, concerned with Latin grammar, and from the time of the student's entrance into grammar school, he was immersed in classical studies. It was here that he first came into educational contact with literature as such. Religion was also emphasized, to be sure, but was usually outside the structure of the liberal arts program itself, and generally without academic "credit" towards a degree. In the Eisleben academy, established after Melanchthon's plan, six days of the week were devoted to the classical curriculum, while the seventh was devoted, not to rest, but to Biblical instruction and study.[35] The English practice in grammar schools was similar, as students were required to attend Sunday sermon and report in Latin on Monday as to what was said.[36] Mark Curtis summarizes the situation at Oxford and Cambridge between 1558 and 1642: "Except for the fact that college and university statutes required attendance at chapel and university sermons, religious instruction for students of the arts might well fall under the heading of extra-statutory learning. An Oxford statute of 1579 did, to be sure, order that each college should engage a catechist who would instruct the members of the college in the beliefs contained in the Thirty-nine Articles, but it did not change the requirements for degrees or provide any systematic way to make achievement in this field a test of a man's qualifications for a degree."[37] Many liberal

[34] T. W. Baldwin, *William Shakspere's Petty School*, Urbana, Illinois: University of Illinois Press, 1943, pp. 30, 32, 163, and 58-59.

[35] Woodward, *op.cit.*, p. 222.

[36] Baldwin, *op.cit.*, p. 84.

[37] Mark H. Curtis, *Oxford and Cambridge in Transition: 1558-1642,*

arts students did, of course, attend the lectures of leading theologians, as when Sir Thomas Bodley attended the lectures of Calvin and Beza in Geneva[38] while in England others flocked to hear the lectures of Cartwright or Andrewes, but such practices mark the rather informal atmosphere of the sixteenth- and seventeenth-century universities, rather than their statutory requirements.

The only conclusion which we are justified in drawing from this evidence is that the Protestant Reformation, in its educational programs, provided the student who had advanced to the level of literary study with an almost totally non-Christian literary fare and with a similar conception of literature. Religious instruction was given, to be sure, but the basic educational fare was in the classics. I know of no reason to suppose that the separation between literature and theology which characterized sixteenth-century Protestant practice both in England and on the continent would have been bridged when it came to interpreting (or writing) Shakespeare's plays.

IV. THE UNDERLYING PROTESTANT THEORY OF THE LIBERAL ARTS

In a typically vivid expression, Martin Luther declared that unless a doctor correctly diagnosed a disease, he would treat it with poison instead of medicine.[39] That saying is closely related to one of the major concerns of the Protestant Reformation—a concern with the operative differences between nature and grace. To confuse the two realms might

---

Oxford: Oxford University Press, 1959, p. 185. For further evidence to the same effect, see pp. 122ff. and Chapter Two, *passim*, in Curtis' definitive study.

[38] Borgeaud, *op.cit.*, p. 57.

[39] Luther, Serm. on Gal. 4.1-7, Weimar ed., vol. 49, p. 11.

lead to damnation in the world to come and to barbarism or chaos in the present order. When men are led to believe that they can merit salvation by their own unaided thoughts and works, they are in mortal danger of missing salvation altogether. On the other hand, if they assume that the secular order can be preserved without both thought and work, they are in imminent danger of degenerating to the level of "Tartars or wild beasts." Thus it is of tremendous importance to determine which disease is being treated— the disease of sin and spiritual death, or the disease of ignorance and cultural barbarism—before a wise physician can prescribe the proper medicine. That distinction is central to our interests here and forms the basis for the Protestant "laicization of art" to which I have already referred.

The concern of all the arts and sciences is primarily with *this* life, with man's existence in the secular order. In his exposition of Isaiah, Luther spoke as follows: "Cicero wrote and taught brilliantly about virtues, prudence, and other matters; likewise Aristotle about ethics, brilliantly and learnedly. The works of both are certainly very useful and very necessary for the conduct of this life. But however excellent they are, the true wisdom cannot be learned from their writings. . . . They cannot show the way to God into the kingdom of heaven."[40] Luther and the other Reformers repeatedly referred to the differences between that grace which leads "into the kingdom of heaven" even those who

[40] Luther, Exp. Isa. 9.2, Plass anthol., vol. 2, 3337. Luther's attitude toward Aristotle was ambiguous—favorable to his purely this-worldly value, unfavorable to his influence on theology. He had great enthusiasm for Cicero, all things considered, and considerably preferred him to Aristotle. For a clear and summarizing view of these matters, see B. A. Gerrish, *Grace and Reason: A Study in the Theology of Luther*, Oxford: Clarendon Press, 1962, pp. 34f. and 40f.

fail most miserably in "the conduct of this life," and those arts which "are certainly very useful and very necessary for the conduct of this life." In terms of this basic distinction, what we call the arts and the sciences were grouped together by the Reformers, as representing the learning and skill which man could develop from within himself, regardless of whether or not he was among the elect. Within this context, Melanchthon wrote that "the Gospel is very different from all other knowledge, religion, and sects. Other knowledge such as computation and measuring, would be developed by the natural understanding of man, even though they were not found in the scripture. But the divine promise of grace is not a light that is born in us, as is computation or law."[41] By saying that computation and law are "born in us," Melanchthon of course does not mean that we have a mature knowledge of such subjects at birth, but rather that we are born with capacities to develop these subjects, whereas we simply cannot generate grace by and for ourselves.

Thus we do, as men, carry within us an ability to understand natural law and a conscience to obey that law, and yet we cannot save ourselves by the law, for our obedience to it (however full that obedience may be) is nonetheless marred by our self-seeking. As sinners, we attempt to obey the law so as to escape punishment, whether here or in hell, and to find reward, in this life or in heaven. Thus our greatest virtues are but splendid vices, for they carry within themselves a love of the self and a seeking of personal advantage rather than a love of God and a seeking to do his will. We are thus enslaved to ourselves, are in prison, as it were, to

[41] Clyde L. Manschreck, *Melanchthon: The Quiet Reformer*, New York: Abingdon Press, 1958, p. 156.

our own self-assertive efforts, so that even the effort after humility becomes a gesture of spiritual pride and the seeking of heaven for our own delight involves us in condemning ourselves to hell. From this impasse there is no escaping by our own exertions: we must be redeemed by God's grace or we remain condemned by our own sin.

This all-too-brief sketch of the classical view of sin and grace may serve to clarify the Reformers' strong rejection of the works of the natural man as qualifying him for salvation. Readers who wish to know more of the Protestant view of the operation of grace and of the plan of salvation may find fuller accounts of that subject elsewhere,[42] but our specific concern here is with the realm of the secular and we must return to it.

All the major Reformers held that the law could not "justify" man; in other words, it could not provide him either with salvation or with the possibility of meriting salvation. Yet they denied that the law was for that reason to be regarded as useless. Luther pointed out the false logic of such conclusions by adducing parallels: "For just as the conclusion is not valid: money does not justify, therefore it is worthless; the eyes do not justify, therefore they must be torn out; the hands do not justify, therefore they must be cut off, so this conclusion is not valid: the law does not justify, therefore it is worthless. One must ascribe to everything its proper office and use."[43] What Luther says here

[42] For a fuller account of these matters see my *God, Man, and Satan*, Princeton: Princeton University Press, 1960, pp. 42-91.

[43] Luther, Exp. of Gal. 3.19, Plass anthol., vol. 2, 2343. It is interesting to compare Plass's translation here, which captures the authentic verve of Luther, with the somewhat less lively version in Erasmus Middleton's translation. Both, of course, should be considered in connection with the original in Weimar ed., vol. 40I, p. 475f.

of the law applies with the same force to the whole range of humanly accessible arts and sciences—including the art of literature. Such arts are not worthless simply because they do not justify man before God, and for Christians to expect secular art to perform a justifying function would be to violate "its proper office and use."

The distinction which Luther makes in his particularly graphic way is presented in somewhat more philosophic form by John Calvin. In this passage from the *Institutes*, the point is inescapable:

". . . to perceive more clearly how far the mind can proceed in any matter according to the degree of its ability, we must here set forth a distinction. This, then, is the distinction: that there is one kind of understanding of earthly things; another of heavenly. I call 'earthly things' those which do not pertain to God or his Kingdom, to true [i.e., divinely acceptable] justice, or to the blessedness of the future life; but which have their significance and relationship with regard to the present life and are, in a sense, confined within its bounds. I call 'heavenly things' the pure knowledge of God, the nature of true righteousness, and the mysteries of the Heavenly Kingdom. The first class includes government, household management, all mechanical skills, and the liberal arts. In the second are the knowledge of God and of his will, and the rule by which we conform our lives to it."[44]

In the realm of "earthly things" (Calvin's phrase here corresponds to what we are referring to as the secular), man can achieve much, but he cannot attain to a saving knowledge of God by his own efforts. For our redemption, it is necessary that God either give us new eyes or open the eyes we have

[44] Calvin, *Inst.* 2.2.13.

blinded by our sin, for otherwise "all is darkness," spiritually speaking. The natural man "is able to understand God's mysteries only in so far as he is illumined by God's grace. He who attributes any more understanding to himself is all the more blind because he does not recognize his own blindness."[45]

With skill in the arts, the situation is quite different. Though such skill is not equally a part of the "common discernment" of all men, for some are more gifted than others, Calvin finds that it is clear from experience, from reason, and from revelation that God has not favored Christians more than non-Christians in terms of such natural gifts. Of talent in the arts, he writes: "Now the discovery or systematic transmission of the arts, or the inner and more excellent knowledge of them, which is characteristic of a few, . . . because it is bestowed indiscriminately upon pious and impious, it is rightly counted among natural gifts."[46]

The basic distinction between natural and supernatural gifts must be recognized and remembered, but it can easily be oversimplified to imply an absolute incompatibility between the two. Theologians and historians of Christian thought will be aware of subtleties which I intentionally omit from my analysis here, for my purpose is only to draw the picture in its major outlines. These major outlines may be seen in Professor Torrance's summary of Calvin's views: "All creaturely endowments, such as wisdom and craftsmanship, come directly as gifts from God whether they are in unbelievers or believers."[47] But the temporal truth (equally accessible to heathen men) and the supernatural truth (as

[45] *Ibid.*, 2.2.20-21.
[46] *Ibid.*, 2.2.14.
[47] T. F. Torrance, *Calvin's Doctrine of Man*, Grand Rapids: Wm. B. Eerdmans, 1957, p. 63.

divinely opened to the elect alone) are not *in themselves* conflicting, though man's ignorance or presumption may at times inject an element of conflict where none should exist. Quirinus Breen writes of Calvin that "his view is not that Epicureanism and Cyrenaism are *per se* hostile to the highest good, but that they are *inadequate*"[48] and John T. McNeill summarizes the point that for Calvin there can be "no thought of the concept (best represented by Duns Scotus) of two kinds of truth that are not mutually harmonious. Rather, his [Calvin's] view is of one God-given truth manifested on two levels, one of which is of value for temporal and mundane concerns only. He is on common ground with Lactantius, who says that though the philosophers missed 'the sum of things,' viz., that the world was created by God so that men might worship him, yet each of them saw something of the truth."[49]

To ignore those aspects of truth which are discoverable within the temporal order was, in Calvin's view, to treat with contempt the gifts of God. In this area Calvin, Luther, and Hooker were—for our practical purposes—at one, and though there were differences of emphasis and approach between them, all would have agreed when Arthur Golding objected to those who could find profit only in explicitly Christian writings, for "nothing can digest with them unless it be divine."[50]

Golding's remark is of considerable significance for indicating how sixteenth-century Protestants were taught to react to literature. It also suggests that some did not apply in these matters the doctrine which the leading theologians

[48] Breen, *op.cit.*, p. 112.
[49] McNeill's comment in Calvin's *Inst.*, vol. 1, p. 274, n. 58.
[50] See above, footnote 3.

advocated. Admitting that fact, let us now return to the teachings of the authoritative leaders themselves, for our concern here is to trace the major positions, not the aberrations.

Of the value of non-Christian work in the arts and sciences, Calvin wrote that "if the Lord has willed that we be helped in physics, dialectic, mathematics, and other like disciplines, by the work and ministry of the ungodly, let us use this assistance. For if we neglect God's gift freely offered in these arts, we ought to suffer just punishment for our sloth."[51] There is no hint here, or anywhere else in Calvin, Luther, or Hooker, of the need to "Christianize" the humane arts and sciences before they may become acceptable for Christians to use and enjoy; on the contrary, they are to be accepted on their own terms, without reinterpretation in terms of Christ-figures and of Christian redemption. The liberal arts have their own integrity, Calvin held, for God "hath raised up the humane sciences which are apt and profitable to the guiding of our life and in serving to our profit may also serve to his glory."[52]

No one who is interested in the relations of theology and culture in the Reformation and Post-Reformation periods can afford to ignore such clear statements. Within the broader range of culture covered by the Reformers, our particular interest is in literature and specifically in the relevance of theology for the interpretation of Shakespeare. As the evidence accumulates, it becomes increasingly clear that the major Protestant theologians not only gave no imperative for the theological commandeering of the liberal arts, but that they specifically sought to preserve the in-

[51] Calvin, *Inst.* 2.2.16.
[52] Calvin, *Against Astrology Judicial*, London, 1561, Sig. A5v.

tegrity of those arts. Critics must keep these facts in mind in the face of contentions on the one hand that Shakespeare was concerned with conveying specifically Christian doctrine in his plays, or on the other hand that he was an agnostic because he did not patently build his plays about Christian doctrine. Those among Shakespeare's contemporaries who understood and accepted the theological positions we are outlining here would not have fallen into either of these errors.

Secular writers, concerned with temporal wisdom, beauty, and truth, were not read with a view to finding gems of Christian truth. Of such writers, Calvin advised that we should "let that admirable light of truth shining in them teach us that the mind of man, though fallen and perverted from its wholeness, is nonetheless clothed and ornamented with God's excellent gifts. If we regard the Spirit of God as the sole fountain of truth, we shall neither reject the truth itself, nor despise it wherever it shall appear, unless we wish to dishonor the spirit of God. For by holding the gifts of the Spirit in slight esteem, we condemn and reproach the Spirit himself."[53] Calvin then proceeds to praise the truth and great equity of the ancient jurists, the "fine observation and artful description of nature" of classical thinkers, and the valuable contributions in their different fields of pagan scholars of rhetoric, medicine and mathematics, by all of which we are "compelled to recognize how preeminent they are," and he concludes by observing "how many gifts the Lord left to human nature even after it was despoiled of its true good."[54]

[53] Calvin, *Inst.* 2.2.15. See also Calvin's *Commentary on Titus* (1.12), pp. 300-301.
[54] Calvin, *Inst.* 2.2.15.

Richard Hooker not only did not disagree with such views, but expressed himself in strikingly similar terms: "There is in the world no kind of knowledge, whereby any part of truth is seen, but we justly account it precious; yea, that principal truth [i.e., Christian truth], in comparison whereof all other knowledge is vile, may receive from it [i.e., secular truth] some kind of light, whether it be that Egyptian and Chaldean wisdom mathematical, wherewith Moses and Daniel were furnished; or that natural, moral, and civil wisdom, wherein Solomon excelled all men; or that rational and oratorical wisdom of the Grecians, which the Apostle St. Paul brought from Tarsus; or that Judaical, which he learned in Jerusalem sitting at the feet of Gamaliel: to detract from the dignity thereof were to injury even God himself, who being that light which none can approach unto, hath sent out these lights whereof we are capable, even as so many sparkles resembling the bright fountain from which they rise."[55]

Or again, to the same general effect, Hooker writes: "The bounds of wisdom are large, and within them much is contained. . . . Whatsoever either men on earth or the angels of heaven do know, it is as a drop of that unemptiable fountain of wisdom; which wisdom hath diversely imparted her treasures unto the world. As her ways are of sundry kinds, so her manner of teaching is not merely one and the same. Some things she openeth by the sacred books of Scripture; some things by the glorious works of Nature; with some things she inspireth them from above by spiritual influence; in some things she leadeth and traineth them only by worldly experience and practice. We may not so in any one special kind admire her, that we disgrace her in

[55] Hooker, *Eccl. Pol.* 3.8.9.

any other; but let all her ways be according unto their place and degree adored."[56]

Hooker held as firmly as did Luther, Melanchthon, and Calvin that man's very great capacities within the temporal order would not avail him for eternal life, apart from God's grace,[57] but like his predecessors he too affirmed the integrity of the purely humane arts and sciences, apart from any necessary connection with Christian revelation.

The technical differences between the theologies of Luther, Calvin, and Hooker are of no direct concern to our particular inquiry, though they have considerable significance in the history of theology. What is important to us is the fact that these three men represent and summarize the major forces which converged in the theological climate of Shakespeare's time, and that they emphatically agree in affirming the essential integrity of the liberal arts. In none of these men is there the slightest evidence of the "reading in" of explicitly Christian theology in connection with humane art and science. According to Luther we must "ascribe to everything its proper office and use," and Hooker held that all things must be treated "according to their place and degree." For Hooker, again, the many sparks of truth are all traceable to the same "bright fountain," while Calvin thought of God as "the sole fountain" of all truth. To each of these theologians, it appeared that a violation of the independent orders of God's truth spelled effrontery towards God and danger for man.

The theological influence of Luther, Calvin, and Hooker did not discourage the development of such explicitly Christian works of literature as those of Spenser, Milton, and

[56] *Ibid.*, 2.1.4.
[57] *Ibid.*, 1.12.3, 1.13.3, 3.8.11, and 3.18.18.

Bunyan, and in varying degrees the theologians helped to shape the ideas of these writers, but for our interests the most significant fact is that Luther, Calvin, and Hooker each declared the independence of the liberal arts from theology. When Calvin wrote that "those persons are superstitious who do not venture to borrow anything from heathen authors" he was in effect affirming the right of Christians to read and to write apart from Church dogma, and Luther underscored the same principle when he affirmed the value of the liberal arts "without considering whether they are heathen or Christian."[58]

Now it is generally acknowledged that we have no clear evidence of Shakespeare's own inner convictions as to religion. We do know that he was a conforming member of the Church of England, but this fact tells us little of his personal faith. He may have been essentially pagan, or he may have been a deeply committed Christian, or he may have occupied some intermediate position. This much, however, we do know: it was in a culture shaped by the ideas we have discussed that Shakespeare lived and wrote. It was also in terms of this culture that he expected to be understood. His was an age of great theological excitement, and many subsequent critics have expected to find the influence of theology marked large on his plays. Some critics, holding that theology should be present in the plays but not finding it there on an obvious level, have proceeded by analogic, typological, and even allegorical analysis to inject theological meaning into Shakespeare. At the opposite extreme of opinion, other critics have concluded that since theological material appears in most of the plays only incidentally, then

[58] Calvin, *Commentary on Titus* (1.12), pp. 300-301, and *Luther on Education*, p. 207.

Shakespeare must have written from the standpoint of a non-believer. In the light of the evidence which I have assembled here, I submit that both these critical conclusions are erroneous.

I make no claim to having discovered Shakespeare's personal faith. But I do suggest, in the light of the theological doctrines which we have examined, that convinced and literate Protestant Christians in Shakespeare's time would not have expected from literature any more explicitly Christian theology than Shakespeare patently gave in his works.

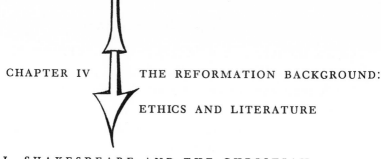

CHAPTER IV   THE REFORMATION BACKGROUND:

ETHICS AND LITERATURE

I. SHAKESPEARE AND THE CHRISTIAN ETHIC

The conception of theology as "the queen of the sciences" is greatly admired by those who see in the Middle Ages a vast and unified culture, beautiful in its harmony and devotion. Whatever may be said, from the historical point of view, of such an idealization of the Middle Ages, it is virtually beyond question that such a view of theology is at once ambiguous and dangerous. It is ambiguous because one is not quite sure whether theology is a queen in the sense of exerting a ruling power over other disciplines, or only in the sense that it treats man's ultimate concerns and possibilities. If the first meaning is accepted, and theology is regarded as exercising suzerainty over other disciplines, then the conception of theology as queen is immensely dangerous, as we can see in the Roman Catholic condemnation of Galileo, in the fundamentalist Protestant condemnation of Darwin, and, if we may say so, in some of the theologizing analyses of Shakespeare which we have examined here. All the evidence we have seen thus far clearly indicates that the major theologians of sixteenth-century Protestantism made no such claims for the suzerainty of theology.

So far as I know, indeed, no major Reformer referred to theology as the queen of the sciences. Scholars, looking back on the Reformation, sometimes have thought of it as effecting a re-enthronement of theology as queen, but if this was so, it was so only in a very restricted sense. As we have seen, the Reformation leaders regarded the subject matter of theology (God's redemption of sinful man) as the most ultimate of all man's concerns, but the eminence of theology was due to the nature of its subject matter, and not to its control of other disciplines and their subject matters. The Reformation attitudes as they affect our concern may be summarized as follows: the truth inherent in each discipline is undergirded by God, and not by theology; thus the worker in every field of man's endeavor is responsible for his performance directly to God, and not to a mediated authority of theology, the theologians, or a clerical hierarchy. The liberal arts were thus enfranchised and granted their own integrity within the temporal order.

Now it is the judgment of most Shakespearean scholars (including this one) that Shakespeare's dramatic interest is almost entirely restricted to what the Reformers called the temporal order. In an earlier chapter we examined the views of a number of critics who in one way or another have denied the essentially secular character of Shakespeare's plays. We considered the claims made by these critics for the presence of numerous redemptive analogues and Christ-figures in Shakespeare, as well as the assignment by these critics of dramatic characters to an afterlife in heaven or hell. We noted that such claims by and large rest on assertions which are not only unsupported by evidence but which may even run contrary to evidence available to us. We therefore concluded, despite the prolific efforts of the school of Knight, that it was wiser to maintain an understanding of Shakespeare's dramatic action as basically restricted to the temporal order. Then, in the chapter immediately preceding this one, we discovered that this secular orientation was precisely what the three major spokesmen of the Reformation taught that men should expect from literature as one of the liberal arts. We thus found that Shakespeare's literary practice of avoiding theological complexities was in accord with the understanding of the liberal arts held by the most influential and representative theologians of his time.

But if literature was judged by the theologians themselves to be free from the necessity of a theological concern, what of its relation to ethics? Though there may be no inevitable involvement of literature with theological doctrines, yet every dramatic or narrative action must deal with human relations and conflicts, and the literary work is thus inextricably involved with the problems of ethics. Dramatic action treats choices on the part of dramatic characters, and choices imply varying degrees of wisdom and folly, good and evil, which are within the province of ethics. Similarly, if the dramatic characters are sufficiently convincing to elicit the audience's interest, they must in some measure elicit from the audience itself certain judgments in terms of choices and sympathies and evaluations, which judgments are also within the field of ethics. Finally, the dramatist himself, if he is to succeed dramatically, must so integrate the choices in action of his characters with the choices in evaluation of his audience as to create a unified effect. Thus the dramatist appeals—though the appeal is usually tacit rather than overt—to some standard of value over and beyond the words and actions of his play, a standard of value by which his audience can understand and appreciate the characters and the plot which he has created. An audience may find its sympathies divided between rival figures on the stage, or it may find itself preponderantly favoring one particular protagonist, but without evaluation of the dramatic choices and actions there would be no dramatic interest, and the evaluation of men, motives, and actions is by definition ethics. It should be unnecessary to demonstrate the many ways in which the dramatist's concern with ethical problems differs from the philosopher's or the moralist's; my sole point here is that the dramatist must set his action against some background of ethical evaluation, and in making this point I am merely reiterating the overwhelming consensus of critical opinion.

Our major concern now is with the nature of the ethical consensus to which Shakespeare tacitly appealed. Was it by an explicitly Christian standard of ethics that he would have had his dramatic conflicts judged? I do not think it was, and neither do most Shakespearean scholars. Shakespeare's standard of dramatic evaluation was the common ethical consensus of man, as that consensus was understood in his own time. Shakespeare did not any more appeal in his plays to an exclusively Christian ethic than he embodied in them an exclusively Christian theology. With the possible exception of *Measure for Measure* (and I am not convinced that an exception is to be admitted there as any more than a possibility), I find that an explicitly New Testament ethic is less relevant to Shakespeare's plays than an ethic of purely natural law, based equally in the Scriptures and the Greek and Latin classics. It is true that individual characters in the plays often rely upon or refer to elements of the Christian faith (and we will consider these matters in the last part of this book), but the fact remains that Shakespeare's total dramatic structure could as well be supported by the ethics of the virtuous heathen as by those of the Christian church.

What are we to make of this situation? Considering the extent of theological interest and the depth of religious commitments in Shakespeare's time, is it not strange that he makes so little use of the standards of Christian ethics? Some critics, evidently distrusting an affirmative answer to these questions, are willing to distort the plays so as to place them under the dominance of explicitly Christian values, while others, showing no reluctance to answer affirmatively, conclude that Shakespeare avoided appeal to the Christian standards because he himself felt no commitment to Christianity. Both views, in quite different ways, seem to me to miss the mark, and through the rest of this chapter I will attempt to show that Shakespeare's appeal to natural law as the norm for evaluating actions in an exclusively temporal setting was again in full accord with the positions of the major theologians of his own age.

LUTHER AND SECULAR SUFFICIENCY

According to Martin Luther, man does not need to look beyond values accessible in the purely temporal sphere in order to lead his life well within that sphere. "In earthly, human affairs man's judgment suffices," Luther declared in a sermon on Isaiah. "For these things he needs no other light than that of reason."[1] Speaking to the same effect on another occasion, he said that "one needs no Christ, no baptism, no Gospel for human life and relations, for matters which pertain to this temporal life; for by implanted powers

[1] Luther, Serm. on Isa. 60.1-6, Lenker ed., vol. 7, p. 319.

human reason knows and understands how such matters are to be handled and arranged."[2]

Luther repeatedly taught that there was no need for man, in the conduct of life in this world, to look beyond the Roman law, for there was no better or more practical basis available for establishing relations between men. When we recognize that the sixteenth-century originator of the Reformation held this opinion, we will be able to view in much clearer perspective the fact that in Shakespeare's dramas there is rarely any appeal to sanctions beyond those available to the pagan citizens of Rome. Luther's judgments here are worthy of particular attention:

"The imperial law, according to which the Roman Empire still rules today and will continue to rule until the Last Day, is nothing more than heathen wisdom, established and set down before Rome had ever heard a thing about Christians or even about God himself."[3]

Although the Roman law is certainly "no aid to salvation and eternal life," Luther said elsewhere, it nonetheless is "certainly God's ordinance; one must have it and cannot do without it."[4]

[2] Luther, Serm. on Titus 2.13, Plass anthol., vol. 2, 2429. B. A. Gerrish (*op.cit.*, p. 26) summarizes Luther's attitudes in a highly effective paradigm: "If, then, we are to do justice to the complexity of Luther's thought, we must carefully distinguish: (1) natural reason, ruling within its proper domain (the Earthly Kingdom); (2) arrogant reason, trespassing upon the domain of faith (the Heavenly Kingdom); (3) regenerate reason, serving humbly in the household of faith, but always subject to the Word of God. Within the first context, reason is an excellent gift of God; within the second, it is Frau Hulda, the Devil's Whore; within the third, it is the handmaiden of faith."

[3] Luther, Exp. Ps. 101.5, Amer. ed., vol. 13, p. 198. Luther recognized, of course, that the Romans acknowledged "gods," but he denied that they knew God.

[4] Luther, Serm on Luke 2.22-23, Plass anthol., vol. 3, 3894. As high as was Luther's opinion of the Roman law, however, he felt that the Old

Indeed, for the entire conduct of the civil order and of life in this world one need not look beyond the teachings of the great classical authorities. In what is, for our purposes, an extremely significant passage from his exposition of Psalm 101, Luther wrote as follows of the unsurpassed value of standards devised by the wise heathen for life in the temporal sphere:

"Therefore whoever wants to learn and become wise in secular government, let him read the heathen books and writings. They have truly painted it and portrayed it quite beautifully and generously, with both verses and pictures, with teachings and examples; and they became the source for the ancient imperial laws. I am convinced that God gave and preserved such heathen books as those of the poets and histories, like Homer, Virgil, Demosthenes, Livy, and afterwards the fine old jurists—as he has also given and preserved other temporal goods among the heathen and godless at all times—that the heathen and godless, too, might have their prophets, apostles, and theologians or preachers for the secular government. . . . Thus they had their Homer, Plato, Aristotle, Cicero, Ulpian, and others, even as the people of God had their Moses, Elijah, Isaiah, and others; and their emperors, kings, and princes, like Alexander, Augustus, etc., were their Davids and Solomons."[5]

In the judgment of matters concerning the present life, Christians cannot improve upon the wisdom of the ancient Greeks and Romans. Christians should not pattern their relations to God on pagan theology, but in the areas where

---

Testament Jewish laws were more careful to protect the rights of persons, while the Roman law was more careful of the rights of property. Luther thus admired the Mosaic code more. See Mueller, *op.cit.*, pp. 48-49.

[5] Luther, Exp. of Ps. 101.5, Amer. ed., vol. 13, p. 199.

theology does not exercise rule (such as the liberal arts in general and Shakespearean drama in particular), the Christian can find sufficient guidance from the heathen. Luther lauds the manner in which Roman boys were reared, so that by the age of twenty they were completely prepared for life: "Thus they became intelligent, wise, and excellent men, skilled in every art and rich in experience, so that all the bishops, priests, and monks in Germany put together would not equal a Roman soldier. Consequently their country prospered; persons were found capable and schooled in every pursuit."[6]

Though heathen virtue is not saving, it is very great—often much greater, indeed, than anything achieved by Christians: "Nor is this a question about what or how great the works done by Alexander the Great, Hannibal, Julius Caesar, and Scipio are. We know that these men did things that are greater than anything a Christian ever did. For you will not easily find such energy in the conduct of war, such patience, and such endurance of evils and labors in any Christian king, nay, not even in the kings of the Children of Israel, in David, and in others."[7]

Among the heathen it was not only the Greeks and Romans who were singled out for emulation, but Luther found much for Christians to admire and imitate even among the feared and hated Turks. Though the Turks were not only un-Christian but even militantly anti-Christian, Luther told his congregation in one sermon that: "You will observe a courageous, strict, and respectable conduct among the Turks so far as their outward life is concerned. They do not indulge in wine, do not over-indulge in drinking and

[6] *Luther on Education*, p. 181.

[7] Luther, Exp. of Gen. 29.1-3, Plass anthol., vol. 3, 4895.

eating as we do, do not dress so frivolously and lavishly. They do not build with our splendor, nor do they put on the airs we do; and they do not curse and swear so much. Toward their emperor and lord they show great, signal obedience, decorum, and honor. Moreover, they have organized their government and administer it as we should like to have it administered in German lands."[8]

What we have seen thus far should make it clear beyond any possible doubt that Luther saw no more need for the introduction of exclusively Christian ethics in the conduct of secular society than Shakespeare evidently felt for their introduction into the secular drama. But Luther went even further than our evidence has thus far indicated. In his view, society simply could not be organized and maintained on the basis of purely Christian ethics, for there simply were not enough Christians to make such an organization feasible. "A Christian is a rare bird," he said—so rare, indeed, that an attempt to order society on the basis of the Sermon on the Mount rather than of the natural law would lead to nothing but chaos. Granted that true Christians will remain a small minority of any society, the most that Luther can hope for is a society of virtuous heathen (and whether they "profess" Christianity or not is immaterial at this point). "Would to God," he wrote, "that the majority of us were good, pious heathen who kept the Natural Law."[9] In another connection he taught that since *"Herr Omnes* [Mr. Everybody] is no Christian," then "The greatest necessity

[8] Luther, Serm. on War against the Turks, Plass anthol., vol. 3, 3029. Luther also taught that Satan, as the prince of this world, fights the order and authority which God has ordained wherever it may be found, "even the secular authority of the heathen." See Mueller, *op.cit.*, p. 41.

[9] Luther, "A Reply to the Twelve Articles of the Peasants in Swabia," Phil. ed., vol. 4, p. 231.

in the world is a strict temporal power. The world cannot be ruled according to the Gospel, for the sphere of influence which the Word has is too small and limited. The Word lays hold of few; not one man in a thousand will accept it. Therefore you cannot establish an external rule with it."[10]

Thus, Luther said elsewhere, "I have often taught that the world ought not and cannot be ruled according to the Gospel and Christian love."[11]

Now if the secular order cannot be effectively held together by exclusively New Testament standards, neither can drama, whose purpose is to reflect the secular order. What Luther said about man's life in this world is paralleled by Shakespeare's literary treatment of that life: in neither case is the general appeal made to a distinctively Christian ethic. I make no claim in this connection that Shakespeare's dramatic practice was consciously modeled on Luther's teachings, but the evidence does indicate a conformity between the two.

UNIVERSAL ETHIC AND THE REALM OF REASON

It was thus to natural law that Luther looked for the ordering of man's life and society within the temporal order.

[10] Luther, Serm. on I Tim. 1.18-20 and 2.1-2, Plass anthol., vol. 2, 1781. Mueller, *op.cit.*, p. 43, declares that "Luther considers it illusory to want to rule a whole country with the gospel. That would be like a shepherd trying to have within the same stable sheep, wolves, lions, eagles, and like animals. The sheep would indeed keep the peace, but their life would soon be cut off, nor would the other animals be at peace for long," and he quotes Luther as follows: "The world and the multitude is and remains un-Christian though they all be baptized and called Christians. But the true Christians dwell (as they say) far from one another and hence it will not do that one Christian government be in control over the whole world, or even over a single country or large groups of people. For there are always more wicked people than pious folk."

[11] Luther, "On Trade and Usury," Amer. ed., vol. 43, p. 264, and see also Weimar ed., vol. 11, p. 252.

The experience of man and the operation of his reason were sufficient guides for secular affairs, whereas the higher revelation of ethical imperatives by Christ could not maintain decency and order in a world which is overwhelmingly un-Christian, whatever pretensions worldly men may make to the contrary. In worldly affairs and government, Luther wrote, "men must be guided by reason (which is the source of human laws): for God has placed secular government and our physical state under the control of reason, and has not sent the Holy Spirit for that purpose."[12] Within the sphere assigned to it, the establishment of temporal order and well-being through the operation of reason is "an excellent gift of God, who ordained it, and who wishes to have it maintained as indispensable to human welfare; without it, men could not live together in society, but would devour one another like the irrational animals. Therefore . . . it is the function and honor of civil government to make men out of wild animals and to restrain them from degenerating into brutes."[13]

Entirely apart from special revelation, God provided the means for men to live on a civilized and humane plane in this world, and it was in pagan Greece and Rome that these means were most effectively developed and employed. So for secular concerns, man may well look to the classics as a kind of "natural revelation," if we may strain these two words by joining them here to indicate what the Reformers had in mind.

It may be helpful at this point to consider Calvin's distinctions between the three forms of grace. The ultimate and most valuable form was, of course, "saving grace," which releases man from bondage to sin and death and

[12] *Luther on Education*, p. 249.
[13] *Ibid.*, p. 243.

brings him into a true relationship with God and into the life everlasting. This operation of grace is distinctively Christian, and experienced only by the elect. But Calvin held that there were also "inferior operations of the Spirit."[14] Thus "general grace" comes to all men to guide them according to the principles of morality and reason, whereas "special grace" serves to provide those distinctive values and abilities, beyond the reach of ordinary men, which characterize the "break-through" achievements of great leaders in all fields. As to this special grace, Calvin wrote that "the same thing is taught elsewhere with respect to particular actions. Even in Homer, men are said to excel in natural ability not only as Jupiter has bestowed it upon each, but 'as he leads them day by day.' "[15] As God's general grace provides sustenance and guidance for all men, so this special grace singles out those who themselves contribute most remarkably to human well-being. Abraham Kuyper sums up the relevance of Calvin's thinking here for our major concerns: "But if Israel was chosen for the sake of religion, this in no way prevented a parallel election of the Greeks for the domain of philosophy and for the revelations of art, nor of the Romans for the classical development within the domain of Law and of State."[16] Here again we encounter the Reformers' careful preservation of the independence of the classical achievement from any theological dominance.

[14] Quoted from Calvin by McNeill in fn., *Inst.*, vol. 1, pp. 262-63. Note that "inferior" here means less valuable, rather than subject to theological oversight, and recall the treatment of theology as "queen" upon which the present chapter opened.

[15] Calvin, *Inst.* 2.2.17.

[16] Abraham Kuyper, *Calvinism*, Grand Rapids: Wm. B. Eerdmans, 1943, pp. 161-62.

At the same time we see here a difference between Luther and Calvin, for Luther said of the rational ordering of human life that God "has not sent the Holy Spirit from heaven to do this work," but has left it to the natural wisdom of men, whereas Calvin here saw an "inferior operation of the Spirit." The two men agreed, however, that such concerns were within the temporal sphere and that in this area an appeal to distinctively Christian revelation was not only unnecessary but often quite irrelevant. Though there was a difference of theological emphasis at this point, Luther and Calvin were both intent upon maintaining that, even apart from Christianity, men were enabled to lead successful and worthwhile lives and to organize peaceful and admirable societies. In these matters, indeed, the achievements of the heathen exceeded those of Christians and Jews.

When we view Shakespeare's dramatic practice against this background, we cannot demonstrate that he accepted these ideas, but we do say that their presence in the theological milieu of his culture made it unnecessary for him to appeal for dramatic sanction to explicitly Christian ethics. Their presence, indeed, made it quite proper for him to appeal only to the standards of natural law and general grace.

Further support for this conclusion may be found in the writings of Richard Hooker. "The law of Reason or human nature," Hooker declared, "is that which men by discourse of natural Reason have rightly found out themselves to be all forever bound unto in their actions."[17] Then, citing the classics in the manner with which we have become familiar, he continues: "Sophocles observeth concerning a breach of this law: 'It is no child of today's or yesterday's birth, but hath been no man knoweth how long sithence.' It is not

---

[17] Hooker, *Eccl. Pol.* 1.8.8.

agreed upon by one, or two, or few, but by all. . . . This law is such that being proposed no man can reject it as unreasonable and unjust. . . ; this law, I say, comprehendeth all those things which men by the light of their natural understanding evidently know, or at leastwise may know, to be beseeming or unbeseeming, virtuous or vicious, good or evil for them to do."[18]

The laws of reason and of human nature are neither purely human inventions nor purely human conventions arrived at for convenience, but are rather man's discovery by his own efforts of God's will for the best ordering of temporal life. We will recall here Calvin's judgment that for Christians to ignore the great wisdom of heathen man was not only manifest folly but even impiety towards God. In treating the same section of Scripture about which Calvin made those remarks, Hooker spoke as follows: "The Apostle St. Paul having speech concerning the heathen saith of them [Rom. 2.14]: 'They are a law unto themselves.' His meaning is, that by force of the light of Reason, wherewith God illuminateth every one which cometh into the world, men being enabled to know truth from falsehood, and good from evil, do thereby learn in many things what the will of God is; which will himself not revealing by any extraordinary means unto them, but they by natural discourse attaining the knowledge thereof, seem the makers of those Laws which indeed are his, and they but only the finders of them out."[19]

Hooker repeatedly underscored the common origin of the law of nature and the moral law of Scripture. He viewed the Scriptures as "principally delivered for instruction" in

[18] *Ibid.*, 1.8.9.
[19] *Ibid.*, 1.8.3.

man's supernatural relations and duties, but nonetheless, he wrote, Scripture "is fraught even with the laws of nature."[20] Indeed, the "law of nature and the moral law of Scripture are in the substance of law all one."[21] Luther and Calvin held the same view, and Luther declared that the moral law was not first revealed to Moses, but in fact "belongs to the whole world; it was written and engraved in the minds of all human beings from the beginning of the world."[22]

Thus, whether it be mediated through the revelation of Scripture or through the operations of reason, a common moral law is equally accessible to all societies, and all men are equally accountable to it. The Reformers were emphatic and consistent in denying that natural man, because he was shut off from Christian grace and revelation, was therefore shut off from the standards of moral conduct and of reason.[23] Luther makes the point quite clearly: "So far as moral precepts are concerned, one cannot find fault with the industry and earnestness of the heathen."[24] Though Luther, like Calvin and Hooker, denied that man could "come into heaven and God's kingdom" on the basis of temporal virtues, he emphasized that "it is true and undeniable, however, that

[20] *Ibid.*, 1.12.1.

[21] *Ibid.*, 3.9.2.

[22] Luther, "Second Disputation against the Antinomians," Plass anthol., vol. 2, 2311. For a further analysis of Luther's views, see Mueller, *op.cit.*, pp. 58 and 44, and Gerrish, *op.cit.*, pp. 13 and 137. For Calvin's similar views, see *Inst.* 2.2.24.

[23] In connection with all the evidence cited here, let us recall and evaluate the flat assertion of the prominent theologizer Miss M. D. H. Parker that for Luther and Calvin, heathen virtues were non-existent. See Parker's *The Slave of Life: A Study of Shakespeare and the Idea of Justice*, London: Chatto and Windus, 1955, p. 72. Miss Parker's error is a common one, unfortunately.

[24] Luther, Appendix to Exp. of Gen. 9.12-16, in Amer. ed., vol. 2, p. 160.

for himself and by virtue of his own powers a man can accustom himself to decency, respectability, and virtue. . . . There are many pious and honorable people in the world. These people have splendid, beautiful virtues; they do splendid, beautiful works. Everyone should be encouraged to have such virtues and to do such works."[25]

Calvin's position is essentially the same. "There is nothing more common," Calvin wrote, "than for a man to be sufficiently instructed in a right standard of conduct by natural law."[26] Or again: "In every age there have been persons who, guided by nature, have striven toward virtue throughout life. I have nothing to say against them even if many lapses can be noted in their moral conduct. For they have by the very zeal of their honesty given proof that there was some purity in their nature." Indeed, Calvin reiterated, many of the heathen "conducted themselves most honorably throughout life."[27] Man's "total depravity," then, emphatically did not imply that he was totally evil in a temporal sense; it only meant that in all its parts (hence "totally") man's nature was so marred by sin that he could not at any point in his life act so purely as to merit God's grace and the life everlasting. Though man was utterly incapable of reasoning with sufficient clarity to arrive at a true knowledge of God, or of acting out of pure enough motives to achieve

[25] Luther, Serm. on John 3.1-15, Plass anthol., vol. 3, 3891. Gerrish, op.cit., p. 74, summarizes as follows: "But what sort of righteousness can reason, with the law's assistance, attain to? The answer is: 'civil righteousness,' not the kind which avails a man before God. So Luther tries to hold two points together: God approves the righteousness which reason can attain—indeed, not merely approves (approbat), but demands (requirit)—and yet this is not the kind of righteousness which is necessary for justification."

[26] Calvin, Inst. 2.2.22.

[27] Ibid., 2.3.3, and see also 3.14.2.

his own salvation, men could within the civil orders of this world act with sufficient morality and wisdom to warrant great admiration. "We know that men, above all other living beings, have the singular superiority of having been endowed with reason and intelligence, and that they have engraved in their consciences the ability to discriminate between right and wrong."[28] At another point, Calvin underscores the key issues as follows: "To sum up: We see among all mankind that reason is proper to our nature; it distinguishes us from brute beasts, just as they by possessing feeling differ from inanimate things."[29] Thus there "is ample proof that in the arrangement of this life no man is without the light of reason" and "some seed of political order has been implanted in all men."[30]

In conclusion, then, we see that however much men may in fact ignore or distort the directives of reason and however they may disrupt moral order in society, they are rendered inexcusable by the very facts of their nature. Even though man has fallen from all possibility of achieving salvation and life in the heavenly city, he has not so far fallen as to have cut himself off from the possibility of achieving honor, well-being, and admirable virtue in an earthly society. Luther, Calvin, and Hooker were united in the conviction that man could achieve these ends on the basis of following the guidance of nature, reason, and conscience, even apart from a specifically Christian revelation and ethic.

The sixteenth-century Protestant views reconstructed here are of considerable importance for appraising the essentially

[28] Calvin, Exp. John 1.9-10, in *Commentaries*, trans. Joseph Haroutunian, Philadelphia: The Westminster Press, 1958, p. 133. Hereafter, this volume will be referred to as *Commentaries* (Haroutunian).

[29] Calvin, *Inst.* 2.2.17.

[30] *Ibid.*, 2.2.13.

secular character of Shakespeare's drama. The preceding chapter demonstrated that the major Protestant theologians inculcated an understanding of literature and the liberal arts as concerned primarily with temporal matters, and the present chapter has shown how the same theologians taught that for the purely temporal and secular arena, a universal moral law was even more relevant than an ethic distinctively based in the New Testament. The evidence presented here does not put us in a position to determine Shakespeare's own beliefs. It does demonstrate, however, that his dramatic practice of finding sanctions in a universal rather than in an exclusively Christian system of ethical values puts him in close accord with the teachings of the major theologians of the Reformation period.

SUMMARY

Everyone recognizes that in Shakespeare's age literature was expected to teach as well as to delight, but the evidence presented here conclusively shows that such teaching, at least in the judgment of the most representative and influential theologians, was not expected to be restricted to particularly Christian doctrines either in theology or in ethics. On the strength of this evidence we should be careful not to seek for Christian doctrine in the Shakespearean dramas except where there is explicit and unmistakable evidence of its presence. Nor should we exercise ourselves in deciding which of Shakespeare's characters are saved and which are damned. Here we should keep in mind Luther's assertion that "he who would look at an act as such sees no difference between a Christian and a non-Christian," and we should recall that Calvin saw little if any thing to distinguish believers from unbelievers.[31] As for attempting to determine the state in grace of Shakespeare's stage characters on the basis of their righteousness and honesty, we would do well to follow the example of Hooker: "As for those virtues that belong unto moral righteousness and honesty of life, we do not mention them, because they are not proper [i.e., not restricted] unto Christian men as they are Christian, but do concern them as they are men."[32] Even the instances of mercy and pity which Shakespeare so beautifully dramatized do not necessarily indicate any Christian commitment on the part of the stage characters who perform them, and we should be warily suspicious of those critics who try to convince us otherwise. It is well to remember here the teaching of Calvin, as summarized by Ronald Wallace, that even an act of unforced love and kindness "on the part of the rich towards the poor is merely a payment of what is 'due by the law of nature.' It is to be regarded as merely the expression of a natural feeling of humanity that all men should have towards each other. A Christian will take no special pride in discharging such a duty. Even heathen writers teach that all are born for the sake of mankind and that the life of society can be properly cultivated only by the interchange of such good offices among men. God has so ordered human life that no one can be self-sufficient."[33] We have had too much theology "read

[31] Luther, Serm. on Luke 5.1-11, Plass anthol., vol. 3, 4910. This position is related to Luther's teaching that "Ecclesia est abscondita" and travels incognito, as Mueller reminds us, op.cit., p. 10. For a discussion of Calvin's comparable position, see Ronald S. Wallace, *Calvin's Doctrine of the Christian Life*, Grand Rapids: Wm. B. Eerdmans, 1959, p. 84.

[32] Hooker, *Eccl. Pol.* 3.1.7.

[33] Wallace, *op.cit.*, pp. 153f.

into" Shakespeare by critics who have not first read enough out of the theologians. Under these circumstances it may be ironic, but it is surely fitting, that the three most influential and representative Protestant theologians of the sixteenth century should be brought to the defense of Shakespeare's magnificent independence against the theologizing interpretations of modern critics.

PART THREE ✦ SHAKESPEARE'S THEOLOGICAL
REFERENCES: A TOPICAL
ANALYSIS AND APPRAISAL

SHAKESPEARE'S THEOLOGICAL REFERENCES: A TOPICAL ANALYSIS AND APPRAISAL

I. PERSPECTIVE

Thus far in our study of Shakespeare and theology we have dealt primarily with broad approaches and general understandings. We now come to a quite different aspect of the subject: Shakespeare's specific uses of doctrines and ideas which are also to be found in the theologians. There are a great many such uses, more indeed than have sometimes been noticed. It should not surprise us that we find, in a writer whose dramatic concerns are bounded by the temporal order, a considerable number of theological references, for religion has always been an important element of man's existence. Any mirror held up to reflect all of man's life will therefore reflect many instances of theological interest, even though theology does not dominate the dramatic whole or form the ultimate referent of its meanings.

So it is that we find a fairly wide range of theological subjects and materials in Shakespeare. In every instance where these are treated at sufficient length to allow us to judge the author's theological sophistication, I find a rather advanced level of knowledge and understanding, though the knowledge is clearly that of a layman and not of a professional. What is primarily impressive is the aptness of the treatment of doctrine to the dramatic characters involved and to the course of the action. As is true with other subjects upon which Shakespeare drew for his character's speeches, whether in allusion, metaphor, or direct comment, we note a typically Shakespearean facility for turning everything to his dramatic and poetic purposes.

Striking instances of this Shakespearean facility for adapting non-dramatic materials to his dramatic purposes may be seen in the assignment of theological and ethical comments to pagan characters. As usual there are a few anachronisms, and—also as usual—these are minor.[1] Indeed, it is fair to say that in almost no important instance are the pagan characters endowed with more theological insight or spiritual power than was credited to them by one or another of our three representative theologians. I am not suggesting that Shakespeare would have gotten his ideas only from the theologians, for obviously he knew the classics quite well, but it is worthy of note that his own treatment of heathen religion and ethics corresponds with theological observations on the same subject. The parallels with Calvin in this regard are most striking, possibly because Calvin appears to have had more classical learning than either Luther or Hooker and certainly makes more allusions to classical life and culture. When Shakespeare has his pagans pray effectively, refer to God in terms of divine fatherhood and mercy, express faith in life after death, deal mercifully and show pity, he is not (as the theologizers sometimes tell us) adumbrating explicitly Christian doctrines; on the contrary, he is merely mirroring attitudes which classicist and theologian alike credited to the pagan world.[2]

---

[1] See, for example, W.T. 2.3.114f.

[2] For instances of the treatment of these matters by Shakespeare and the theologians, see below under the headings PRAYER, GOD, DEATH, MERCY, and PITY. Recall, too, the opinion of J. A. K. Thomson, expressed in *Shakespeare and the Classics*, London: George Allen and Unwin, Ltd., 1952, p. 253: "There are indications, in *Cymbeline* and elsewhere, that Shakespeare was not unaware of the paganism of some of the sentiments appropriate to his characters." When Thomson continues, however, to say

Nor is there any lack of appropriateness to character in the doctrinal references and statements which Shakespeare assigns to characters under the Christian dispensation. Characterization is sometimes served by the expression of explicitly Christian beliefs and opinions, or by references to them, and where this is the case Shakespeare shows an apt knowledge of the theological doctrines he employs. Shakespeare certainly does not display a professional concern with theology, but at the same time I think it is fair to say that one who is versed in historical theology will be impressed by the extent of Shakespeare's knowledge and the pertinency with which he puts that knowledge to use. Shakespeare does not devote his writings to theological ends, but where doctrines are treated in the plays they are treated with sufficient sophistication to show that Shakespeare had an intelligent and informed lay knowledge of theology.

Concerned as he was with the universally human, Shakespeare found considerable dramatic relevance in the Christian treatments of sin. In the Christian understanding, sin is, after all, a universal element of human experience where saving grace is not, and the theological analyses of sin, guilt, and misery would have seemed to Elizabethans to have a relevance to all human situations. The theology of sin thus appears to have been quite serviceable to Shakespeare, whereas the theology of grace was less so.

I hope it will be borne in mind in connection with such statements, here and elsewhere, that I am referring to the limited dramatic relevance of saving grace. It will be recalled

---

that since Shakespeare was not theologically minded, "we need not suppose that he gave much thought to the matter," he seems to go beyond the evidence. How much thought Shakespeare gave, we can never know, but it was enough to insure considerable aptness to his use of theological references within his dramatic situations.

that there were two other orders of grace: general grace, which applied to all men as men, and special grace, which inspired the particularly gifted to live and think and work at a level above that which was accessible to the majority of men. If we wish to speak in these terms, the two latter orders of grace furnish the principal arena for Shakespeare's dramatic action. We have seen that Calvin and the other theologians made it unmistakably clear that intelligent Christians could not confine their interest or attention only to the area of saving grace and revelation. We thus find the theologians concerned with doctrines and approaches which, strictly speaking, are not originally Christian, or which are not exclusively Christian.

There are thus many areas which might be called intermediate, where the treatment of ideas and the approach to situations might almost equally well be that of a Christian or of a heathen wisdom. Just as the Christian analysis of sin might be aptly applied to non-Christian situations, so too aspects of non-Christian wisdom could be incorporated into the Christian tradition, and such a process of borrowing from pagan sources had been going on since the days of the early church. Christianity found many attitudes already present in the virtuous heathen which corresponded to the ethical teachings of the Mosaic law, and we have seen that Luther, Calvin, and Hooker valued classical ethical systems as quite appropriate to the conduct of society in the temporal sphere. In addition, there were certain distinctively classical ideas—especially those concerned with reason and its operations—which some patristic theologians adapted to Christian purposes and which remained an important part of the Christian tradition thereafter. We treat these intermediate subjects here with the full recognition that they can be traced to non-Christian as well as to Christian sources, but their incorporation within the great theological works makes it proper for them to appear in our analysis.

What follows is an alphabetical list of Shakespeare's treatment of theological subjects, with related comments on the same subjects by the theologians. Some Shakespearean references have been purposely omitted as too obvious to require comment, while others are omitted as too esoteric or doubtful in their intent, and there are probably still others which have been omitted by oversight. Inclusion has been based on the inherent interest of the uses and on an attempt to represent the range of Shakespeare's references, but I make no pretense at providing an exhaustive catalogue.

Treatment of the same themes by one or more of our three basic theologians are given along with Shakespeare's lines, so as to illustrate in some measure the theological currency and meaning of the ideas which Shakespeare employs, and also to throw light or provide perspective on Shakespeare's expression of these ideas. In no sense is this a source study: it is only in isolated instances that we see where Shakespeare may have picked up a few phrases, but even in these cases the association is no more than a possible one, and I make no claims of influence.

Though it seems clear to me that Shakespeare was theologically well-informed, I have not found it possible to trace his theological reading in any definitive way. In the Roman plays we can find clear marks of his having consulted his source in North's Plutarch, and at times there is even an almost word-for-word reproduction of North's phrases. The same or similar close association may also be noted in Shakespeare's use of certain Biblical materials, but so far as I have been able to discover there was no such adherence to any theological source. The ideas Shakespeare employs were usual in theology, and he appears to have written them down out of a familiar understanding. His primary concerns were not theological, and there was no need for him to give close allegiance to any text. His use of Christian theology is thus more nearly conversational—the easy phrasing of well-known doctrines as the need arose—than was true of his treatment of certain other sources.

In providing theological counterpoints to Shakespeare's dramatic use of theological material, I have in general restricted myself to the writings of Luther, Calvin, and Hooker. Since it has not been possible to demonstrate conclusively which were the particular theologians and the precise theological works that influenced Shakespeare, it has seemed best to select these three men, who most fully represent the major currents at work in the religious milieu of Shakespeare's time and culture. Furthermore, I have, with but few exceptions, cited doctrinal material only from these theologians, for unless some limit had been placed on the treatment of the doctrines and ideas listed below, that treatment would have expanded out of all proportion. We are not, after all, interested in tracing the full history of these doctrines (to many of which many volumes have already been devoted), but only in illustrating and illumining Shakespeare's usage. For this purpose, Luther, Calvin, and Hooker are helpful not only because of the influence which they exerted, but also because of the fact that they were carefully preserving what they regarded as basic Christian positions. None regarded himself as originating new doctrines; each was interested in summarizing and applying to his own time essential Christian doctrines which had long since been formulated and which had, through many centuries of Christian teaching, become commonplaces of Western thought and life.

✧ *Affliction*

Affliction and adversity are repeatedly found in Shake-spearean drama, but in considering the relation to theology of their employment by Shakespeare, it is important to remember that affliction and adversity do not in themselves represent marks of salvation. A confusion sometimes occurs here when it is assumed that Lear's noble bearing of afflic-tion means that he is saved, whereas Shakespeare has not used terms which his contemporaries would have regarded as recognizable marks of Christian salvation. Shakespeare simply does not raise the issue of salvation in connection with Lear, and it is therefore wise for us as readers to judge Lear's growth in terms of non-Christian and classical norms, not going beyond such judgments as that expressed by Aeschylus when he remarked that Zeus "has laid it down that wisdom comes alone through suffering."[1]

The theologians repeatedly made clear that suffering as such had no Christian significance. Luther states the point quite clearly when he declares that both the virtuous heathen and also "many reckless villains and rough people" bear pain and death with nobility and patience, but he unequiv-ocally denies that any such patience in affliction produces redemption. To assume that one's noble bearing of pain and death atones for one's sins is to "deny God and his Christ, blaspheme his grace and pervert his gospel."[2] Whereas we sometimes hear Lear's reference to his "crosses"[3] cited as an indication of his redemption, Luther stated quite emphati-cally of the sufferings which men bear that "our cross does not save us."[4]

It is true, of course, that there are such things as Christian affliction and the growth in grace through affliction, and we will treat these matters in connection with the afflictions of Richard II under the entry entitled HEAVEN. There is, in addition, a brief reference to affliction as a means of saving grace in the hybrid play *Henry VIII*, where Griffith describes Cardinal Wolsey's end in these terms:

> His overthrow heap'd happiness upon him;
> For then, and not till then, he felt himself
> And found the blessedness of being little.
> And, to add greater honors to his age
> Than man could give him, he died fearing God.[5]

[1] Aeschylus, *Agamemnon*, 177f., trans. Richmond Lattimore, in *The Complete Greek Tragedies: Aeschylus*, Chicago: University of Chicago Press, 1959, p. 40.

[2] Luther, Serm. on Luke 18.31-43, Lenker ed., vol. 11, pp. 127f.

[3] *Lear* 5.3.278.

[4] Luther, Serm. on day of Helena's finding of the cross, May 3, 1522, Weimar ed., vol. 10 III, p. 119.

[5] *Henry VIII* 4.2.64ff.

✦ *Atonement*

The Atonement holds a central place in Christian theology, but, as we have already seen, Christians were not accustomed to seeing it given such a place in literature. We do not find that Shakespeare has treated the subject in more than passing references, and of these three may be taken as the fullest of his expressions.

In *2 Henry VI* Warwick addresses to the King what Suffolk aptly describes as "a dreadful oath, sworn with a solemn tongue," used to underscore an accusation:

> As surely as my soul intends to live
> With that dread King that took our state upon him

To free us from his Father's wrathful curse,
I do believe that violent hands were laid
Upon the life of this thrice-famed duke.[1]

In *Richard III* Clarence uses a reference to the Atonement
to solemnize an appeal to his murderers:

I charge you, as you hope to have redemption
By Christ's dear blood shed for our grievous sins,
That you depart, and lay no hands on me.[2]

The appeal is an apt one under the circumstances, for
Clarence is suggesting to the murderers that by slaying him
they would wilfully exclude themselves from the benefits
of the Atonement. Another apt appeal to the Atonement
comes in Isabella's plea that Angelo show mercy to her
brother, a plea which is placed against the background of
Christ's redemption of man:

Why, all the souls that were, were forfeit once;
And he that might the vantage best have took
Found out the remedy.[3]

In each of these instances, the treatment of the Atonement
is appropriate to the immediate dramatic situation of character and plot, and in each the reference is in terms of such
commonplace ideas as not to require theological commentary here. In no instance do we find the Atonement given
more detailed attention in the plays than in these quite restricted uses. As for the tendency among theologizing critics
to read the afflictions of men and women in Shakespearean
drama as though they somehow represented atonements
for sin, nothing could be more futile, theologically speaking.
A certain civil and temporal purification and even ennoble-
ment may come from human affliction, rightly borne, but

we should not confuse these effects so as to suppose that the plays were concerned with Christian salvation. (See above, under AFFLICTION), Luther warns us against such a confusion of civil and theological categories: "the human race has no satisfaction for sins except the civil one, which the state requires. But this satisfaction has nothing to do with theology. *It* has only one Sacrifice: Christ, our Lord, who rendered satisfaction to the wrath of God."[4] Shakespeare makes only quite rare, and even then quite restricted, references to this sacrifice and satisfaction.

[1] *2 Henry VI* 3.2.153ff.   [2] *Rich. III* 1.4.194ff.
[3] *M. for M.* 2.2.73ff.
[4] Luther, Exp. Gen. 42.6-7, Plass anthol., vol. 3, 4569.

✦ Autonomous Man

An essential element of sin is the creature's assertion of independence from the Creator, and from normative relations with other creatures. In the world of Milton's *Paradise Lost*, this assertion takes a predominantly theological form, when Lucifer denies that he was created by God;[1] in Shakespeare's plays, it takes a predominantly ethical form, when the dramatic characters assert their independence from each other. Thus Coriolanus, even in making an assertion of autogeny not unlike that of Milton's Lucifer, is not thinking of his relations to God, but of his relations to his mother and family. As his wife, mother, and son approach, he repudiates them all:

> But out, affection!
> All bond and privilege of nature, break! . . .
> . . . I'll never
> Be such a gosling to obey instinct, but stand

As if a man were author of himself
And knew no other kin.[2]

Shakespeare's point is clear within the drama, for Coriolanus' temporary denial of his familial ties puts him on
the brink of the ultimate destruction of order. Luther
affirmed the common consensus that without order and
obedience in the home, there could be no peace or stability
in city or nation, for the family bond is the most basic of
all the bonds of civilized society.[3] It is of course true that a
child may be absolved from allegiance to a parent under
certain circumstances, as for example with Jessica and
Shylock, but in general the family tie is basic to what is
humane in life. In *King Lear* much can be said of the old
king's folly, but that folly never went so far as to justify the
inhuman response to him on the part of Regan and Goneril,
and Albany summarizes the case against the autonomous
pretension when he speaks to Goneril:

> I fear your disposition.
> That nature which contemns it origin
> Cannot be bordered certain in itself.
> She that herself will sliver and disbranch
> From her material sap, perforce must wither
> And come to deadly use.[4]

The same ethical point is made by Calvin: "Now it is an
ugly and unnatural thing that the child should not know
those by whom he came into the world, and by whom he
was nourished and brought up. Therefore if the child dis-
dain his father or his mother, he is a monster and every man
will abhor him."[5] In quite similar terms, Albany sees Goneril's "vile offences" as implying that

> Humanity must perforce prey on itself,
> Like monsters of the deep.[6]

The autonomous pretense appears quite clearly in Richard III, who repudiates all the bonds of nature relating him to other men:

> I have no brother; I am like no brother.
> And this word "love," which greybeards call divine,
> Be resident in men like one another,
> And not in me![7]

If Richard's denial of fraternal relation to other men were treated in terms of a complete system of theology it would include within itself a denial of relationship to God, but again Shakespeare's dramatic focus is on relationships within the temporal order. The consequences upon himself of Richard's repudiation of such relationships are in keeping with the theologians' tracing of the consequences of sin. Commenting on Isaiah 58:7 ("And that thou hide not thyself from thine own flesh"), Calvin writes: "Here we ought to observe the term *flesh*, by which he means all men universally, not one of whom we can behold without seeing, as in a mirror, 'our own flesh.' It is therefore a proof of the greatest inhumanity to despise those in whom we are constrained to recognize our own likeness."[8] The progress of sin runs its full course in Richard, until he declares

> Alas, I rather hate myself,

and

> I myself
> Find in myself no pity to myself.[9]

The dramatic degeneration of Richard follows the traditional conception of the course of sin, which Calvin summarizes as follows: "man cannot injure man, but he becomes an enemy to his own flesh, and violates and perverts the whole order of nature."[10]

[1] John Milton, *Paradise Lost*, v, 860-64.
[2] *Coriol.* 5.3.24f. and 34ff.
[3] Luther, Serm. for Nov. 5, 1525, Weimar ed., vol. 16, p. 500.
[4] *Lear* 4.2.31ff.
[5] Calvin, *Sermons on Deuteronomy* (5.16), Golding trans., London, 1583, p. 213.
[6] *Lear* 4.2.49f.   [7] *3 Henry VI* 5.6.80ff.
[8] Calvin, *Commentaries on Isaiah*, vol. 4, p. 234.
[9] *Rich. III* 5.3.190 and 203f.
[10] Calvin, *Commentary on Genesis* (37.25-27), vol. 2, p. 270.

✦ Beasts, Beastliness, and Humanity

The concern for man's relationship to the beasts is ancient and widespread. We find here one of the overlapping areas between the Graeco-Latin and the Biblical traditions, for in both traditions man was regarded as occupying a middle ground between the beasts of the field and the heavenly creatures, though the distinctions were variously made. The classical and Scriptural understandings buttressed each other here, and their merging in the patristic period was reinforced in the Renaissance and Reformation. Zwingli, the humanist scholar, friend of Erasmus, and early Protestant leader, summarized the issue as it was understood generally in his age: "we are set here between the hammer and the anvil, half beast and half angel."[1]

Shakespeare makes frequent use of this classical and Christian conception of man, and repeatedly refers to it at critical points in his dramas. It is fair to say that, though he rarely introduces references to the God-man as savior, he consistently refers to the man-beast as specter. His treatment of the relation between human and animal nature is often quite similar to that of the theologians, as we will see by comparison between his words and theirs. This comparison will not yield any substantively new understanding, for Lovejoy and others have amply clarified the significance of the great chain of being, but it may indicate the spread of these ideas along an axis which has not been so fully explored. Again, we are not engaged in a source study, and I am not suggesting that Shakespeare's expressions derived from this or that theologian, but only that there is a close consistency between Shakespearean and theological usage when both treat this aspect of man's relation to other creatures.

Theologians, like other Renaissance men, made much of reason and language as distinguishing marks between man and the beasts. When the Wittenberg student Hamlet says that a beast "wants discourse of reason,"[2] he joins reason and language in a fashion typical of the sixteenth century, as does the Wittenberg professor Luther, who says of "the faculty of speech" that "by this activity alone man is set apart from all animals,"[3] and also that reason is "the essential difference by which man is distinguished from animals and other things."[4] Though reason is limited, clouded with ignorance, and unable to reach unaided to God, it is essential to the life of man in this world, as we have seen in earlier chapters. "Alienated from right reason," Calvin declares, "man is almost like the cattle of the field."[5] Again Calvin defines man as "a rational being, differing from brute beasts, because he is endowed with understanding"[6] and writes that when men turn from "a true judgment" they "become brutish in themselves," while we are reminded in *Hamlet* that if we are separated from "fair judgment" then "we are pictures or mere beasts."[7] Related to this distinguishing quality is Hamlet's reference to "that capability and godlike reason," which will be treated below under the entry REASON.

Though man has about him a godlike quality, he can readily reduce himself to the bestial level. Hooker asks: "Is it not wonderful that base desires should so extinguish in men the sense of their own excellency, as to make them willing that their souls should be like to the souls of beasts, mortal and corruptible like their bodies?"[8] Hamlet raises a similar question:

> What is a man,
> If his chief good and market of his time
> Be but to sleep and feed? A beast, no more.[9]

With Hamlet and Hooker, these questions are essentially rhetorical, as both have answers ready for the questions as soon as they are asked.

In *King Lear*, however, such problems are raised with far greater urgency, even when they are not stated in the technical form of a question. In one sense, the entire tragedy is concerned with questioning the relation between human and animal nature. Gloucester recalls Tom o'Bedlam as a fellow "which made me think a man a worm" and Edgar himself had earlier chosen this particular disguise so as

> To take the basest and most poorest shape
> That ever penury, in contempt of man,
> Brought near to beast.[10]

Edgar's brother Edmund chose to follow a nature goddess in whom are apotheosized all the more vicious and animalistic qualities, as the play presents to us varied and catalytic views of man's relation to nature as a whole, to his own human nature, and to the animal nature which he finds both without and also within himself.

It is Lear, of course, who strips the matter to its heart, and of Tom he declares that "unaccommodated man is no more but such a poor, bare, forked animal," and we recall Calvin's declaration that "as to body there was no real difference between men and the dumb beasts."[11] Lear is passionately concerned with the significance of this identity in body between "unaccommodated man" and "a poor, bare, forked animal." He assumes that there is more to man, and reproaches his daughters accordingly:

> Allow not nature more than nature needs,
> Man's life is cheap as beast's.[12]

Calvin makes a similar assumption (and admits that Christians were not the only ones to make it) when he attacks those who would regard man as no better than the beasts: "Let them, then, if they will, make a living soul common to man and to the brutes, since in so far as the body is concerned they have all the same life, but let them not employ this as an argument for confounding the soul of man with the brutes."[13]

Goneril, Regan, and their adherents act on the assumption, contrary to Lear's hope, that man's life is as cheap as beast's, with results which are admirably summarized in Albany's words:

> If that the heavens do not their visible spirits
> Send quickly down to tame these vile offences,
> It will come,
> Humanity must perforce prey on itself,
> Like monsters of the deep.[14]

Albany's reference to the intervention of "the heavens" will be treated under the entry on Providence, but what concerns us here is Albany's concern for a predatory humanity. It was a commonplace among authorities on ethics that where power was disjoined from order and law, man would be reduced to an animal-like existence. "Those who take [civil order] from man deprive him of his very humanity," according to Calvin,[15] while Luther warned that where force is held to be ultimately decisive (as with Goneril, Regan, and Edmund) "it will result in a life like that in the wild woods among irrational animals, where one animal devours another: the fox devours the rabbit, the wolf the fox, and the bear usually tears apart the wolf. So it would be among men under a government of mere force."[16] Tyrants and rebels are alike—and we should recall that Goneril and Regan were both rebels against their father and tyrants over others—in that both reduce humanity to an animal level. Of those "that are disobedient to lawful superiority" Calvin wrote that they "are as enemies to God and nature, and to all mankind: yea, they be as monsters whom all men ought to abhor," while Luther wrote of the lawless ruler that "because he has the opportunity to do evil and go unpunished, he sets off on this course and acts like a wild beast . . . , does only what pleases himself" and, though he may be a prince in name, is in reality a "savage animal."[17] In these expressions, as in many others we quote, Luther and Calvin were but voicing the opinion of a long tradition, which in this instance found dramatic expression in Albany's fear that "Humanity must perforce prey on itself, Like monsters of the deep."

---

[1] Ulrich Zwingli, "Of the Education of Youth," in *Zwingli and Bullinger,*

G. W. Bromiley trans., Philadelphia: The Westminster Press, 1953, p. 106.

[2] *Ham.* 1.2.150.

[3] Luther, *Table Talk*, Plass anthol., vol. 2, 2264.

[4] Luther, "Disputation Concerning Man," Amer. ed. vol. 34, p. 137.

[5] Calvin, Serm. on Gen. 6.3, quoted in Torrance, *op.cit.*, p. 102.

[6] Calvin, *Inst.* 2.2.12.

[7] *Ham.* 4.5.85f., and Calvin, Serm. on Deut. 4.3f., quoted in Torrance, p. 103.

[8] Hooker, *Eccl. Pol.* 5.2.1.   [9] *Ham.* 4.4.33ff.

[10] *Lear* 4.1.36 and 2.3.4ff.

[11] *Lear* 3.4.112 and Calvin, Exp. Mal. 1.2-6, in *Commentaries* (Haroutunian), p. 292.

[12] *Lear* 2.4.269f.

[13] Calvin, *Psychopannychia* in *Tracts*, vol. 3, p. 451.

[14] *Lear* 4.2.46ff.   [15] Calvin, *Inst.* 4.20.2.

[16] Luther, Exp. of Deut. 1.13, Plass anthol., vol. 2, 1794.

[17] Luther, Exp. of Magnificat, *Reformation Writings*, vol. 2, p. 188, and Calvin, *Sermons on Deuteronomy* (5.16), p. 217b. It may be of interest to some readers to compare Calvin's condemnation of disobedience to "lawful superiority" in this passage with his approbation of the right of "lesser magistrates" to oppose the unlawful actions of even a duly constituted ruler. See *Inst.* 4.20.30-32.

✦ Bible

Shakespeare's knowledge of the Bible, and his use of Biblical allusions for dramatic purposes, have been so thoroughly studied by Richmond Noble that no direct attention is given to these matters here, and the reader has already been referred to Noble's book, *Shakespeare's Biblical Knowledge and Use of the Book of Common Prayer.*

✦ Contentment

Contentment and happiness are subjects of universal human concern and as such are treated both by classical and by Christian thinkers. To a considerable extent their conclusions overlap, whereas at other points the Christian attitude appears to be distinctive. Old Gaunt's advice to his banished son Bolingbroke could as well be Greek as Christian:

> All places that the eye of heaven visits
> Are to a wise man ports and happy havens.[1]

Similarly, Calvin's remark could as well be that of a pagan wise man: "This mockery of fools for reposing in the slippery and fleeting 'blessings' of the world shows in the first place that the wise should seek a far different kind of happiness."[2] Lady Macbeth's lament is equally universal:

> Naught's had, all's spent,
> Where our desire is got without content.[3]

In a parallel vein, Calvin's comment again is that of a general human wisdom when he writes of the prosperity of the wicked: "While they live so turbulent a life, even though they may be lords of the earth a hundred times over, having everything, they possess nothing."[4]

In *Richard II*, we find a different and more distinctively Christian analysis of contentment in terms of possessing nothing. In prison, the degraded and newly humbled Richard speaks of himself as follows:

> But whate'er I be,
> Nor I, nor any man that but man is,
> With nothing shall be pleas'd till he be eas'd
> With being nothing.[5]

"God is the God of the humble," Luther writes, "and of those that are brought even to nothing," while on another occasion he declares that God's "way is to make something out of nothing—life out of death, righteousness out of sin, honor out of shame, riches out of poverty."[6] It may be, of course, that Richard here is merely referring to death, and is saying only that man will not be content so long as he is alive, but if he is (as I think more likely in his case) speaking in more decidedly Christian terms, then we may find the whole tradition to which he refers summarized when Calvin quotes Augustine quoting Cyprian: "For what else does this statement of Cyprian mean which Augustine so often repeats: 'We ought to glory in nothing, because nothing is ours,' except that man, rendered utterly destitute in his own right, should learn to depend wholly on God?"[7]

[1] *Rich. II* 1.3.276f.   [2] Calvin, *Inst.* 2.10.17.   [3] *Macb.* 3.2.5f.

[4] Calvin, Exp. Matt 5.5, *Commentaries* (Haroutunian), p. 337.

[5] *Rich. II* 5.5.38ff.

[6] Luther, Exp. Gal. 3.19, *Commentary on Galatians*, trans. Erasmus Middleton, London: William Tegg and Co., 1850, p. 244, and Serm. on Matt. 11.25-30, Plass anthol., vol. 2, 2093.

[7] Calvin, *Inst.* 2.2.9.

✦ Death

We have already had occasion to consider, in an earlier chapter, Robert Stevenson's accurate appraisal of Shakespeare's deathbeds.[1] Although there are a few characters who meet death in the plays with some indication of Christian faith and hope, most do not give us any such indication. It is equally true, furthermore, that most of the comments on death by Shakespeare's characters could as well be made by Greeks or Romans as by Christians. This is not to say that such comments are therefore un-Christian, for Christianity contains not only unique features but many elements common to human wisdom everywhere. The point to be emphasized is that Shakespeare was not writing plays which can be theologically categorized as pro-Christian or anti-

Christian, but that he was primarily concerned with the life of man within the secular order, where Christian and non-Christian ideas frequently overlap and coincide.

Most of us would expect that characters in Shakespeare's pre-Christian plays would not talk Christian doctrine, and we find this expectation to be correct, whatever attempts may be made by the theologizers to convert common wisdom into exclusivist dogma. Pericles declares of death:

> For death remembered should be like a mirror,
> Who tells us life's but breath, to trust it error.[2]

The thought sounds eminently pious, as indeed it is on any count, but its piety is not exclusively Christian, as Calvin reminds us: "And even the Paynims have said, that there is not anything but death which showeth how small a thing man is. . . . So then death showeth us what we be, and what is our nature; and yet nevertheless ye shall see many strive against that necessity."[3] The fact that such an admirable thought was not uniquely Christian did not disturb Calvin; by the same token I suggest that it would not have disturbed Shakespeare's Jacobean audiences, nor would it have set them to thinking of Pericles in Christian terms. The same observation applies to Hermione's contempt for death in *The Winter's Tale* when she declares in her distress:

> Tell me what blessings I have here alive
> That I should fear to die.[4]

A remark of Luther's is apropos here in which he points out that the wise heathen feared death little, indeed "highly and honorably esteemed it," and though for Luther as a preacher this observation served as a point of departure for Christian exhortation, we have already seen that Luther

himself did not expect such Christian exhortation in literature.[5] That Hermione often speaks and acts with piety and
wisdom is true, but it does not follow that she should for
these reasons be considered a type of Christ.

It is not only the pre-Christian characters who speak of
death in universal terms. Compare Richard II's famous remarks on death,

> Nothing can we call our own but death
> And that small model of the barren earth
> Which serves as paste and cover to our bones[6]

with Calvin's citation of heathen agreement to the effect
that though our greed for power and wealth could "swallow
up the whole earth," yet nevertheless when "we be once
dead, we must have no more ground than our own length,
wherein to rot and consume away to nothing."[7] A similar
reference comes in Warwick's dying recognition that there
"is nothing left me but my body's length."[8] Such expressions are essentially commonplaces both of the classical
and the Christian traditions, as are most of Shakespeare's
treatments of death.

The references to expectation of the Christian heaven are
few, and in their dramatic treatment they are so muted as
to suggest that Shakespeare wished to provide this particular
stroke of characterization within the limits of a stage play
without attracting the attention of his audience beyond
the bounds of his major concern for dramatizing the temporal order. Had Shakespeare wished us to extrapolate our
interest in his characters beyond the final lines he wrote
about those characters and the final lines of the plays in
which they figure, he would surely have done more to direct
our attention to the afterlife. References to heaven are not

only rare but exceedingly brief, as a few examples will remind us: There is Warwick's "Warwick bids you all farewell, to meet in heaven,"[9] and King Edward's expectation of an embassage "From my Redeemer to redeem me hence,"[10] while even Richard II says only:

Mount, mount, my soul! thy seat is up on high;
Whilst my gross flesh sinks downward, here to die.[11]

Such expressions are essentially commonplaces, varied from immemorial usage only enough to make poetic what might otherwise have been a mere cliché or platitude. This judgment applies even to the most famous of such sentiments in Shakespeare, Horatio's address to the dead Hamlet:

Good night, sweet prince,
And flights of angels sing thee to thy rest![12]

The "Good night" refers to the conception of death as sleep which we have already discussed,[13] while the remainder of the expression picks up various conceptions which had long since passed into common usage from Biblical references to angelic choirs and to the angels who carried Lazarus to Abraham's bosom. For centuries the Latin burial service (still in use among sixteenth-century Roman Catholics and also employed at the burial of that original Anglican, Henry VIII) had familiarized Englishmen with phrases which, translated, read: "May the angels lead thee into Paradise. . . . May the choir of angels receive thee and with Lazarus, once a beggar, mayest thou have eternal rest." This Latin service may scarcely be regarded in any conclusive way as Shakespeare's direct source, however, for phrases similar to Horatio's are so widely scattered throughout sixteenth- and early seventeenth-century usage as to indicate that Shakespeare's words were merely a poetic synthesis of time-worn and virtually universal expressions.[14] In contemplating heaven, Luther confidently refers to "my guides, the holy angels" who know the way well, Calvin writes of "a soul unspeakably precious, which is carried by angels to a blessed life," and Bullinger declares that our translation to heaven "is brought to pass by angels carrying up our souls with a most swift flight," while the popular English preacher Matthew Griffith refers to our souls as "immediately carried" to heaven by angels, and the layman Richard Brathwait promises the dying Christian that "the whole host of heaven [will] conduct thee to the palace of eternity."[15] Paul N. Siegel helpfully refers us to the ending of *Everyman*, where Knowledge speaks as follows over Everyman's grave: "Methinks that I hear angels sing, And make great joy and melody, Where Everyman's soul shall received be."[16]

To summarize, then, we see that Shakespeare's references to death are most often made against the background of universal human experience. On the rare occasions when he refers to the Christian conception of heaven, the references are almost always confined within one or two lines and consist of commonplaces. There is no reason, either literary or theological, to assume that such references were intended to constitute the focal point of the plays.

The longest and best-known treatment of death in the plays is the Duke's famous counsel to Claudio in *Measure for Measure*, and although J. V. Cunningham tells us that we find "the experience of Christian resignation" to have been "fully explored" in this speech, I see no possibility of finding in it even a single attitude which is distinctively Christian.[17] The more I study the relations between Shakespeare and the Christian tradition, the more convinced I become that

Shakespeare knew that tradition far better than many critics who hold that he epitomized its views, and concomitantly I become increasingly sure that when he wanted a character to express a Christian idea, he was able to make the expression obvious to his own audience and derivatively to us, if we approach his works in terms of historical theology. When we view his works in this perspective, we see that as a rule he chose to speak in terms of general human wisdom. The results are in keeping with the theological attitudes toward the liberal arts which we have already studied.

An interesting example of Shakespeare's effective use of distinctions between explicitly Christian and other attitudes toward death may be found in the reference to death in *King Lear*, in which Edgar declares that "ripeness is all" and the similar statement by Hamlet that "readiness is all."[18] Taking these two phrases—in themselves virtually identical—Shakespeare places them in contexts which are strikingly and distinctively appropriate to Edgar as a virtuous heathen and to Hamlet as a Christian prince who was educated at the university made famous by Martin Luther. Let us examine first Edgar's advice to his father, who is again thinking longingly of death:

> What, in ill thoughts again? Men must endure
> Their going hence, even as their coming hither;
> Ripeness is all. Come on.[19]

George Seibel regards this speech as being no more appropriate to a Christian than to Omar Khayyám—but he ignores the fact that this is as it should be, since Edgar is a pre-Christian character—and George Orwell refers to it as "an un-Christian sentiment." Without disputing the obvious fact that much stoic wisdom has been blended with Christian attitudes, this remark of Edgar's remains more nearly stoic than Christian, and so the comments of Seibel and Orwell have point.[20] In the bleak world of *King Lear*, there is great force to Edgar's affirmation of human endurance and virtue in the face of birth and death which are at once uninvited and inevitable. But as Edgar states his case to his father, the emphasis is on fortitude and not on faith.

With Hamlet, the context is decisively different, as indeed it should be, for Shakespeare has not only chosen to place Hamlet in a Christian society (though grossly degenerated) but has repeatedly referred to Christian attitudes throughout the play. For Hamlet, the context of readiness is essentially and explicitly Christian. In response to Horatio's advice that he "obey" his misgivings about the coming match with Laertes, Hamlet declares:

> there's a special providence in the fall of a sparrow.
> If it be now, 'tis not to come; if it be not to come,
> it will be now; if it be not now, yet it will come: the
> readiness is all.[21]

With Hamlet, the "readiness" is not only linked to but even seems to summarize the declaration of his reliance upon New Testament promises. It is on this basis, Luther declares, that the Christian does not greatly care about death.[22] Christians, as Luther puts it, "should behave as those who are at every moment ready for death," while Calvin writes that "we should always be ready" and that "we ought to live as if we were every moment about to depart from this life."[23] Hooker's advice is essentially the same, that we should "provide always beforehand that those evils overtake us not which death unexpected doth use to bring upon careless men, and that although it be sudden in itself, nevertheless in regard of our prepared minds it may not be sudden."[24]

When viewed within the total dramatic contexts and in terms of the preceding lines, the phrase "ripeness is all" is appropriate for Edgar in the world of *Lear*, which is at best illumined by human kindness and at most by a hopeful fatalism, and so too "readiness is all" suits the later character of Hamlet as a prince who professes the grounds of Christian hope. In neither instance, however, is our attention directed towards theological speculation and away from the reaction of individual characters to the immediate situations in which they are placed on the stage. Shakespeare could have created his own version of *The Divine Comedy* or of *Pilgrim's Progress*, and could have placed Edgar and Hamlet in such a new world, but he did not do so. As critics, we should use relevant evidence from all sources (including the theological) which may help us to understand the meaning of lines and the development of character and action upon Shakespeare's stage, but we are not invited to go beyond the limits of that stage so as to speculate upon what has traditionally been assumed to be the quite different stage of the afterlife.

[1] See above, pp. 51f.   [2] *Per.* 1.1.45f.

[3] Calvin, *Sermons on Job* (1.20-22), A. Golding trans., London, 1574, p. 30b, line 21.

[4] *W.T.* 3.2.107f.

[5] Luther, *Table Talk*, William Hazlitt trans., London: George Bell and Sons, 1902, entries 141 (p. 60) and 788 (p. 314).

[6] *Rich. II* 3.2.152ff.

[7] Calvin, *Sermons on Job* (1.20-22), Golding trans., p. 30b, lines 21ff.

[8] *3 Henry VI* 5.2.26.   [9] *3 Henry VI* 5.2.49.   [10] *Rich. III* 2.1.3f.

[11] *Rich. II* 5.5.111f.   [12] *Ham.* 5.2.370f.   [13] See above, pp. 54ff.

[14] See Brother Baldwin Peter, "*Hamlet* and *In Paradisum*," *Shakespeare Quarterly*, vol. 3, pp. 279-80. Brother Peter admits that other sources are possible, but suggests that "the particular form in Shakespeare, however,

links it with *In Paradisum*" (*ibid.*, p. 279n.) While there is surely a link in terms of the commonplaces involved, the evidence is not such as to allow us to assume that Shakespeare's immediate or exclusive source for Horatio's words was *In Paradisum*.

[15] Luther, Third Sermon on Angels: Michaelmas, 1531, Weimar ed., vol. 34 II, 28of.; Calvin, Exp. Luke 16.22, *Commentary on the Gospels*, vol. 2, p. 186; Bullinger, *Decades*, vol. 4, p. 388; Matthew Griffith, *Bethel*, London, 1634, p. 525; Richard Brathwait, *A Spiritual Spicerie*, London, 1638, pp. 465-66.

[16] Siegel, *op.cit.*, p. 92.

[17] J. V. Cunningham, *Woe or Wonder*, Denver: University of Denver Press, 1951, pp. 10-11.

[18] *Lear* 5.2.11 and *Ham.* 5.2.233.   [19] *Lear* 5.2.8ff.

[20] Seibel, *op.cit.*, p. 70 and George Orwell, *Shooting an Elephant and other Essays*, New York: Harcourt, Brace and Co., 1950, p. 48.

[21] *Ham.* 5.2.230ff.

[22] Luther, Exp. Eccl. 3.2, Weimar ed., vol. 20, p. 60.

[23] Luther quoted in Quistorp, *op.cit.*, p. 107n.; Calvin, *Commentary on I Corinthians* (7.29), p. 257; and Calvin, Exp. Rom. 14.7-9, *Commentaries* (Haroutunian), p. 318.

[24] Hooker, *Eccl. Pol.* 5.46.3. Bertram Joseph, apropos of Hamlet's remark, cites Latimer's admonition that God "would have us ready at all times." See Joseph's *Conscience and the King*, London: Chatto and Windus, 1953, p. 141.

✧ *Devil*

"Evil as evil cannot be desired," Hooker writes; "if that be desired which is evil, the cause is the goodness which is or seemeth to be joined with it."[1] The conception summarized in these words extends back through Christianity to the Greeks. It was linked with the Biblical treatment of the devil who could, according to the apostle Paul, appear as an angel of light, and the conjoined traditions provided an understanding of evil as operating through deceit and disguise.[2] This conception finds repeated expression in Shakespeare. Most famous, perhaps is Macbeth's depairing repudiation of

> th' equivocation of the fiend,
> That lies like truth.[3]

There are many similar references, though not necessarily in the same mood. In *Twelfth Night*, Shakespeare makes Viola's almost mock-serious reflections serve the uses of comedy:

> Disguise, I see thou art a wickedness
> Wherein the pregnant enemy does much.[4]

On the other hand, the mood is one of great urgency when Hamlet, in his confrontation of Gertrude, demands of her:

> What devil was 't
> That thus cozen'd you at hoodman-blind?[5]

Hamlet earlier referred to the devil's power "T'assume a pleasing shape," and for Hamlet such references are always made in a tone of deep concern.[6] In a lighter vein is the remark of Berowne in *Love's Labour's Lost* that "Devils soonest tempt, resembling spirits of light,"[7] for Shakespeare can treat the subject in both of the traditional moods of Christian reference to the devil: the light and humorous mode or that of utmost seriousness. Our concern now will be with a few examples of the serious references to the devil on the part of Shakespeare's characters.

Edgar, in his madman's role in *King Lear*, makes repeated references to various diabolical spirits and their operations, but his analysis is summarized when he declares that "the foul fiend . . . hurts the poor creature of earth."[8] The phrase epitomizes the demonic. Melancholy and "all the maladies which afflict mankind" are produced by the devil, Luther writes.[9] Again Luther teaches that the devil "does not want one little blade of grass or a little leaf to grow."[10] It is in the unrelieved and undeviating joy in destruction, the infliction of pain, and the fomenting of strife that the devil differs from man, even at his most sinful. "But to be so wicked as to find one's pleasure and delight only in the misfortune of other people, in their lingering hunger, thirst, misery, and want, in the perpetration of nothing but bloodshed and treason, especially in the lives of those who neither have done nor could do one any harm, this is the hellish and insatiable rage and fury of the wretched devil, of which human nature is incapable."[11]

Human nature is incapable of continuous and undeviating evil of this sort, but it may approach such evil, as when Macbeth destroys Macduff's family "who neither have done nor could do" him any harm. Though human beings may not be devils (recall here Othello's glance at Iago's feet), they may still do the devil's work. "We still see," Luther said of the devil, "that he is the lord and prince of the world and speaks not only through animals but also through human beings, nowadays for the greater part through the latter."[12] Within this context, the precise identity of the weird sisters in Macbeth is of only secondary importance, for whether as women or as lesser demons they do the work of what Macbeth calls "juggling fiends."[13]

The relation of very wicked men to the devil is sooner or later displayed in their behavior, Calvin declares, so that they are "rightly recognized to be the children of Satan from his image, into which they have degenerated."[14] A character such as Iago may for a time conceal from other characters his relationship to evil, but the audience is given ample hints not only through his soliloquies but through his actions. The course of evil as historically understood in the Christian tradition and as embodied in Shakespeare's major villains has been copiously reported by Bernard

Spivack,[15] but in relation to Iago at least one of Luther's remarks may be added to Spivack's evidence, as this remark so clearly applies to Iago's indefatigable cunning: "The devil [not that Iago is the devil, but only reacts "in his image"] . . . is not idle, and has no rest. If he is struck down once, he will rise again; if he cannot enter at the front door, he sees to it that he enters at the rear; if he cannot effect an entrance in this way, he breaks in through the roof or digs his way through underneath the doorsill, toiling until he effects an entrance, employing all manner of cunning and schemes. If one way fails, he tries another and perseveres until he succeeds."[16] Thus, to add a relevant comment from Calvin, the devil "obscures the light with darkness, he entangles men's minds in errors, he stirs up hatred, he kindles contentions and combats," just as does that human "demi-devil," Iago.[17] Men acting in the devil's interest carry on his work for him.

The demonic agents eventually destroy themselves, of course, for the devil both uses and abuses his own adherents, and it is the nature of evil to work its infection most completely in those who are most closely associated with it. What Macbeth gets from his bargain is the sere, the yellow leaf, and a life which consists merely in an endless and meaningless succession of days, but he does not recognize the ultimate duplicity of evil until even these things are to be taken from him. Faced with Macduff's exposure of his last protecting "charm," he declares:

> And be these juggling fiends no more believed,
> That palter with us in a double sense,
> That keep the word of promise to our ear
> And break it to our hope![18]

In *Richard II*, Exton comes to a similar recognition after his assassination of the king:

> O, would the deed were good!
> For now the devil, that told me I did well,
> Says that this deed is chronicled in hell.[19]

But even where there are such clear references to hell, I do not judge that Shakespeare is focusing our attention upon the rewards and punishments of the afterlife, any more than in the references to heaven which we discussed under DEATH, above. That Macbeth degenerated into a viciously evil man, there can be no doubt, and it is also true that we can clearly trace in his degeneration the patterns of the course of sin which the theologians taught. Macbeth represents as fully drawn a portrait of human sin as anything in Bunyan or Milton or Dante, and I find no essential difference between Shakespeare's view of the devil's operation and theirs, but there is this crucial difference between the focus of his work and theirs: In their treatment of the devil and sin, they do not allow us to forget for long the presence of judgment in an afterlife, and though Shakespeare gives dramatic acknowledgment to that eternal judgment, his concern in the plays is for the judgments which are passed upon evil in this life. Shakespeare's treatment of evil is entirely in keeping with the traditional Christian understanding of the demonic, but Shakespeare does not write theology and his focus remains upon the temporal operation of the devil's kingdom.

The devil's work may be described as the conflation of good and evil, the transvaluation of values, after the pattern followed by Milton's Satan when he declared, "Evil, be thou my good."[20] That, essentially, is the creed of hell, and so too is the chant of the weird sisters:

Fair is foul, and foul is fair.[21]

Luther says of the devil that he "defiles what is good and even turns it into evil,"[22] but Luther is also careful to note that the "heathen philosophers" were not unaware that this transvaluation of values represented the ultimate peril for man: They knew, he observes, that "as long as immorality is still considered vice and sin, help and remedy are possible; but when it is regarded as right, one cannot help."[23] Speaking of his own time, Luther preaches that "nearly all vices have now unfortunately turned into virtues . . . [and] are made to appear as virtues. . . . And so a sinner no longer exists in the world; but, God have mercy on us, the world is full of 'saints.' Seneca says: *Ibi deest remedii locus ubi vitia honores fiunt*, 'where vices become honorable virtues, the situation defies remedy.' "[24]

The convergence between Luther and Seneca here brings us back to the common ground, to the great ethical consensus of human wisdom in terms of which Shakespeare's drama is conducted. Seneca and Luther would have disagreed as to how Macbeth could have been "saved" in an eternal sense, but they would have been in essential agreement as to how he was damned within the temporal order, and that agreement furnishes the standard of values in terms of which our favorable sympathies are aroused and our adverse judgments are made. It is true that characters within the plays are often tempted by and even accept an evil as a good, or a good as an evil, but the total dramatic action would lose both interest and significance were the audience to do so. Banquo warns Macbeth that

> oftentimes, to win us to our harm,
> The instruments of darkness tell us truths,
> Win us with honest trifles, to betray 's
> In deepest consequence.[25]

Shakespeare creates and develops the character of Macbeth in terms of such a betrayal, but were the audience similarly betrayed, its reaction to the drama would be like Macbeth's to life, and the tragedy would appear merely as

> a tale
> Told by an idiot, full of sound and fury,
> Signifying nothing.[26]

It is against that reduction of order to chaos that both drama and society are protected by the broad ethical consensus of such men as Luther and Seneca.[27]

[1] Hooker, *Eccl. Pol.* 1.7.6. [2] II Cor. 11.14. [3] *Macb.* 5.5.43f.
[4] *T.N.* 2.2.28f. [5] *Ham.* 3.4.76f. [6] *Ham.* 2.2.628.
[7] *L.L.L.* 4.3.257. [8] *Lear* 3.4.120ff.

[9] Luther, *Table Talk*, Hazlitt trans., entry 597 (p. 256). See also entry 577 (p. 250).

[10] Luther, *Table Talk*, Plass anthol., vol. 1, 1187.

[11] Luther, Serm. on Eph. 6.10-17, Plass anthol., vol. 1, 1156.

[12] Luther, Serm. on Gen. 3.1-6, Plass anthol., vol. 1, 1153.

[13] *Macb.* 5.8.19.   [14] Calvin, *Inst.* 1.14.18.

[15] Bernard Spivack, *Shakespeare and the Allegory of Evil*, New York: Columbia University Press, 1958.

[16] Luther, Serm. on John 4.47-54, Lenker ed., vol. 14, p. 267.

[17] Calvin, *Inst.* 1.14.15.   [18] *Macb.* 5.8.19ff.

[19] *Rich. II* 5.5.115ff.   [20] Milton, *Paradise Lost*, IV, 110.

[21] *Macb.* 1.1.11.

[22] Luther, Exp. John 6.69-71, Plass anthol., vol. 1, 1150.

[23] Luther, Serm. on I Thess. 4.1-7, Plass anthol., vol. 2, 4146.

[24] Luther, Serm. on Luke 16.19-31, Plass anthol., vol. 2, 4201.

[25] *Macb.* 1.3.123ff.   [26] *Macb.* 5.5.26ff.

[27] This is certainly not to suggest that such a consensus was total, but is merely intended to refer back to the analysis given in Chapter Four.

Questions of election were not much discussed by Shakespeare's characters, a fact which is explicable both in terms
of the secular limits of his art and also in terms of strong
theological admonitions against curiosity in this matter. Predestination was a labyrinth into which one was well advised
not to wander, and only Cassio does wander into it, in his
maudlin discussion with Iago: "there be souls must be
saved, and there be souls must not be saved," and "the
Lieutenant is to be saved before the ancient."[1] Now this is
an extremely funny episode in any terms, and it would have
seemed even more amusing to an audience which would
have recognized more readily than we do the seriousness of
the subject into which Cassio has stumbled in his drunken
abandon. Calvin declares that "those who seek their or
others' salvation in the labyrinth of predestination, while
they move out of the way of faith set before them, are insane."[2] Luther goes even further, and writes that "just as
murder, theft, and swearing are sins, so it is also sinful to
try to investigate such matters [as one's own election]; and
the devil is at the root of this, as he is of all other sins."[3]
With Cassio, the devil at work is the amusing "devil drunk-
enness,"[4] and we have one of the oldest of stock comic
situations: the not-quite-sensible discussion of a serious
subject by a tipsy stage character. Thus, in view of the
context and of evidence both literary and theological, it
scarcely seems that we can take Cassio's remarks as an indication of his salvation, as at least one critic has invited
us to do. The incident does indeed provide another indication of Shakespeare's ability to put theological material to

dramatic use, but it is not the kind of use the theologizers would have us find.

1 *Oth.* 2.3.106ff.

2 Calvin, Exp. John 6.40, *Commentaries* (Haroutunian), p. 303.

8 Luther, "Letter to Someone Unknown: Aug. 8, 1545," *The Letters of Martin Luther*, Margaret A. Currie trans., London: Macmillan and Co., 1908, p. 462.

4 *Oth.* 2.3.297.

✦ *Eschatology*

Characters in Shakespeare's plays make occasional references to the last judgment and the dissolution of the earth, but these references, where direct, are generally brief and of no great structural importance to the plays. There is one long speech, however, which is cast in terms quite similar to those of eschatology, and it may be of some value to point out the possible parallels. I say that the parallels are "possible" rather than inescapable, for Prospero's great speech cannot be restricted to a treatment of the last things, though it may allude to them. Upon receiving news of Caliban's approach, Prospero concludes the wedding masque in *The Tempest* in words of almost mystic tone. We have already examined his reference to "our little life" as "rounded with a sleep,"[1] and our present interest is in the following lines on the conclusion of the little play:

> And, like the baseless fabric of this vision,
> The cloud-capp'd towers, the gorgeous palaces,
> The solemn temples, the great globe itself,
> Yea, all which it inherit, shall dissolve,
> And, like this insubstantial pageant faded,
> Leave not a rack behind.[2]

The reference to human life and to this world in terms of a passing vision may be paralleled in Calvin's reference to our life as "only a show or phantom that passes away"[3] and to "the whole world" as "a form which quickly vanishes away . . . as evanescent as smoke,"[4] for "the shape of this world passeth away and all the things therein do glide and vanish away."[5] Commenting upon Paul's teaching that men should "use this world as not abusing it, for the fashion of this world passeth away," Calvin writes: "By these words the Apostle excellently noteth the vanity of the world. Nothing, sayeth he, is firm or sure, for it is only a vision or outward show. But he seemeth to have alluded to pavillions or halls, in the which when the tapestry and costly hangings are pulled down, and wrapped up in a moment, there appeareth another show: and those things which pleased the eyes of the beholders, are by and by taken from their sight."[6] As was his frequent practice, Calvin was here summarizing a long and widespread tradition, and it is quite possible that much closer parallels could be found to Prospero's words at other points within that tradition. The focus of our interest, however, is not in an exhaustive history of doctrinal usage, but rather in noting the shape of ideas to which allusions are made. Such an allusion as has been suggested here would not be at all inappropriate to the characterization of Prospero as one who in his first appearance expresses his faith in "providence divine" and who in his last appearance vows that "every third thought shall be my grave."[7]

[1] See above, p. 54.   [2] *Temp.* 4.1.151ff.
[3] Calvin, *Commentary on Psalms* (103.15-16), vol. 4, p. 138.
[4] *Ibid.*, p. 121.
[5] Calvin, *Commentary on Job* (1.20-22), Golding trans., p. 31b, line 2.
[6] Calvin, *Commentary upon St. Paul's Epistles to the Corinthians* (I Cor. 7.30f.), T. Tymme trans., London, 1577, folio 87.
[7] *Temp.* 1.2.159 and 5.1.311.

✦ Fear

"Fear in itself," Hooker writes, "is a thing not sinful. For is not fear a thing natural and for men's preservation necessary, implanted in us by the provident and most generous Giver of all good things, to the end that we might not run headlong upon those mischiefs wherewith we are not able to encounter, but use the remedy of shunning those evils which we have not ability to withstand?"[1] To ignore such faultless and valuable fear is to court disaster, as Enobarbus recognizes that Antony is doing:

> Now he'll outstare the lightning. To be furious
> Is to be frighted out of fear, and in that mood
> The dove will peck the estridge . . .
> . . . When valor preys on reason,
> It eats the sword it fights with.[2]

The point may be summarized in the words of Cressida:

> Blind fear that seeing reason leads, finds safer
> footing than blind reason stumbling without fear.
> To fear the worst oft cures the worse.[3]

This observation is balanced against Trolius' "crossing" proverb, "Fears make devils of cherubims; they never see truly,"[4] for it is possible to play almost endlessly upon the connotations of the word "fear."

For our purposes here, there are two primary senses connected with the word. Fear may be godly—that is, it may indicate reverence for God—or it may be a very different thing, a kind of fright and dread. Luther clarifies the two meanings in this way: "Being afraid of God is different from fearing God. The fear of God is a fruit of love, but being afraid of him is the seed of hatred. Therefore we should not be afraid of God but should fear him so that we do not hate him whom we should love."[5] The fear of God which "is a fruit of love" will lead men to respect God's will for themselves and others, as does Banquo in *Macbeth*, who, because he stands in the great hand of God, can declare to the Weird Sisters that he neither begs nor fears their favors or their hate.[6] Luther describes an attitude much like that of Banquo when he writes that "I may have a good, and divine pride, commanded by God and demanded of me and all others. This says: 'I must not give way to the devil; I will not give consideration to the devil or follow him. . . .' This is really praiseworthy pride."[7] Macbeth himself is not far removed from such an attitude when he is still able to declare, in the first act, that

> I dare do all that may become a man.
> Who dares do more is none.[8]

The "fear" which Macbeth displays here, and for which his wife taunts him, is the kind which, according to Luther, makes us "guard ourselves against sin and serve our neighbor, while we live here upon earth."[9]

But then there is another fear, the fear which arises from acting in defiance of the moral law, of God and man, and from the consequent life of guilt. It is a form of this fear which Richard III feels:

> What do I fear? Myself? . . .
>
> . . . .
> Then fly. What, from myself?[10]

Calvin declares that though the wicked "be a terror to every man, yet must they be fain to run away themselves."[11] The same fear, in other forms, plagues Macbeth after his murder of Duncan, so that throughout the second and third acts he seems to be almost completely in its grip. Tyrants, according to Calvin, "be so troubled in their minds" that "they themselves are afraid, not only of men, but also of every leaf that shaketh upon a tree" for it seems universally true that "when we set aside the fear of God, a mere nothing fills us with trepidation" just as Macbeth finds of himself that "every noise appals me."[12] Hooker holds, like Calvin, that "the fears and suspicions which improbity" breeds in the wicked are "strengthened by every occasion."[13]

Yet there is a more frightful state than that of guilt-inspired fear, as Hooker reminds his congregation in one of his sermons: "we are to stand in fear of nothing more than the extremity of not fearing."[14] At that point, a man's conscience no longer makes a coward of him, because his conscience is dead, and it is to this point that the conscience-haunted Macbeth rushes so that he

> may tell pale-hearted fear it lies
> And sleep in spite of thunder.[15]

Whether he is ever totally free of conscience and its fears may be debated, but after his second visit to the Weird Sisters there is no more of the earlier preoccupation with "saucy doubts and fears" and in the last act he can declare that "I have almost forgot the taste of fears."[16] After Acheron, Macbeth seems to live in what Hooker calls "that pit wherein they are sunk that have put far from them the evil day, that have made a league with death and have said, 'Tush, we shall feel no harm.' " This is the pit "wherein souls destitute of all hope are plunged."[17]

---

[1] Hooker, Serm. IV, Keble ed., vol. 2, p. 376.

[2] A. and C. 3.13.195ff. [3] T. and C. 3.2.76ff. [4] T. and C. 3.2.74.

[5] Luther, Serm. on Ecclus. 15.1-8, Plass anthol., vol. 1, 1525.
[6] *Macb.* 1.3.60f.
[7] Luther, Serm. on John 2.17, Amer. ed., vol. 22, p. 232.
[8] *Macb.* 1.7.45f.
[9] Luther, Exp. I Pet. 1.17-21, Lenker ed., vol. 3, p. 71.
[10] *Rich. III* 5.3.183 and 186.
[11] Calvin, Serm. on Job 27.19 to 28.9, *op.cit.*, 475a, line 16.
[12] Calvin, *ibid.*, p. 277b, line 38; Serm. on Matt. 26.69-75 in *Commentaries* (Harouthunian), p. 322; and *Macb.* 2.2.58.
[13] Hooker, *Eccl. Pol.* 6.6.14.   [14] Hooker, Serm. IV, *op.cit.*, p. 377.
[15] *Macb.* 4.1.85.   [16] *Macb.* 3.4.25 and 5.5.10.
[17] Hooker, Serm. IV, *op.cit.*, p. 377.

✦ *Flattery and Counsel*

In *As You Like It*, Duke Senior speaks of the hardships of exile in terms of an ancient distinction:

> This is no flattery; these are counsellors
> That feelingly persuade me what I am.[1]

In *Timon of Athens* the same distinction is made:

> O, that men's ears should be
> To counsel deaf, but not to flattery.[2]

The contrast between flattery and counsel—the one being deceitful, the other speaking true—is not distinctively Christian, being a part of general human wisdom, but much was made of this contrast by the theologians. Here, indeed, we have one of the clearest of many possible instances of the use of general human wisdom for a distinctively Christian purpose, and the reformers, especially, repeatedly underscored the dangers into which men allowed themselves to be betrayed when they accepted a flattering view of their sins and when, as a consequence, they assumed their own "desert" of heaven. Luther makes the point, quoting Jerome: "Jerome saith, that he had seen many which could suffer great inconveniences in their body and goods, but none that could despise their own praises," while elsewhere he writes that "*Philautia,* or the notion of our own wisdom, is the most dangerous of vices; for it keeps our hearts from accepting reproof and improvement; rather they are intent only on being admired by others."[3] Calvin speaks in the same terms: "Whoever, then, heeds such teachers as hold us back with thought only of our good traits will not advance in self-knowledge, but will be plunged into the worst ignorance" and again "since, therefore, a man is far from being benefited by such flatteries, let us not, to our ruin, willingly delude ourselves."[4]

For the theologians, such references were usually employed with the intent of leading people to acknowledge their sins, to repent, and to lead a new life. For Shakespeare, on the contrary, the references are usually to a more secular form of self-knowledge, but he could also on occasion dramatize an appeal as distinctively Christian as that of the theologians. We find such an appeal in Hamlet's words to Gertrude:

> Mother, for love of grace,
> Lay not that flattering unction to your soul,
> That not your trepass but my madness speaks.
> It will but skin and film the ulcerous place,
> Whiles rank corruption, mining all within,
> Infects unseen.[5]

Hamlet's purpose throughout his appeal to Gertrude is not only to win her to his side in the conflict with Claudius, but also to lead her to acknowledge her sin (that "you may see the inmost part of you")[6] and to follow the Christian practice of confession and reform:

Confess yourself to heaven;
Repent what's past; avoid what is to come.[7]

We will say more of the aptness of these appeals when we come to the entry on repentance, but our concern here is for the distinction between flattery and counsel. When Hamlet appeals to Gertrude, he appeals as a Christian counsellor who repudiates flattery. He follows the plan which he had devised earlier to speak to her in terms of kindness, as well as of harsh reality:

I will speak daggers to her, but use none.
My tongue and soul in this be hypocrites—
How in my words somever she be shent,
To give them seals never, my soul, consent![8]

The attitude is that appropriate to Christian rebuke, for as Luther advised, "you should so inflict the wound that you can both mitigate and heal it; you should be so severe as not to forget to be kind."[9] It was in this spirit that Hamlet both acted and spoke:

I must be cruel, only to be kind.[10]

Had G. B. Shaw recognized Hamlet's encounter with Gertrude in these terms, he might not have regarded the scene as "unnatural" and Hamlet's reproach as "repulsive."[11]

Though Shakespeare's customary reference to the difference between counsel and flattery is not so closely associated with the theologians' major concern as it is in *Hamlet*, the *form* of the reference is generally the same whether it is employed by the theologians or the dramatist. The expression of such attitudes by the theologians certainly reinforced and perhaps even popularized a distinction to which Shakespeare repeatedly recurred. Thus in *Twelfth Night*, the fool declares that he does "the better for my foes and the worse for my friends," because the friends "praise me and make an ass of me; now my foes tell me plainly I am an ass: so that by my foes, sir, I profit in the knowledge of myself, and by my friends I am abused."[12]

A similar treatment is found in *Timon of Athens*, as Alcibiades confronts the embittered Timon:

Tim.	If I hope well, I'll never see thee more.
Alcib.	I never did thee harm.
Tim.	Yes, thou spokest well of me.
Alcib.	Call'st thou that harm?
Tim.	Men daily find it.[13]

Luther analyzes the subject in substantially the same form: "All are deceived who are praised, and all who praise are deceivers. Who then should not tremble at being praised? Who should not wish to be dispraised? Are those, then, the only ones who lead and teach us rightly, who reprove all our actions and call us miserable? Indeed, such is the case."[14]

[1] *A.Y.L.* 2.1.10f.   [2] *T. of A.* 1.2.256f.

[3] Luther, *Commentary on Galatians* (5.25), Middleton trans., p. 445, and Exp. Isa. 5.21, Plass anthol., vol. 2, 1972.

[4] Calvin, *Inst.* 2.1.2 and 3.12.5.   [5] *Ham.* 3.4.144ff.

[6] *Ibid.*, 3.4.20.   [7] *Ibid.*, 3.4.149f.

[8] *Ibid.*, 3.3.414ff.

[9] Luther, Exp. Gal. 4.16, Weimar ed., vol. 2, 546. The original reads: "Sic enim vulnus infligere oportet, ut scias et mitigare et sanare: sic severum esse, ut benignitatis non obliviscaris."

[10] *Ham.* 3.4.178.

[11] G. B. Shaw, "Preface to *The Dark Lady of the Sonnets*," in *Selected Plays with Prefaces*, New York: Dodd, Mead and Co., 1948, vol. 3, p. 843.

[12] *T.N.* 5.1.13ff.   [13] *T. of A.* 4.3.171ff.

[14] Luther, Exp. Ps. 5.12. I have altered the translation found in Lenker ed., vol. 1, p. 325, to accord more closely with the original Latin of Weimar ed., vol. 5, p. 196.

✦ Freedom *Free Will*

The problems involved in the question of free will are at best exceedingly and exceptionally complex, and are further complicated by the ambiguity of the term itself, as well as by the emotional connotations which it arouses. For these reasons, Luther declares, "I would wish that the words 'free will' had never been invented"[1] and Calvin comments that "few have defined what free will is, although it repeatedly occurs in the writings of all."[2] Calvin cites the scholastic distinctions, and states his agreement with them: "Now in the schools three kinds of freedom are distinguished: first from necessity, second from sin, third from misery. The first of these so inheres in man by nature that it cannot possibly be taken away, but the two others have been lost through sin. I willingly accept this distinction."[3] Man in effect, then, is free from acting out of necessity, but he is not free from sin and misery. In every major theologian's treatment of freedom from this point on (and sometimes even before), the analysis becomes increasingly technical. Fortunately, we do not need to follow the intricacies of this matter, for Shakespeare did not employ them, and so we may turn to the theologians' practical teachings on freedom.

Luther denied that man was free to establish by his own will a saving relationship with God, but affirmed that he was free to act in secular relations, so that "we may still in good faith teach people to credit man with 'free will' in respect, not of what is above him, but of what is below him."[4] In a somewhat similar fashion, Calvin saw two answers to the question of man's freedom, and he would affirm or deny freedom depending upon the context of the question. "Indeed," he wrote, "if we ponder the direction of external things, we shall not doubt that to this extent they are left to human judgment. But if we lend our ears to the many testimonies which proclaim that the Lord also rules men's minds in external things, these will compel us to subordinate decision itself to the secret impulse of God."[5] When he was discussing the area of grace and of faith, Calvin would emphasize the election of God; when he was discussing the area of human decision, he called for action in the assumption of responsible decision between good and evil: "Choose in which group you would prefer to be numbered."[6] As for Hooker, he tells his Puritan critics that if they will read him and Calvin impartially, no difference will be found between them.[7] Whether Hooker was correct in his assumption of essential agreement with Calvin I am not sure, but for our purposes in analyzing the relation between Shakespeare and the sixteenth-century theological milieu, I am confident that such differences as might have existed at this point between our three major theologians are not pertinent to the questions before us.

Dramatic characters act in terms of practical choices, and both Shakespeare and his audience had to be able to agree that the stage characters were morally responsible for those choices. To such an understanding of moral responsibility, the theologians contributed unequivocal support: In terms of moral choice, men could do what they willed to do, and were responsible for the results of their actions. Without some such understandings, the drama would lose direction and meaning.

Nowhere is the necessity for moral responsibility clearer than in the cases of Iago and Edmund. If these two great villains were not responsible for their actions, an audience could scarcely regard them as being, in any meaningful sense, villainous. Shakespeare thus has each of them repudiate any notion that men must act as they do out of necessity: both, in other words, affirm the individual's responsibility for his actions. And, in view of our concern here, the interesting thing is that both do this in terms which are strikingly reminiscent of similar affirmations by the theologians. Thus, though Shakespeare was not intent upon dramatizing the Christian tradition, he could and did appeal to important elements of that tradition in constructing his actions and characters.

The speeches of Iago and Edmund are long, and are so familiar that there is no need for us to quote them in full here.[8] The gist of both is that men are responsible for their actions, and have no grounds for blaming their evildoings upon forces external to themselves. The same point is central to the theologians' judgment of sin. According to Luther, "a man without the spirit of God does not do evil against his will, under pressure, as though he were taken by the scruff of the neck and dragged into it, like a thief or foot pad being dragged off against his will to punishment; but he does it spontaneously and voluntarily."[9] Calvin too deplores the "excuses" which men make to relieve themselves of responsibility, for he says that "men cannot allege that the evil cometh from anywhere else than themselves," while Hooker deplores "that secret shame wherewith our nature in itself doth abhor the deformity of sin, and for that cause [men] study by all means how to find the first original of it elsewhere."[10] These remarks summarize the personal accountability insisted upon by the Christian tradition and accepted by Iago when he tells Roderigo that "'Tis in ourselves that we are thus or thus . . . the power and corrigible authority of this lies in our wills."[11] The latter phrase sums up a commonplace idea which Calvin also expresses when he declares that "all sin results from our own will and inclination,"[12] while Edmund's ridicule of the notion that "we were villains on necessity, fools by heavenly compulsion" or "by a divine thrusting on" similarly recalls a number of theological expressions. Calvin teaches that "if we sin, it does not happen from compulsion, as though we were constrained to it by an alien power" and that "people with a bad conscience gain nothing by pushing forward the providence of God as a screen for their misdeeds,"[13] while we have already noted Luther's caustic denial that we do evil "unwillingly and by compulsion" as though . . . taken by the scruff of the neck and dragged into it." Like Edmund's, too, is Calvin's attack on the astrological notion that "all the evils wherewith the stars threaten us do proceed from the order of nature, [so that] we must needs conceive this phantasy that our sins are not the cause,"[14] a treatment which in turn reminds us of Cassius' famous words in *Julius Caesar*:

> The fault, dear Brutus, is not in our stars,
> But in ourselves, that we are underlings.[15]

Shakespeare's characters do not, to be sure, always affirm their own freedom of action. In *The Winter's Tale*, Florizel expresses an almost mechanistic determinism:

> But as th' unthought-on accident is guilty
> To what we wildly do, so we profess
> Ourselves to be the slaves of chance and flies
> Of every wind that blows.[16]

The thought is eminently un-Christian, which is not inappropriate when we recall that Shakespeare does not pretend to make Florizel a Christian character. It might be interesting, however, to note how explicitly such words run counter to theological doctrine. Calvin writes that "we do not, with the Stoics, contrive a necessity out of the perpetual connection and intimately related series of causes, which is contained in nature," while Hooker teaches that "whatsoever we work as men, the same we do wittingly work and freely; neither are we according to the manner of natural agents any way so tied, but that it is in our power to leave the things we do undone."[17]

The Christian teaching holds that while the faithful man should rely upon God's grace in the ordering of life in this world, he should not expect God to do everything for him. Indeed, man is placed in the world to *act*, and even those who most emphasized the sovereignty and providence of God (for example, Calvin) also most urgently insisted upon human activism. God has provided us with the means to use in shaping our own lives and societies: to neglect those means is sin. This doctrine of the free use of the means provided by God forms a very important part of Shakespeare's theological milieu, and the doctrine is explicitly and comprehensively, though briefly, stated by Shakespeare's characters at several points. Let us look first to Hamlet's treatment of the matter.

Hamlet's references to theological doctrines are rather frequent, and display a theological acumen quite appropriate to one whose education Shakespeare has ascribed to that original seat of Protestant learning, Wittenberg. In the treatment of reason, Hamlet comes particularly close to a passage in one of Luther's Wittenberg lectures. In discussing men's free use of the means which God has provided, Luther singles out reason as one of these, and comments:

"for God certainly did not give us our reason and the advice and aid which it supplies in order to have us contemptuously disregard them," while Hamlet soliloquizes in strikingly similar terms:

> Sure he that made us with such large discourse,
> Looking before and after, gave us not
> That capability and godlike reason
> To fust in us unus'd.[18]

Hamlet's use may be regarded as theology bettered by poetry, but whether or not the direct influence upon this passage in the play is from Luther's lectures, the passage does show the adaptation of theological materials in a dramatic speech.[19]

In two other speeches, Shakespearean characters treat this doctrine of the free use of means with precision and at the same time with a comprehensiveness which takes account of both elements in the traditional theological usage: God's will and man's. In *All's Well that Ends Well*, Helena combines references to the power of heaven and to man's freedom, as also does the Bishop of Carlisle in *Richard II*. The bishop's remark is, quite appropriately, the fuller and more admonitory of the two, as he advises Richard both to trust God and to bestir himself:

> Fear not, my lord. That power that made you king
> Hath power to keep you king in spite of all.
> The means that heaven yields must be embrac'd,
> And not neglected; else, if heaven would,
> And we will not, heaven's offer we refuse,
> The proffered means of succour and redress.[20]

Helena's soliloquy stresses the same points:

Our remedies oft in ourselves do lie,
Which we ascribe to heaven: The fated sky
Gives us free scope; only doth backward pull
Our slow designs, when we ourselves are dull.[21]

"The means that heaven yields must be embrac'd, And not neglected," says Shakespeare's bishop, while Luther declares that "Means are not to be neglected, but we are to employ those means which it is possible for us to use."[22] Or again— and these quotations are all from the same series of Wittenberg lectures just quoted in connection with Hamlet's treatment of reason—Luther teaches that "this life rests on God's providence and on your faith, since he has promised to be your God and to sustain you. Therefore you should not say: No matter what I do, I cannot hinder the will of God so that because of my conduct less happens than God has determined. For this is the language of the devil, and it is forever damned. Rather you should go on in simple faith, and when you are in danger and trouble, you use whatever means you can, lest you tempt God."[23] Here as with Carlisle, the admonition is that man should use all means at his disposal, lest "heaven's offer we refuse."

The same observation is found in Calvin: "For he who has set the limits to our life has at the same time entrusted to us its care; he has provided means and helps to preserve it," and the conclusion is also the same as with Luther, Helena, and Carlisle: "Now it is very clear what our duty is: thus, if the Lord has committed to us the protection of our life, our duty is to protect it; if he offers helps, to use them; if he forewarns of dangers, not to plunge headlong; if he makes remedies available, not to neglect them."[24] It is true that the Christian "will ever look to [God] as the principal cause of things," but it is equally true for Calvin that the Christian "yet will give attention to the secondary causes in their proper place."[25] This doctrine applies especially "with reference to future events," and Calvin teaches that the Christian "will count it among the blessings of the Lord, if he is not destitute of human helps which he may use for his safety. Therefore he will neither cease to take counsel, nor be sluggish in beseeching the assistance of those whom he sees to have the means to help him; but, considering that whatever creatures are capable of furnishing anything to him are offered by the Lord unto his hand, he will put them to use as lawful instruments of divine providence."[26] In sum, then, it is an essential part of faith in God's providence that Christians should act vigorously, making free use of those means which God has provided, for otherwise "the fated sky" will "backward pull Our slow designs, when we ourselves are dull."

[1] Luther, Defense and Explanation of all the Articles, Amer. ed., vol. 32, p. 94.

[2] Calvin, Inst. 2.2.4.   [3] Ibid., 2.2.5.

[4] Luther, The Bondage of the Will, eds. J. I. Packer and O. R. Johnston, London: James Clarke and Co., 1957, p. 107.

[5] Calvin, Inst. 2.4.6.   [6] Ibid., 3.8.6.

[7] Hooker, "Fragments of an Answer," Keble ed., vol. 2, p. 31.

[8] See Oth. 1.3.322ff. and Lear 1.2.133ff.

[9] Luther, The Bondage of the Will, p. 102.

[10] Calvin, Serm. on Deut. 31.14-17, Golding trans., p. 1086a, and Hooker, "Fragments of an Answer," op.cit., p. 44.   [11] Oth. 1.3.322ff.

[12] Calvin, quoted in Wilhelm Niesel, The Theology of Calvin, Philadelphia: The Westminster Press, 1956, p. 86.

[13] Ibid., and Exp. Gen. 45.8, Commentaries (Haroutunian), p. 274.

[14] Calvin, Against Astrology Judicial, Sigs. C7-C7v.

[15] J.C. 1.2.140f.   [16] W.T. 4.4.551ff.

[17] Calvin, Inst. 1.16.8, and Hooker, Eccl. Pol. 1.7.2.

[18] Ham. 4.4.36ff., and Luther, Exp. Gen. 32.6-8, Plass anthol., vol. 2, 2437.

[19] For a bit more on these particular lines from Hamlet, see below under Reason.

[20] *Rich. II* 3.2.27ff.   [21] *All's Well* 1.1.231ff.
[22] Luther, Exp. Gen. 32.6-8, *loc.cit.*
[23] Luther, Exp. Gen. 43.1-5, Plass anthol., vol. 3, 4118.
[24] Calvin, *Inst.* 1.17.4.   [25] *Ibid.,* 1.17.6.   [26] *Ibid.,* 1.17.9.

✧ God and the Gods Hamlet-Lear

References to God, the gods, and derivative or compound words fill twelve columns in Bartlett's *Complete Concordance of Shakespeare.* Most of these are virtual clichés, ranging from conventional piety to conventional expletive, and do not require theological commentary. There are also a number of quite interesting remarks, from the standpoint of historical theology. There are, for example, such references to God's justice as Claudius' "There is no shuffling; there the action lies In his true nature,"[1] while Claudio acknowledges that justice is defined by heaven rather than by man: "on whom it will, it will; On whom it will not, so; yet still 'tis just."[2] Yet the nature of God is not to be understood only in terms of justice, as Isabella says:

> Why, all the souls that were were forfeit once,
> And he that might the vantage best have took
> Found out the remedy.[3]

The divine "finding out of the remedy" through the incarnation and atonement was a unique event, but there are also daily rescues and continuous care, which Hamlet affirms when he speaks of "a special providence in the fall of a sparrow,"[4] while the aged Adam in *As You Like It* prays that

> He that doth the ravens feed,
> Yea, providently caters for the sparrow,
> Be comfort to my age![5]

All of this and more can be found in the speeches of Shakespeare's characters who live in a Christian society and think within the framework of Christian meaning. In no instance, however, did Shakespeare attempt to provide a comprehensive understanding of God. References to the deity contribute to the development of character and action within particular dramatic contexts. Characters refer to God only as they feel themselves related to him in their own situations, not as he is in himself, and this observation applies regardless of whether the characters are good or evil. Claudius in *Hamlet* finds that he cannot effectively pray because he does not fully repent and make restitution, so that his words fly up while his thoughts remain below.[6] Throughout Claudius' soliloquy on prayer there is much of what theologians would regard as a valid understanding of God, but Shakespeare's attempt is not to characterize God: it is to characterize the guilty king. Similarly, when the eminently just character Banquo declares that

In the great hand of God I stand,[7]

we may discern behind his remark a faith that God would have men stand both under his protection and in loyalty to his moral commands, but the major enlightenment which Shakespeare provides in this line is as to Banquo, not as to God. That Shakespeare's recorded interests should have been focused in this fashion does not mean, as some would perhaps like to believe, that he was not a Christian. It merely means that he was a dramatist.

It also provides one further indication that he understood the Christian tradition rather intimately, for when he has his characters speak of God, they do so within the context of their own immediate involvement in some particular problem or decision; they do not philosophize about God, do not theorize about him, but relate the practical problems of their existence to their thoughts of God, and vice versa. If we would study the deepest insights of Shakespeare's characters into God, we can best do so through noting their remarks about their own problems and their decisions involving mercy and justice, prayer, providence, and repentance. Under each of those headings, more will be said about the implications of various characters' understandings of God.

Thus far we have been discussing remarks about God which are made by characters who are either presumably Christian themselves or who surely speak within the context of a Christian society. There are two other contexts for the references to God in Shakespeare's plays. The first of these is the context of general grace, where the words may appear to be Christian, for Christians also speak in a similar fashion, but where in fact the references are equally appropriate to the pious heathen. Since it is important for us not to interpolate Christian theology into situations where Shakespeare has not introduced it, it is necessary for us to make clear the propriety of the theology which he assigns to his pagan characters. Thus we will now turn to the consideration of this context, showing that remarks made by non-Christians which are compatible with Christianity are yet not exclusively Christian, after which we will proceed to analyze those treatments of God which are quite incompatible with Christianity, and even antithetical to it.

It would be a great mistake to assume that if a Shakespearean character makes a pious remark about God or the gods, that character is therefore to be interpreted in terms of Christian salvation, even though Shakespeare may have placed the action of the play prior to the Christian dispensation. It really should be unnecessary to suggest that characters whom Shakespeare has carefully shown to be pre-Christian are in fact to be interpreted as such, but it will probably do no harm to indicate here as well as elsewhere that the religious insights which Shakespeare grants to his pagan characters had theological warrant for being within the reach of pagan men.

There is no point in finding Christian significance in Lear's much-noted remark to Cordelia after the defeat of her army that

> Upon such sacrifices, my Cordelia,
> The gods themselves throw incense,[8]

for, as Calvin reminds us, it was "of course" a commonplace among pagans "that God is not pleased with sacrifices unless sincerity of intention accompany them."[9] Similarly, faith in the outworkings of divine justice was not unknown among the Greeks, with their emphasis upon nemesis and retribution, and there is no exclusively Christian insight in such remarks as Albany's:

> This shows you are above,
> You justicers, that these our nether crimes
> So speedily can venge![10]

Even among those who know nothing whatever of Christianity, some demonstrably believe no less than Albany, so that as Calvin observes they "confess that there is a God reigning in heaven who executeth such justice as never was looked for."[11]

The presence of clear recognitions of just retribution in *Lear* does not render it a "Christian play." Neither do the prayers, for as Calvin says, "the door [of prayer] is not open to a few but to all mortals," and even unbelievers often find that their prayers "are not denied."[12] Hooker teaches that "every good and holy desire [recall Lear's near-prayers] though it lack the form, hath notwithstanding in itself the substance and with him [God] the force of a prayer, who regardeth the very moanings, groans, and sighs of the heart of man."[13] It is within this context that we can most properly understand, for what it is, Edgar's "Well pray you, father."[14]

Even the general conception of God as merciful in himself and desiring mercy from men is not beyond the reach of non-Christian religion, a fact which Calvin acknowledges when he writes that among all men, whether or not they are Christian, "the feeling is somehow ingrained in them that God is merciful to all who seek him."[15] When Tamora pleads with Titus to imitate the gods by being merciful, she is not exceeding the limits of pagan wisdom:

> Wilt thou draw near the nature of the gods?
> Draw near them then in being merciful.[16]

The evidence simply does not allow us to regard such remarks as indicative of the dramatist's intent to give expression to Christian ethics, for as Calvin observes, not only "pagan philosophers" but even "the worst despisers of godliness" have "confessed openly that we are never so like God as when we do that which is good."[17] Tamora's remark is perfectly fitting, within such an understanding of paganism.

To take these passages, or others like them, as material for theologizing and analogizing is at best gratuitous and at worst distorting. It is clear from the evidence that men may talk good sense, good ethics, and moving piety without being therefore either Christian, or types of Christ, or even types of Christians. There can be little doubt that Shakespeare respects his pagan characters enough to give their paganism its due. That we should do so too seems advisable from the standpoint alike of historical theology and of literary criticism.

Shakespeare has his characters refer to God not only within a Christian context, and within a context shared by Christians and the virtuous heathen, but also within a context quite antithetical to Christian doctrine. When Edmund addresses the goddess nature, and dedicates his services to her, he is clearly linking himself with the wild and ruthless aspects of the universe:

> Thou, nature, art my goddess; to thy law
> My services are bound.[18]

There is no point in underscoring the obvious, and discussing the many ways in which Edmund's words and actions stand opposed to Christian faith and teachings, but it is interesting to compare Edmund's prayer to nature with Luther's remarks on nature and the idolatry of nature, for Luther's remarks might well stand as a kind of commentary on the characterization of Edmund:

"Nature . . . sets before itself no other object than the self, to which it is moved and directs itself; it sees only and seeks only itself and aims at itself in everything; everything else, even God himself, it bypasses as if it did not see it, and turns to itself. . . . [So nature] puts itself in the place of everything, and even in the place of God, and seeks only its own and not what is God's. Thus it idolizes and absolutizes itself . . . , regards everything it sees as worthless unless it serves to its advantage and makes itself available to it. It values only what it can use for its own enjoyment, advantage, and benefit."[19]

Viewed in some such terms as these, Edmund's dedication of his services to the nature goddess has considerable significance in the dramatic development of his character. Again, however, the view of the gods held by a character is not presented for its own sake, but rather for its relevance to our understanding of dramatic characters and actions.

I suspect that the gods whom Edmund calls upon to "stand up for bastards" are the referents of Gloucester's despairing words,

> As flies to wanton boys, are we to th' gods.
> They kill us for their sport.[20]

Certainly Gloucester's view of the gods at this point fits the gods whom Edmund serves, and both conceptions clearly contradict the Christian view of the deity. This contradiction may be classified under two heads: first, concerning the divine plurality; second, the divine nature. Of these, the first is the least serious, for there was a strong tradition in Christian theology to the effect that many pagan references to the plurality of gods could be taken as semantic devices, behind which there was in effect the admission of a single supreme deity. This view was not unanimously held among Christian theologians, but it had a strong advocate in the sixteenth century in the person of Calvin, who cited Justin Martyr's demonstration "by very many testimonies that the unity of God has been engraved upon the heart of all," and added that "Tertullian likewise proves the same point by phrases in common use."[21]

Other competent theologians would of course have disagreed at this point, but as to the divine nature there could be no doubt that any view of God as the afflictor of mortal flies was utterly wrong. Calvin describes a situation rather like that in which Gloucester is placed when he writes that "men curse their life, loathe the day of their birth, abominate heaven and the light of day, rail against God, and as they are eloquent in blasphemy, accuse him of injustice and cruelty" because of their afflictions.[22] The purpose of those afflictions, Calvin teaches, is that men "may learn in calamities to accuse and loathe their own worthlessness rather than to charge God with unjust cruelty."[23] Relevant here is what we have already seen[24] of what the theologians regarded as men's inclination to evade responsibility for their own troubles and sins. "It is a wicked sacrilege," Calvin writes, "to transfer to God the blame for their own misfortunes, which lay in themselves" and it is a mark of impiety to "complain that God with unbridled power abuses his miserable creatures for his cruel amusement."[25]

What Calvin says along these lines is in no sense peculiar to him, but summarizes a general Christian consensus on such views as those which Gloucester expresses. I am not implying that Shakespeare's audience, standing under the strong influence of the Christian tradition, would have turned against Gloucester with a shudder. Such revulsion would not have fitted the dramatic situation as Shakespeare has developed it, nor would it have expressed a proper reaction in terms of Christian charity. What I am suggesting is that Shakespeare has here utilized a kind of tension between Christian attitude and dramatic expression for the purpose of heightening interest in the development of a sympathetic stage character in the setting of pre-Christian

Britain. In terms of situation, character, and setting, the words have great dramatic force.

We have now treated certain representative instances in which Shakespeare's characters make significant references to God. We have grouped these references according to whether they were made on Christian grounds, on a shared common ground between Christianity and paganism, or on grounds quite incompatible with the Christian faith. In each instance and on whatever grounds, it seems clear that Shakespeare was employing familiarity with Christian teachings for the effective development of dramatic action and character. A familiar understanding of Christian doctrine in historical perspective thus contributes to a fuller appreciation of Shakespeare's art, but Shakespeare's art is not devoted to theologizing the theater.

[1] *Ham.* 3.3.60f. [2] *M. for M.* 1.2.126f. [3] *Ibid.*, 2.2.73ff.
[4] *Ham.* 5.2.229. [5] *A.Y.L.* 2.3.43ff. [6] *Ham.* 3.3.38 and 97.
[7] *Macb.* 2.3.136. [8] *Lear* 5.3.20f. [9] Calvin, *Inst.* 2.2.24.
[10] *Lear* 4.2.78ff.
[11] Calvin, Serm. on Job 12.17-25, Golding trans., p. 224a, line 31.
[12] Calvin, *Inst.* 3.20.13 and 15. [13] Hooker, *Eccl. Pol.* 5.48.2.
[14] *Lear* 4.6.223.
[15] Calvin, Exp. Ezek. 18.23, *Commentaries* (Haroutunian), p. 402.
[16] *Titus* 1.1.117.
[17] Calvin, Exp. Matt. 5.43-46, *Commentaries* (Haroutunian), p. 333.
[18] *Lear* 1.2.1f.
[19] Luther, *Lectures on Romans* (8.3), Wilhelm Pauck trans., Philadelphia: The Westminster Press, 1961, pp. 219-20.
[20] *Lear* 1.2.22 and 4.1.38f. [21] Calvin, *Inst.* 1.10.3.
[22] *Ibid.*, 3.7.10. [23] *Ibid.*, 2.5.11.
[24] See, above, the entry on FREEDOM.
[25] Calvin, *Inst.* 2.5.11 and 3.24.14.

✧ Guilt

God's justice operates in a number of ways for the punishment of sin, and the sense of guilt is one of these ways. It is thus that the Ghost speaks in *Hamlet*, warning Hamlet that he should contrive nothing against Gertrude:

> Leave her to heaven,
> And to those thorns that in her bosom lodge
> To prick and sting her.[1]

The fact that Gertrude seems to feel no such pricks and stings until Hamlet forces her to see herself as in a mirror will be discussed in the entry on SELF-KNOWLEDGE, but what concerns us here is the normal operation of the human conscience, plaguing the wrong-doer.

As the devil's enticements are couched in terms of deceit, the sinner is rarely aware of the full measure of what lies in store for him. Thus Exton declares, after murdering Richard II:

> O, would the deed were good!
> For now the devil, that told me I did well,
> Says that this deed is chronicled in hell.[2]

Luther speaks in similar terms of the operation of sin which "is not felt" while it is being acted; for if it were actively felt at the time "we would be warned by the ill effects which sin brings on and we would draw back."[3] Like Exton, Macbeth does not seem fully aware of the consequences of Duncan's murder; he certainly does not foresee the turmoil of guilt, sleeplessness, fear, and anguish from which he later suffers. He does see that there will be consequences, but he envisions these as the spread of "bloody instructions" among subjects who will seek to "plague the inventor" as he plagues Duncan.[4] What he finds, however, is much, much more. Menteith describes his condition with fair accuracy:

> Who then shall blame
> His pester'd senses to recoil and start,
> When all that is within him does condemn
> Itself for being there?[5]

Calvin treats various Old Testament references to the plague of an evil conscience, and writes that it is "as though God had said, 'If I were even to be silent and not take upon me the office of a judge, and if there were no other accuser, and no one to plead the cause, yet stand against thee will thy wickedness, and fill thee with shame.' "[6] In the same vein Luther declares that "to no one is a wicked person as unbearable and ruinous as to himself."[7] Many of Shakespeare's characters express such an experience of the operations of guilt. In *Hamlet*, Claudius declares

> The harlot's cheek, beautied with plast'ring art,
> Is not more ugly to the thing that helps it
> Than is my deed to my most painted word.
> O heavy burden![8]

Richard III suffers from a similar affliction:

> O no! Alas, I rather hate myself
> For hateful deeds committed by myself.[9]

In *The Tempest*, Alonso admits to a like experience:

> O, it is monstrous, monstrous!
> Methought the billows spoke and told me of it;
> The winds did sing it to me; and the thunder,
> That deep and dreadful organpipe, pronounc'd
> The name of Prosper. It did bass my trespass.[10]

As Calvin put it, "fierce people are so uneasy inside as to be their own disturbers," and seem even "to be always in a state of panic."[11] The most striking single image of guilt is Macbeth's "O, full of scorpions is my mind, dear wife," which is parallel to Hooker's comment that "the remorse of sin is in [the heart] as the deadly sting of a serpent."[12]

There is also the quieter response of despair, as when Lady Macbeth recognizes that "our desire is got without content."[13] Apropos here is Luther's question: "Even if [the wicked] were to gain possession of everything that they wished, what sweet and pure enjoyment could they have if their conscience was not at rest? Is there an evil more cruel than the unrest caused by a mordant conscience?"[14] Hooker preaches that though "it may seem a paradox, it is a truth, that no wicked man's estate is prosperous, fortunate, or happy."[15] It is against such a background that Shakespeare has Lady Macbeth come to feel "'Tis safer to be that which we destroy" and Macbeth himself to declare it better to "be with the dead" than to continue in such "doubtful joy" and "restless ecstasy."[16] Calvin writes that "the more stout-hearted the wicked are in their contempt of God, the weaker they become, so as to tremble at their own shadow; and this condition is far more wretched than to be cut off at a single blow."[17]

Similar experiences of guilt are treated in other plays, as when Gertrude in *Hamlet* declares that

> To my sick soul (as sin's true nature is)
> Each toy seems prologue to some great amiss.
> So full of artless jealousy is guilt
> It spills itself in fearing to be spilt.[18]

We may summarize here with two references from the theologians. In whichever direction these sinners turn their eyes, Luther writes, "everything becomes black and horrible," and Calvin declares that even "while the unbelievers flourish, they do not know what is waiting for them on the next day; therefore, they must always live in turmoil because of perplexity and fear; neither can they enjoy the smile of fortune without, one way or another, stupefying themselves."[19]

[1] *Ham.* 1.5.86ff.   [2] *Rich. II* 5.5.114ff.

[3] Luther, Exp. Gen. 3.7, Amer. ed., vol. 1, p. 163.

[4] *Macb.* 1.7.7ff.   [5] *Ibid.*, 5.2.22ff.

[6] Calvin, *Commentary on Jeremiah* (2.19), vol. 1, p. 104.

[7] Luther, Exp. Ps. 37.9, Plass anthol., vol. 3, 4632.

[8] *Ham.* 3.1.51ff.   [9] *Rich. III* 5.3.190f.   [10] *Temp.* 3.3.95ff.

[11] Calvin, Exp. Matt. 5.5, and Exp. Heb. 10.36-38, *Commentaries* (Haroutunian), pp. 337 and 252.

[12] *Macb.* 3.2.40, and Hooker, *Eccl. Pol.* 6.6.14.   [13] *Macb.* 3.2.6.

[14] Luther, "Comforts for the Weary and Heavy Laden," *Reformation Writings,* Woolf ed., vol. 2, p. 36.

[15] Hooker, Serm. iv, Keble ed., vol. 2, p. 374.

[16] *Macb.* 3.2.7f and 19ff.

[17] Calvin, Exp. Lev. 26.39, *Commentaries on the Pentateuch,* p. 239.

[18] *Ham.* 4.5.17ff.

[19] Luther, Exp. Gen. 4.10, Amer. ed., vol. 1, p. 287, and Calvin, Exp. Matt. 19.27-29, *Commentaries* (Haroutunian), p. 207.

✧ *Happiness: See Contentment*

✧ *Hatred*

It is obvious, according to Biblical doctrine, that hatred is a sin, though many Christians continue to commit it. Shylock in *The Merchant of Venice* shows considerable familiarity with the Bible, and his words exemplify the basic objection to hate: that it is a kind of thought-murder. He makes his point with a question:

Hates any man the thing he would not kill?[1]

I suspect that Jewish doctrine on this matter is the same as Christian, but, however that may be, the linking of hatred with murder has strong theological warrant. Thus Luther finds "the root of anger" to be "the spirit that wants to kill,"[2] while Calvin declares that "where there is either anger or hatred, there is the intent to do harm" and asks: "See whether you can be angry against your brother without burning with desire to hurt him."[3] Such expressions represent commonplace doctrine.

While Shylock hates one man, Timon hates all men. In view of this fact, it is particularly puzzling to find Timon referred to by the theologizers as a type of Christ. Timon of course represents something of a special case, because there are so many unsolved problems in connection with this particular drama, but there can scarcely be any question that hatred is a basic element in what Alcibiades calls Timon's "latter spirits."[4] Timon prays to the gods that they may

> grant, as Timon grows, his hate may grow
> To the whole race of mankind, high and low![5]

Later, he says that

> I am Misanthropos, and hate mankind,[6]

and he advises his faithful steward Flavius to

> Hate all, curse all, show charity to none.[7]

If it is at all relevant to make theological commentary on Timon, it will certainly not be that he is a type of Christ. He will scarcely even appear to be a type of normal humanity, if we apply Calvin's summary of Christian teaching to the effect that "it is therefore a proof of the greatest inhumanity to despise those in whom we are constrained to recognize our own likeness."[8] As for Timon's hatred of life in general, we might also recall Calvin's summary of Christian doctrine that though we should hate the sin which distorts life, "life should not be hated as such, because it is rightly regarded as among God's chief blessings."[9] Though it cannot be denied that Timon was abused by men, and even if we strain the evidence to accept the claim of his epitaph that he was one "who, alive, all living men did hate,"[10] the fact remains that his later life was as antithetical to Christian ideals as were the lives of Iago and Edmund, though in a different way. A passage from William Tyndale states the issue succinctly: "When thy neighbor hath showed thee more unkindness than God hath love, then mayest thou hate him, and not before."[11]

[1] *Merch.* 4.1.67.

[2] Luther, *Serm. on Ten Commandments*, Plass anthol., vol. 1, 74.

[3] Calvin, *Inst.* 2.8.39.   [4] *T. of A.* 5.4.74.   [5] *Ibid.*, 4.1.39f.

[6] *Ibid.*, 4.3.53.   [7] *Ibid.*, 4.3.533.

[8] Calvin, *Commentaries on Isaiah* (58.7), vol. 4, p. 234.

[9] Calvin, *Inst.* 3.9.3, and Exp. John 12.25, *Commentaries* (Haroutunian), p. 318.

[10] *T. of A.* 5.4.72.

[11] Tyndale, *Expositions of Scripture*, p. 47.

✧ *Heaven*

In the entry for DEATH, we have already analyzed a number of Shakespeare's references to heaven, but I have reserved for separate treatment here two remarks in which Richard II refers to preparing himself for heaven. Before discussing these, however, I would like to suggest again that Shakespeare uses references to the life everlasting for the purpose of characterization within the limits of the "two hours' traffic" of his stage. Even though the dying

Richard declares that his soul's "seat is up on high,"[1] we do not find Shakespeare going beyond this brief line to focus our attention on the everlasting fate of Richard's soul.

The major dramatic value of Richard's remarks lies in the fact that they provide a focus for the development of his character under affliction. In his last meeting with his queen, he tells her that

Our holy lives must win a new world's crown,
Which our profane hours here have stricken down.[2]

Later, in his prison soliloquy, he declares that

I wasted time, and now doth time waste me.[3]

Calvin's words are applicable here: "God by prolonging time to each [person], sustains him that he may repent. . . . This is a very necessary admonition, so that we may learn to employ time aright, as we shall otherwise suffer a just punishment for our idleness."[4] Thus the deposed monarch, whom "waste of idle hours hath quite thrown down," prepares himself for heaven by the disciplines of humility and affliction.[5]

Suffering and time provide the opportunity for Richard to win a new world's crown. Luther expresses the commonplace doctrine when he writes that "lest the sinner fall into spiritual sleep or become secure and even boast in a way about having done well, God comes with a rod of iron. . . . Why? Not that a man should render satisfaction for sin by enduring such sufferings, for God is not satisfied by such inflictions (*poenis*) and does not look at our 'satisfactions.' Rather he strikes (*punit*) to keep the sinner from snoring securely or even from glorying in the evil deeds he has committed."[6] Through such discipline, it is God's purpose, as

Calvin puts it, "even that we ought to strive after newness of life," for "heaven is our home and in the school of suffering we must prepare ourselves for our final departure."[7]

Richard II is one of the rare characters whom Shakespeare treats in such a way as to indicate the relevance of the kind of theological doctrines of the afterlife which we have cited here. Even so, however, it remains true that Shakespeare's focus is upon characterization and action in the theater, rather than in heaven and hell.

[1] *Rich. II* 5.5.111.   [2] *Ibid.,* 5.1.24f.   [3] *Ibid.,* 5.5.49.

[4] Calvin, Exp. II Pet. 3.9, *Catholic Epistles,* p. 419.

[5] *Rich. II* 3.4.66. For an analysis of Richard's references to his reduction to "nothing," see the entry on Contentment.

[6] Luther, Exp. Gen. 37.18-20, Plass anthol., vol. 3, 4238.

[7] Calvin, Exp. I Pet. 3.10, *Catholic Epistles,* p. 420, and Exp. Rom. 8.30, quoted in Quistorp, *op.cit.,* p. 35.

✦ *Honor*

It is a fact that striving after honor has always been regarded with suspicion in the Christian tradition, though it is also a fact that concern for one's good name is not repudiated as sinful. In view of these two facts, confusion easily arises, and it is difficult to know what relevance (if any) Christian doctrine may have in a particular situation. The very ambiguities which we encounter here should be instructive, and it is for that basic reason that I will develop them in some detail.

There are several points, of course, at which the reference is unmistakably clear and we should turn first to these. Take for example Wolsey's admonition against "too much honor:"

O, 'tis a burden, Cromwell, 'tis a burden
Too heavy for a man that hopes for heaven![1]

Similarly, we find the classical apotheosis of honor in Antony's remark that

If I lose mine honor,
I lose myself.[2]

Calvin summarizes the classical and Christian conceptions when he writes that "the heathen philosophers do not condemn every desire of glory, but among Christians, whoever is desirous of glory departs from true glory."[3] Antony thus reflects the views inculcated by "heathen philosophers," as Wolsey reflects the Christian tradition. Among Shakespeare's other characters who speak on this subject, Iago comes as close as Wolsey to summarizing one valid element of Christian teaching, though he is of course speaking in his deceitful role as "honest Iago" when he treats Othello to the following commonplace:

Good name in man and woman, dear my lord,
Is the immediate jewel of their souls.
Who steals my purse steals trash. . . .[4]

Here Iago is merely elevating to the level of poetry an analogy which was repeatedly used in connection with a good name and the slanderer. Calvin gives similar expression to this popular thought: "For if a good name is more precious than all riches (Prov. 22.1), we harm a man more by despoiling him of the integrity of his name than by taking away his possessions."[5] When Shakespeare wishes religious and ethical references to be clear and unambiguous to his audience, he knows how to make them so.

But what are we to do with Cassio's remarks? After his cashiering by Othello, he cries out to Iago:

> Reputation, reputation, reputation! O, I have lost
> my reputation! I have lost the immortal part of
> myself, and what remains is bestial![6]

This sounds like the kind of concern for honor against which Wolsey warned, and of which Calvin wrote that whereas our purpose in life should be to seek God's glory rather than our own, "if we lose our purpose of living for the sake of life—that is, if we desire too much to live in the world— we set aside the purpose of life."[7] Perhaps such a criticism of excessive concern for life in this world would be the proper theological counterpart to Cassio's concern for reputation as "the immortal part of myself." On the other hand, reputation is indispensable to leadership, it is what the leader leaves behind him in the world, and Cassio may merely be expressing a proper regard for his own good name. Or again, even if Cassio's remark is seen as excessive and a vice, there is another aspect of the traditional Christian understanding of honor, also summarized by Calvin when he writes that some vestige of concern for God's honor "remains imprinted in [man's] very vices. For whence comes such concern to men about their good name but shame? And whence comes shame but from regard for what is honorable? The beginning and cause of this is that they understand themselves to have been born to cultivate righteousness, in which the seed of religion is enclosed."[8]

I have made a good deal of the ambiguity of Cassio's remark, not because I think it is incumbent upon us to arrive at a theological evaluation of every character, but for the very different reason that I think it is impossible to do so. To state categorically, as has been done in recent years, that Cassio is saved is to make an assertion which is at least as dubious from the theological as from the literary perspective. We have already examined, under the entry on election, the significance of Cassio's maudlin discussion of his own salvation and that of Iago, and we saw there how weak a reed that discussion provides as foundation for any assurance that Cassio would have appeared to Elizabethans to be in a state of grace. Clarity of analysis requires us to admit both theological irrelevance and theological ambiguity wherever they exist. It is safe to assume that Shakespeare knew theology sufficiently well that when he wished to use it in explicit ways, he was able to do so without confusion, as we have repeatedly seen. Conversely, we may assume that when he did not make theological references clear in his writings, he did not expect us to read them in.

[1] *Henry VIII* 3.2.383ff.   [2] *A. and C.* 3.4.22f.
[3] Calvin, *Commentary on Galatians* (5.26), p. 170.
[4] *Oth.* 3.3.155ff.   [5] Calvin, *Inst.* 2.8.47.   [6] *Oth.* 2.3.262ff.
[7] Calvin, Exp. Dan. 3.16-18, *Commentaries* (Haroutunian), p. 242.
[8] Calvin, *Inst.* 1.15.6.

✦ Hypocrisy

Among Shakespeare's many references to hypocrisy, those which refer to religious hypocrisy are of particular interest to us. Here as elsewhere, we find that Shakespeare has given poetic expression to commonplaces of theology. In *The Merchant of Venice* Bassanio refers to the cloaking of error and grossness by citations from Scripture:

> In religion
> What damned error, but some sober brow

Will bless it, and approve it with a text,
Hiding the grossness with fair ornament?[1]

Luther employs the same widespread idea in a sermon when he declares that "no devil, heretic, or schismatic spirit will step forth and declare: 'I devil, or I heretic, am preaching my own doctrine.' No, they all claim: 'It is not my teaching; it is God's word.' Everyone wants to have the reputation of preaching God's word."[2] Calvin observes that "In all ages the irreligious affectation of religion, because it is rooted in man's nature, has manifested itself and still manifests itself,"[3] and remarks could indeed be found from all ages to the same effect. In Shakespeare, the fullest portrayal of explicitly religious hypocrisy is found in Richard III, who says of himself in a soliloquy:

But then I sigh, and, with a piece of Scripture,
Tell them that God bids us do good for evil;
And thus I clothe my naked villainy
With odd old ends stol'n forth of holy writ,
And seem a saint when most I play the devil.[4]

Apropos here are such expressions as Calvin's that "all those who go around draped with a false sanctimoniousness do it by the devil's prodding," and Luther's to the effect that man-made godliness is "mere blasphemy of God and the greatest of all sins man commits."[5] As one final example of Shakespeare's dramatic references to religious hypocrisy, we recall Polonius' words which give so "smart a lash" to Claudius' conscience:

We are oft to blame in this,
'Tis too much prov'd, that with devotion's visage

And pious action we do sugar o'er
The devil himself.[6]

[1] *Merch.* 3.2.77ff.
[2] Luther, Serm. on John 7.16, Amer. ed., vol. 23, p. 225.
[3] Calvin, *Inst.* 2.8.5.   [4] *Rich. III* 1.3.334ff.
[5] Calvin, Exp. I Tim. 4.1-5, *Commentaries* (Haroutunian), p. 345, and Luther, Exp. I Pet. 1.18-19, Lenker ed., vol. 3, p. 73.
[6] *Ham.* 3.1.46ff.

✣ *Image of God: See Man*

✣ *Inconstancy*

Our preceding entry on religious hypocrisy treated matters which have been universally recognized and emphasized throughout the Christian tradition. No such uniform treatment was accorded to inconstancy, though it has not been ignored in the theological analysis of man, particularly in connection with man's creation and fall. In *The Two Gentlemen of Verona,* Proteus refers to inconstancy in a way which may perhaps be reinforced by recalling the theological usage:

> O heaven, were man
> But constant, he were perfect! That one error
> Fills him with faults, makes him run through
>   all th' sins.[1]

"Nothing is more inconstant than man," Calvin declares, and he continues to say of Adam's created nature that "in this integrity man by free will had the power, if he so willed, to attain eternal life. . . . Therefore Adam could have stood if he wished, seeing that he fell solely by his own will. But it was because his will was capable of being bent to one side or the other, and was not given the constancy to persevere, that he fell so easily."[2] In his plays, Shakespeare surely had no intent to teach theology, nor was Proteus attempting to do so, but in these words on man's inconstancy Shakespeare might have sought by allusion to religious ideas to illumine a particular situation in the secular drama, just as his references to nature and other subjects serve a similar purpose. In this connection we should also recall that a repudiation of human inconstancy is in no sense distinctive of Christianity, but may just as well be traced through the intellectual history of Greece and Rome.

[1] T.G.V. 5.4.110ff.   [2] Calvin, *Inst.* 1.15.5. and 8.

✣ Ingratitude

Ingratitude is another sin which was castigated by classical and Christian writers alike. "The heathen," according to Luther, "have said that unthankfulness is the greatest vice. Therefore you have given the severest rebuke to a man if you have charged him with ingratitude."[1] In *Twelfth Night*, Viola declares that

> I hate ingratitude more in a man
> Than lying, vainness, babbling, drunkenness,
> Or any taint of vice whose strong corruption
> Inhabits our frail blood.[2]

At this point, as at so many others, the classical and Christian analyses of particular vices are the same. Agreeing with the classical authorities and with Viola's opinion, Luther advises that "unthankfulness is the greatest and most shameful vice. Because of it the spring dries up whence flow all faithfulness and benefactions among men."[3]

[1] Luther, Exp. Luke 17.11-19, Plass anthol., vol. 3, 4551.
[2] T.N. 3.4.388ff.   [3] Luther, *op.cit.*

✦ *Integrity*

Sixteenth-century theology recognized two basic types of integrity: that of the natural man within the natural order who has achieved such integrity as he possesses by his own works, and that of the Christian within the order of grace whose integrity originates in the gift of God and rests in his providence. Both types are represented in Shakespeare's characters. We will begin with the pagan understanding and move toward the Christian.

We find the integrity of the natural man asserted, as we would expect, in the Roman plays. Thus Pompey declares of his war against the triumvirate:

> If the great gods be just, they shall assist
> The deeds of justest men.[1]

Later, Pompey's response to the suggestion that his guests be assassinated indicates that his sense of justice is at best quite superficial and easily shaken by self-interest. We have already cited sufficient evidence to show, in the chapter on ethical backgrounds, that sixteenth-century theology recognized the ethical potential of men within the secular order. In the character of Brutus, in *Julius Caesar*, we see that ethical potential realized at its highest level. Like Pompey, Brutus refers to his personal integrity, but he can of course make a far better claim to such integrity than Pompey can:

> There is no terror, Cassius, in your threats;
> For I am arm'd so strong in honesty,
> That they pass me by as the idle wind,
> Which I respect not.[2]

Calvin's comment is pertinent both to Brutus and to Pompey: "Even the pagans say that true glory consists in an upright conscience. Now, this is true but it is not the whole truth. Since all men are blinded by too much self-love, we are not to be satisfied with our own judgment of our deeds."[3] With Brutus, there would seem to be a minimum of self-deception in his confidence; with Pompey, on the other hand, the margin of self-deception is large. Much the same judgment would seem to apply to Polonius, when his own life is viewed in terms of his famous advice to Laertes:

> This above all—to thine own self be true,
> And it must follow, as the night the day,
> Thou canst not then be false to any man.[4]

In Christian terms, the fault with such integrity as Polonius recommends is that it places man's reliance entirely upon himself, without reference to God, for, as Luther writes, whoever is satisfied "with his own truth and wisdom is incapable of comprehending the truth and wisdom of God."[5] Polonius' rather pompous reference to integrity, though spoken in a Christian age, is actually far closer to Pompey's than to Brutus', for Brutus' honesty is genuine.

All self-assurance is not un-Christian, of course. Thus Luther writes of a good, godly pride, which God requires of everyone. This proper pride says: "I must not give way to the devil; I will not look at the devil and follow him."[6] Such was the spirit of Banquo's "In the great hand of God I stand" and on such terms he addressed the weird sisters:

> Speak then to me, who neither beg nor fear
> Your favors nor your hate.[7]

This Christian sense of assurance is even more explicit in the pious King Henry VI, whose assurance is that "God, our hope, will succour us" and who therefore could declare:

> What stronger breastplate than a heart untainted?
> Thrice is he armed, that hath his quarrel just,
> And he but naked, though locked up in steel,
> Whose conscience with injustice is corrupted.[8]

A Christian confidence in their own integrity is shared by Banquo and King Henry VI, but there are also marked differences between the two men, especially in that Banquo never claims that reliance upon God will save him from earthly disasters, while Henry seems to feel that because he is safe in God he will therefore be safe from men. The naïveté of the pious king can be put in Christian perspective if it is seen in terms of the Christian's duty to use all the means available to him in the secular realm, which we have already discussed in the entry on FREEDOM, above. Sixteenth-century theologians would not, however, have seen anything un-Christian in the nature of the assurance expressed by Banquo and Henry VI. The point may be seen in terms of one of Hooker's sermons: "Judge thyself. God hath left us infallible evidence, whereby we may at any time give true and righteous sentence upon ourselves. We cannot examine the hearts of other men; we may our own. 'That we have passed from death to life, we know it,' saith St. John, [1 John 3.14] 'because we love our brethren'; and 'know ye not your own selves, how that Jesus Christ is in you, except ye be reprobates?' [2 Cor. 13.5] I trust, beloved, we know that we are not reprobates, because our spirit doth bear us record, that the faith of our Lord Jesus Christ is in us."[9]

Judged in those terms, there would not appear to be anything presumptuous about Richmond's prayer addressing God as "O thou, whose captain I account myself,"[10] for his reliance is clearly upon God rather than upon himself alone. Also in keeping with sixteenth-century theology was Richmond's appeal to his troops before the battle against Richard III, who

> hath ever been God's enemy:
> Then if you fight against God's enemy,
> God will in justice ward you as his soldiers.[11]

Relevant here are the words of Calvin concerning just men, that by "comparing their good cause with the evil cause of the wicked, they thence derive confidence of victory, not so much by the commendation of their own righteousness as by the just and deserved condemnation of their adversaries."[12]

[1] A. and C. 2.1.1f.   [2] J.C. 4.3.66ff.
[3] Calvin, Exp. II Cor. 10.17, Commentaries (Haroutunian), p. 320.
[4] Ham. 1.3.78ff.
[5] Luther, Lectures on Romans (3.7), Pauck ed., p. 70.
[6] Luther, Serm. on John 2.17, Amer. ed., vol. 22, p. 232.
[7] Macb. 2.3.136 and 1.3.60f.   [8] 2 Henry VI 4.4.55 and 3.2.232ff.
[9] Hooker, Serm. v, par. 13, Keble ed., vol. 2, p. 389.
[10] Rich. III 5.3.109.   [11] Ibid., 5.3.253ff.
[12] Calvin, Inst. 3.14.18.

✦ Justice and Judgment

What the theologians would have regarded as a proper attitude towards the execution of justice by a ruler finds expression in the words of Henry V:

Touching our person, seek we no revenge,
But we our kingdom's safety must so tender,
Whose ruin you have sought, that to her laws
We do deliver you.[1]

The common theological position may be represented by Calvin's statement: "it is the duty of all magistrates here to guard particularly against giving vent to their passions even in the slightest degree. Rather, if they have to punish, let them not be carried away with headlong anger, or be seized with hatred, or burn with implacable severity. Let them also (as Augustine says) have pity on the common nature in the one whose special fault they are punishing."[2] But, human nature being polluted with sin, perfect justice is impossible to achieve on earth. "One should not permit sin," Luther says. "Yet one should exercise mercy, for we are all made of the dough of which prostitutes and fornicators are made. If we stand, we stand by grace alone; otherwise our piety stands on a wisp of straw and soon collapses."[3] Lear speaks in related terms, and though he never refers to grace he is concerned with "the common dough" of human sin. "The rascal beadle" who whips the whore, Lear says, "hotly lusts to use her" in the way for which he is whipping her,[4] while Luther writes that the executioner before performing his office should pray, "Dear God, I kill a man unwillingly, for in thy sight I am no more godly than he."[5] Lear's attention was focused upon lust, and Luther's upon godliness, but on both accounts the imperfection of humanly administered justice is underscored.

In *Macbeth*, young Macduff concludes that "liars and swearers" are fools to allow honest men to hang them, "for there are liars and swearers enow to beat the honest men and hang up them,"[6] while Luther declares that "if all those were hanged that are thieves and yet would not be called so, the world would soon be desolate, and there would not be either hangmen or gallows enough."[7] Though there are not enough honest men to punish the evil-doers (recall Hamlet's "to be honest, as this world goes, is to be one man pick'd out of ten thousand"),[8] the evil-doers in effect punish themselves. Luther puts it this way: "As men all rob and cheat each other, God manages in a masterful way that one thief shall punish the other, elsewhere would we find gallows or ropes enough?"[9]

Whatever failures in justice may accompany the human administration of the positive law, however, evildoers cannot escape the justice of God, as Henry V tells the soldier Williams: "If these men have defeated the law and outrun native punishment, though they can outstrip men, they have no wings to fly from God."[10] God's judgment will surely be pronounced at the final Doom, but it may also come in this life, whether in terms of outward calamities and punishments visited upon the wicked, or in terms of inner anguish and guilt of mind (for which see the entry entitled GUILT). The timing of such divine judgment cannot be predicted by man. "The powers, delaying (not forgetting)," as Ariel tells the "three men of sin" in *The Tempest,* will nonetheless certainly visit retribution for evil.[11] "God exercises his judgments freely, in his own way and order," as Calvin writes, "so that some receive their punishment immediately, whereas others are allowed for a while to enjoy their ease and pleasure in peace," while Hooker says that "the judgments of God do not always follow crimes as thunder doth lightning, but sometimes the space of many ages cometh between."[12]

There is obviously a difference, the Christian tradition holds, between the justice of earthly and heavenly tribunals. Nowhere is that difference more graphically described than in Claudius' soliloquy:

> In the corrupted currents of this world
> Offence's gilded hand may shove by justice,
> And oft 'tis seen the wicked prize itself
> Buys out the law; but 'tis not so above.[13]

Calvin speaks to the same effect: "God judges in a different manner from men; for the hidden tricks and wicked arts, by which wicked men are accustomed to deceive and take advantage of the more simple, are not taken into account by men; or if they are taken into account, they are at least extenuated, and are not estimated according to their just weight." But, as Claudius says, "'tis not so above":

> There is no shuffling; there the action lies
> In his true nature, and we ourselves compell'd,
> Even to the teeth and forehead of our faults,
> To give in evidence.[14]

Calvin, too, continues his analysis along the same lines: "But God, dragging forth to light those very men of dazzling reputation, who under specious pretences had been in the habit of concealing their unjust practices, plainly declares that they are murderers."[15] To Hamlet himself, this point is quite clear:

> For murther, though it have no tongue, will speak
> With most miraculous organ.[16]

[1] *Henry V* 2.2.174ff.   [2] Calvin, *Inst.* 4.20.12.
[3] Luther, Exp. Matt. 20.20-23, Plass anthol., vol. 3, 4263.
[4] *Lear* 4.6.164ff.

⁵ Luther, quoted by Roland Bainton, *Here I Stand*, New York: Abingdon Press, 1950, p. 241.

⁶ *Macb.* 4.2.55ff.

⁷ Luther, Exp. Seventh Commandment in *The Greater Catechism, Luther's Primary Works*, eds. Henry Wace and C. A. Buchheim, London: Hodder and Stoughton, 1896, p. 72.

⁸ *Ham.* 2.2.178f.

⁹ Luther, Exp. Seventh Commandment, *op.cit.*, p. 76.

¹⁰ *Henry V* 4.1.177.   ¹¹ *Temp.* 3.3.73 and 53.

¹² Calvin, Exp. Luke 13.1-3, *Commentaries* (Haroutunian), p. 281, and Hooker, Serm. IV, Keble ed., vol. 2, p. 374.

¹³ *Ham.* 3.3.57ff.   ¹⁴ *Ibid.*, 3.3.60ff.

¹⁵ Calvin, *Commentary on Isaiah* (1.15), vol. 1, p. 62.

¹⁶ *Ham.* 2.2.621f.

✦ *Kingship*

Shakespeare's kings are not, by and large, very pious or even very moral men. There are exceptions, of course, but the general rule stands, and it is a rule to which the major theologians would have agreed. Hooker puts the matter as tactfully as he can, but though his expression could not have offended the crown his opinion is clear enough: "Devotion and the feeling sense of religion," he writes, "are not usual in the noblest, wisest, and chiefest personages of state."[1] Luther, as usual, expresses himself with more directness and verve: "O, what a rare bird will a lord and ruler be in heaven," while on another occasion he declares that power always has been and always will be "more often given to the Pilates, Herods, Annases, and Caiaphases than to the pious Peters, Pauls, and the like."[2] "You must know," he says, "that from the beginning of the world a wise prince is a rare bird indeed; still more so a pious prince. They are usually the greatest fools or the worst knaves on earth. Therefore one must constantly expect the worst from them and look for little good from them, especially in divine matters which concern the salvation of souls."[3] In Luther's judgment, to which Calvin and Hooker agree, it would be foolish to regard a ruler as disqualified by a lack of piety: "To be qualified to rule, it is not enough to be pious. A jackass is also pious. Ability and experience are required in order to rule."[4] In fact, if one had to choose between a pious and an able ruler, Luther's choice would be clear-cut: if both qualifications cannot be had, in the magistrate, "it is better for him to be prudent and not good than good and not prudent."[5]

No matter how bad or ineffective the prince might be, Luther could see no justification for rebelling against him: "I am and always will be on the side of those against whom insurrection is directed, no matter how unjust their cause; I am opposed to those who rise in insurrection, no matter how just their cause, because there can be no insurrection without hurting the innocent and shedding their blood."[6] The official doctrine of the Church of England was in accord with Luther at this point, and Hooker holds that "unto kings by human right, honor by very divine right is due."[7]

With these views, Calvin to a large extent agrees, but only to an extent. He emphatically forbids private persons to rebel against kings under any circumstances and he warns all citizens that wickedness and impiety in rulers do not disqualify them from rule. But for the "lesser magistrates"— that is, for those who hold duly constituted authority but whose authority is less than that of the prince—there is another obligation. If rulers are so neglectful or tyrannous in office that freedom be "in any respect diminished, far less be violated" then "they are faithless in office, and traitors to their country."[8] Though Calvin feared a mob as much as Luther and Hooker, and though he carefully and repeatedly warned against resistance to authority except in cases of extreme provocation, there were points beyond which he was unwilling to go in forbidding resistance to the prince.

To the Bishop of Carlisle's question in *Richard II*—"What subject can give sentence on his king?"[9]—Luther would certainly have answered "none," and Hooker would probably have agreed. Calvin, on the other hand, would have pointed to the lesser magistrates, of whom he wrote in one of the most famous passages in *The Institutes* that "I am so far from forbidding them to withstand, in accordance with their duty, the fierce licentiousness of kings that, if they wink at kings who violently fall upon and assault the lowly common folk, I declare that their dissimulation involves nefarious perfidy, because they dishonestly betray the freedom of the people, of which they know that they have been appointed protectors by God's ordinance."[10] But though Calvin would have disagreed in principle with Carlisle's view that none could judge the king, his practical view of such actions as those of Bolingbroke would probably have been in accord with Carlisle's.

I have developed these differences here because they were historically important, as the seeds planted by Calvin's political doctrine were beginning to take root and grow in England, especially among the parliamentarians who saw themselves as vested with the powers of the lesser magistrate. As for Shakespearean drama, however, the relevance of Calvin's dissent is tenuous. None of the rebels in Shakespeare's history plays, whether English or Roman, quite seem to fit the case as Calvin describes it, though both Brutus and Bolingbroke would have qualified to the extent that they were lesser magistrates. It is of course quite true that Shakespeare could not possibly have risked royal displeasure to the extent of dramatizing a consistently admirable and morally justified rebel, and there is no reason to think that he ever wanted to do so.[11] But it is just possible—though surely no more—that when the Essex conspirators paid Shakespeare's company to stage *Richard II* on the eve of their rebellion, they may have been seeking to invoke something which has since been lost to us: a dramatic portrayal of a relatively sympathetic "lesser magistrate" rising against the crown. It is certainly true that Essex was far from possessing either the character or the justification of a Bolingbroke, and that Bolingbroke's actions themselves would have been highly questionable even in Calvin's eyes. On the other hand, Essex's followers may have gambled upon pointing up similarities which not only seem quite obscure to us today but which obviously failed to elicit the desired response in London.

Whatever may be said of Essex's attitude, however, it is clear from the evidence that Shakespeare's company had no intention whatever of abetting revolution, and virtually all scholars agree that Shakespeare himself gives every indication of the most undeviating support for the establishment. Even Luther could have asked for no more.

[1] Hooker, *Eccl. Pol.* 7.24.15.

[2] Luther, "Open Letter to the Christian Nobility," Phil. ed., vol. 2, p. 163, and "Treatise Concerning the Ban," *ibid.*, p. 49.

[3] Luther, "Secular Authority: To What Extent it Should be Obeyed," Phil. ed., vol. 3, p. 258.

[4] Luther, Exp. Ex. 19.7, Plass anthol., vol. 2, 1773.

[5] Luther, Exp. Deut. 1.13-16, Amer. ed., vol. 9, p. 19.

[6] Luther, "Against Insurrection and Rebellion," Amer. ed., vol. 45, p. 63.

[7] Hooker, *Eccl. Pol.* 8.2.6.   [8] Calvin, *Inst.* 4.20.8.

[9] *Rich. II* 4.1.121.   [10] Calvin, *Inst.* 4.20.31.

[11] The case of Richmond in *Richard III* does not constitute an exception to this general rule, for Richmond, as founder of the Tudor dynasty, was

regarded not as a rebel but as the rightful heir to the throne who came to depose the usurping tyrant Richard III.

✦ *Man*

It is a truism to say that man, simply as a human being, has been invested with more significance in the Greek and Hebrew traditions than in most others. As these two traditions merge in Christianity, we find repeated references to man's unique value, and as the Renaissance and Reformation re-emphasize both classical and Biblical outlooks, we find a new and exuberant recognition of human dignity. Luther expresses a common theme when he says that "men-servants, maids, and everybody ought to interest themselves in this high honor and say: I am a human being; this is certainly a higher title than being a prince, for God did not make a prince; men made him. But that I am a human being is the work of God alone."[1] Shakespeare's age was pervaded by such attitudes, and apart from them, I for one find it difficult to conceive of the development of Shakespearean drama, with its respectful and even awesome concern for each individual character.

Underlying such attitudes, from the Christian point of view, is the doctrine of the image of God in man. This doctrine was not a merely abstract affirmation, isolated from life, but had the most practical implications. "We are not to consider what men merit of themselves," Calvin teaches, "but to look upon the image of God in all men, to which we owe honor and love."[2] Nowhere do we find clearer expression of this concern by a Shakespearean character than in King Edward's rebuke of the murder committed by certain of his subjects:

> your carters or your waiting vassals
> Have done a drunken slaughter and defac'd
> The precious image of our dear Redeemer.[3]

The theological understanding which underlies these words is summed up by Calvin: "Now, if we do not wish to violate the image of God, we ought to hold our neighbor sacred. And if we do not wish to renounce all humanity, we ought to cherish his as our own flesh."[4]

Man's basic worth and dignity, then, consists in the fact of his humanity, bearing the image of God. In the Christian view, man's originating sin (from which all others spring) consists in the fact that he is unwilling to remain content with his inherent dignity, and that he overreaches himself. It is in these terms that Wolsey advises Cromwell:

> Cromwell, I charge thee, fling away ambition!
> By that sin fell the angels. How can man then
> (The image of his Maker) hope to win by it?[5]

Luther speaks in the same vein: "This lust for honor poisoned man when the devil in Paradise moved Adam and Eve to desire to be like God; and it is still sticking to us."[6] The plague continues, as Isabella observes in *Measure for Measure*:

> But man, proud man,
> Drest in a little brief authority,
> Most ignorant of what he's most assur'd
> (His glassy essence), like an angry ape,
> Plays such fantastic tricks before high heaven
> As make the angels weep.[7]

Man thus refuses to know himself, refuses to see his own condition as in a mirror ("his glassy essence"), while, in

Antony's words, "we strut To our confusion."[8] In Antony's classical view the heavens laugh at the results, whereas in Isabella's Christian view they weep. This difference is but another example of Shakespeare's careful characterization.

Shearing away all pretenses, man needs to look at himself again, needs to strip himself of his additions and "leavings" to see himself simply as a man. "As men arrogate to themselves more than is right," Calvin declares, "and even inebriate themselves with delusions, [God] strips them naked, that after having known that all they think they either have from nature, or from themselves, or from other creatures, is a mere phantom, they may seek true glory."[9] Lear comes to acknowledge this truth when he sees naked Tom:

> Is man no more than this? Consider him well.
> Thou ow'st the worm no silk, the beast no hide, the
> sheep no wool, the cat no perfume. Ha! Here's
> three on 's are sophisticated! Thou art the thing
> itself; unaccommodated man is no more but such
> a poor, bare, forked animal as thou art.[10]

Now recognizing his own condition, Lear tears at his clothes to strip off all the superfluities. Lear had to be brought to this condition by suffering, but Shakespeare endows Henry V with a similar understanding when he makes him say of himself as king, that "his ceremonies laid by, in his nakedness he appears but a man."[11] Henry's recognition is so effortless that it appears less valuable than Lear's, but both at least speak to the same point, and it was a point equally accessible to pagan and to Christian in terms of self-knowledge, when judged within the secular order.

A response to common humanity quite different from that of Lear and Henry is displayed by Timon of Athens after the collapse of his fortunes, a response characterized rather by hatred of all men than by any recognition of his natural bond with even the worst and poorest. We have already discussed Timon's misanthropy under the entry on HATRED, but something more should also be said here. Timon sees nothing but evil in man:

> All's obliquy;
> There's nothing level in our cursed natures
> But direct villany. Therefore be abhorr'd
> All feasts, societies, and throngs of men!
> His semblable, yea, himself, Timon disdains.
> Destruction fang mankind![12]

The treatment of human nature by major sixteenth-century theologians was in one sense similar to Timon's, but in an even more basic sense it was radically different. Thus Luther teaches that "one must trust no human being insofar as he is a human being, even though one finds his conduct beyond reproach." In the next breath, however, Luther adds: "Yet there must be no hate; no matter how evil one considers him, one must not for this reason abandon him or despair of his improvement."[13] All men, after all, display the image of God, all are brothers, and all are involved in the same sin. Hooker thus declares that it is a part of men's natural endowment that their duty is "no less to love others than themselves," due to the "relation of equality between ourselves and them that are as ourselves."[14] Timon utterly ignores this aspect of his relation to others, though it was accessible to him through natural reason, even apart from revealed theology. Thus his view was distorted, even when judged by the standards of one who like Hooker holds that man's best deeds are so flawed as to need the pardon of

God, and who teaches that "our nature . . . inclineth only unto evil."[15] Calvin writes to similar effect on man's sin, and yet he too warns that we should not despise mankind, for he teaches that many examples among pagans as well as Christians "warn us against adjudging man's nature wholly corrupted,"[16] while in another place he teaches that "he who truly worships and honors God will be afraid to think slanderously of man."[17] Our three major theologians thus agree that every man was so deeply involved in sin as to be quite incapable of pleasing God, that none could rescue himself from this condition so that none had any pretense of preeminence in virtue, and that each should recognize the image of God in his fellowmen. The example of Timon, flying to the wilderness, may be interestingly compared with Calvin's ironic words: "It is a goodly thing to play the philosopher in wilderness far from the company of men: but it agreeth not with Christian gentleness as it were for hatred of mankind to fly into desert and solitariness, and therewithal to forsake those duties which the Lord hath chiefly commanded."[18]

It may seem to be out of keeping with our general practice to examine the pre-Christian Timon so closely by the standards of Christian theology. There are several reasons for doing so. In the first place, the theologizers' interpretation of Timon as a type of Christ needs to be set in the perspective of historical theology. In the second place, a close analysis clearly demonstrates the differences between Timon's misanthropy and the theological understanding of man as fallen but still a child of God, and thus once again illustrates the care with which Shakespearean characterization was developed. Finally, the analysis of this particularly un-Christian view of man should serve to set in perspective the more Christian views of man which we will discuss below and under the entry on SIN.

Timon's basic error consists in focusing entirely upon one side of man's nature while ignoring the other, so that he is totally lacking in balance. It is quite otherwise with Hamlet, who keeps both aspects of human nature clearly in focus:

> What is a man,
> If his chief good and market of his time
> Be but to sleep and feed? A beast, no more.
> Sure he that made us with such large discourse,
> Looking before and after, gave us not
> That capability and godlike reason
> To fust in us unus'd?[19]

We have already noted in the entry on BEASTS, that theologians would have agreed with Hamlet's suggestion that man differs from the lower animals in that he has been endowed with "discourse of reason."[20] The same point arises in the first three lines quoted above, where Hamlet categorizes a life which is devoted only "to sleep and feed" as that of "a beast, no more," whereas Calvin speaks to the same effect when he observes that "men have not only life, so that they can eat and drink," but that they also "have understanding and reason."[21] Calvin summarizes the popular renaissance conception of reason's operation in terms similar to Hamlet's "large discourse, Looking before and after," when he refers to "the nimbleness of the mind of man, which vieweth the heaven and earth and secrets of nature, and comprehending all ages in understanding and memory, digesteth everything in order, and gathereth things to come by things past."[22] Finally, Hamlet's rhetorical question as to whether God gave us such reason "To fust in us unus'd" is paralleled by Luther's "for God certainly did not give us our reason and the advice and aid which it supplies in order to have us contemptuously disregard them."[23] We thus see that Hamlet's remarks about man at this point are quite in keeping with Christian doctrine, but we must not for this reason jump to the conclusion that Hamlet's soliloquy on Fortinbras' army is a Christian statement. Though it incorporates a clear understanding both of man's animal nature and of his God-given rationality, the speech as a whole indicates a preoccupation with revenge, ambition, and bloody thoughts. Hamlet is as yet far removed from his later reliance on the "special providence in the fall of a sparrow."[24]

[1] Luther, Serm. on Creed, Plass anthol., vol. 2, 2733.

[2] Calvin, *Inst.* 3.7.6. [3] *Rich. III* 2.1.121f.

[4] Calvin, *Inst.* 2.8.40.

[5] *Henry VIII* 3.2.440ff. Though some scholars regard these lines as un-Shakespearean, I treat them here because they are often cited, and refer the reader to the various theories of the joint authorship of *Henry VIII*.

[6] Luther, Serm. on Luke 2.14, Plass anthol., vol. 2, 2064.

[7] *M. for M.* 2.2.117ff. [8] *A. and C.* 3.13.114f.

[9] Calvin, *Commentary on Jeremiah* (9.24), vol. 1, pp. 498-99.

[10] *Lear* 3.4.107ff. [11] *Henry V* 4.1.110.

[12] *T. of A.* 4.3.18ff.

[13] Luther, *Lectures on Genesis* (12.11-13), Amer. ed., vol. 2, p. 301.

[14] Hooker, *Eccl. Pol.* 1.8.7.

[15] Hooker, Serm. II, par. 7, Keble ed., vol. 2, p. 302, and "Fragment of an Answer," *ibid.*, p. 29.

[16] Calvin, *Inst.* 2.3.3.

[17] Calvin, Exp. Jas. 3.9, quoted in Torrance, *op.cit.*, p. 84. The translation appears to be Torrance's.

[18] Calvin, *Inst.* 4.13.16, Norton trans.

[19] *Ham.* 4.4.33ff. [20] *Ham.* 1.2.149.

[21] Calvin, Exp. Job 10.7f, quoted by Torrance, *op.cit.*, p. 69.

[22] Calvin, *Inst.* 1.15.2, Norton trans.

[23] Luther, *Lectures on Genesis* (32.6-8), Plass anthol., vol. 2, 2437.

[24] *Ham.* 5.2.230f.

✦ Mercy

Mercy is referred to by Shakespeare's characters in two ways. At times it is treated within a distinctively Christian context, while at other times the context is equally accessible to Christians and to the virtuous heathen. We have already seen in the entry on God that the Roman Tamora's plea for mercy on the grounds that it is "near the nature of the gods" was quite appropriate even within a pre-Christian society. According to Calvin, "Even to pagans, deprived of the Law and the Prophets, some taste of this truth has always been given."[1] Nor is Tamora the only one to make so generalized an appeal, for in *Measure for Measure* Isabella at least once speaks in the same terms:

> No ceremony that to great ones 'longs,
> Not the king's crown nor the deputed sword,
> The marshall's truncheon nor the judge's robe,
> Become them with one half so good a grace
> As mercy does.[2]

Such references are equally Senecan and Christian, as Calvin notes when he describes clemency as "that best counselor of kings and surest keeper of the kingly throne . . . which by a certain writer of antiquity [i.e. Seneca] was truly called the chief gift of princes."[3]

If the appeal for mercy is not exclusively Christian, neither is the repudiation of an excessively rigorous justice. Shakespeare's contemporaries knew enough of the classics (their education being almost entirely classical) so that they would have recognized more readily than most modern readers what was a product of common human insight, and what was uniquely Christian. Furthermore, an age which included so much serious theological reading and instruction would know too much theology to "read in" Christian analogues and allusions after the indiscriminate fashion of certain modern critics. Thus, in connection with mercy and justice, it is well to note that a condemnation of excessively rigorous justice was not an exclusive prerogative of Christianity, as leading Christian theologians recognized. In this connection, Luther reminds us that it has been well said "by a certain heathen: *Summum ius, summa iniustitia,* that is, the most extreme justice is the greatest injustice. Ecclesiastes 7.16 also warns: 'Be not righteous overmuch, neither make thyself overwise.' "[4] What is uniquely Christian is the denial of man's ability to be sufficiently just to satisfy God, along with the corollary doctrine that man's only ultimate hope is in the mercy of God.

The most famous appeals for mercy made by Shakespeare's characters refer to these distinctively Christian doctrines. Let us begin with Portia's words to Shylock:

> Though justice be thy plea, consider this—
> That, in the course of justice, none of us
> Should see salvation.[5]

Of relevance here is Luther's remark: "A lawyer says: Let justice be done though the world perish. A theologian says: Let sin be forgiven and the world saved, for justice is not done, but sin is always done."[6] The undergirding theological assumption is that man's justice is quite insufficient to merit salvation, for as Hooker preaches, the little righteousness we have "is, God knoweth, corrupt and unsound; we put no confidence at all in it, we challenge nothing in the world for it, we dare not call God to a reckoning, as if we had him in our debt-books," while he says elsewhere that by our own efforts we can bring forth "nothing in [God's] sight acceptable, no, not the blossoms or least buds that *tend to the fruit of eternal life.*"[7] Calvin's judgment accords with Luther's and Hooker's, as with Portia's, when he writes that "we are received into the grace of God out of sheer mercy. . . . Since we see that every particle of our salvation stands thus outside of us, why is it that we still trust or glory in works?"[8]

Shylock emphatically repudiates all such appeals, declaring that "I stand for judgment," "I stand here for law," and "My deeds upon my head."[9] When the Duke asks, "How shalt thou hope for mercy, rend'ring none?" Shylock counters with another question, "What judgment shall I dread, doing no wrong?"[10] Shylock's characterization is thus clearly developed in terms of the Old Testament legalism which the New Testament repudiates. Shylock's reliance upon the letter of the law brings into focus the sixteenth-century religious contention over the sufficiency of human justice and works, which sufficiency Hooker calls "a strange and strong delusion . . . wherewith the man of sin hath bewitched the world."[11] Calvin of course also denies the possibility of an impeccable uprightness: "Let one of Adam's children come forward with such uprightness. If there is no one, they must either perish out of God's sight or flee to the shelter of his mercy."[12] It is on the basis of such theological doctrines that Isabella appeals to Angelo in *Measure for Measure*:

> How would you be,
> If he which is the top of judgment should
> But judge you as you are? O, think on that!
> And mercy then will breathe within your lips,
> Like man new made.[13]

Such appeals may be quite effectively linked with the petition in the Lord's Prayer that God "forgive us our trespasses as we forgive those who trespass against us," and it is in these terms that Lord Say pleads for mercy in 2 *Henry VI*:

> If, when you make your pray'rs,
> God should be so obdurate as yourselves,
> How would it fare with your departed souls?[14]

Portia somewhat naïvely makes the same appeal to Shylock, though he is presumably not accustomed to using the Lord's Prayer:

> We do pray for mercy
> And that same prayer doth teach us all to render
> The deeds of mercy.[15]

The point is obvious, and none of the relevant theological comments differ essentially from Calvin's: "we ought not to seek forgiveness of sins from God unless we ourselves also forgive the offenses against us of all those who do or have done us ill. If we retain feelings of hatred in our hearts, if we plot revenge and ponder any occasion to cause harm, and even if we do not try to get back into our enemies' good graces, by every sort of office deserve well of them, and commend ourselves to them, by this prayer we entreat God not to forgive our sins."[16] In one sense, the true praying of the Lord's Prayer consists in the practice of mercy.

Portia's last direct appeal to Shylock—"Then must the Jew be merciful"—is countered by Shylock's question "On what compulsion must I? Tell me that," and this exchange ushers in one of the most famous of Shakespeare's set pieces:

The quality of mercy is not strain'd;
It droppeth as the gentle rain from heaven
Upon the place beneath.[17]

Portia thus appeals for mercy as a spontaneous act, not as compulsion, and this appeal again accords with long-established theological doctrines which may be summarized in Luther's advice that "if you want to practice mercy, its water must rise from the spring and fountainhead," and his consistent position that God is pleased only by acts of spontaneous love.[18]

Whereas Christian doctrine consistently questions the worth of justice without mercy, it is also important to note that it denies the validity of mercy isolated from justice. The two should be kept not only in balance, but even in union. Zwingli summarizes the traditional teachings: "goodness is both mercy and justice. Deprive mercy of justice, and it is no longer mercy, but indifference or timidity. But fail to temper justice by kindness and forbearance and at once it becomes the greatest injustice and violence."[19] Thus Angelo in *Measure for Measure*, though he is a hypocrite, or perhaps even because he is a hypocrite, is appealing to a well-known principle of ethics when he replies to Isabella's appeal for mercy:

I show it most when I show justice;
For then I pity those I do not know,
Which a dismiss'd offence would after gall,
And do him right that, answering one foul wrong,
Lives not to act another.[20]

Whatever may be said of the death sentence placed upon Claudio by the equally guilty Angelo, the ethical principal cited by Angelo was well established. Luther writes of the magistrate that he "sins as greatly against God if he does not punish and protect and does not fulfil the duties of his office as does one to whom the sword has not been committed when he commits a murder. If he can punish and does not—even though the punishment consists in the taking of life and the shedding of blood—then he is guilty of all the murder and evil which these fellows commit, because, by willful neglect of the divine command he permits them to practice their wickedness, though he can prevent it and is in duty bound to do so."[21] The same position is expressed by Escalus, who can speak without the hypocrisy of Angelo, when he declares that

> Mercy is not itself that oft looks so,
> Pardon is still the nurse of second woe.[22]

Finally, the principle is also cited by the Prince in *Romeo and Juliet* in reference to the feuding houses of Montague and Capulet:

> Mercy but murders, pardoning those who kill.[23]

Again, a remark of Luther's is relevant: ". . . a good physician, when a disease is so bad and so great that he has to cut off a hand, foot, ear, eye, or let it decay, does so in order to save the body. Looked at from the point of view of the member that he cuts off, he seems a cruel and merciless man; but looked at from the point of view of the body, which he intends to save, it turns out that he is a fine and true man and does a work that is good and Christian, as far as it goes."[24]

Mercy and justice must thus be kept together, for neither can fully exist without the other. Calvin summarizes the Christian doctrines with balance and inclusiveness: "Yet it is necessary for the magistrate to pay attention to both [mercy and justice], lest by excessive severity he either harm more than heal; or, by superstitious affectation of clemency, fall into the cruelest gentleness, if he should (with a soft and dissolute kindness) abandon many to their destruction. For during the reign of Nerva it was not without reason said: it is indeed bad to live under a prince with whom nothing is permitted; but much worse under one by whom everything is allowed."[25] Calvin's reference to the Emperor Nerva affords a glimpse into a classical precedent for the situation in Shakespeare's *Measure for Measure*, which has so often been treated as a uniquely Christian play. It also brings us full circle, back to the area of a universal human wisdom where Christian and classical ethics interlock and overlap.

[1] Calvin, Exp. Ezek. 18.23, *Commentaries* (Haroutunian), p. 402.

[2] *M. for M.* 2.2.59ff.   [3] Calvin, *Inst.* 4.20.10.

[4] Luther, Serm. on Phil. 4.4-7, Lenker ed., vol. 7, p. 101.

[5] *Merch.* 4.1.198ff.

[6] Luther, *Table Talk*, Plass anthol., vol. 1, 1578.

[7] Hooker, Serm. II, par. 7, Keble ed., vol. 2, p. 302, and "Fragments of an Answer," *ibid.*, p. 29.

[8] Calvin, *Inst.* 3.14.17.   [9] *Merch.* 4.1.103, 142, and 206.

[10] *Ibid.*, 4.1.88f.

[11] Hooker, Serm. VI, par. 21, Keble ed., vol. 2, p. 398.

[12] Calvin, *Inst.* 3.17.15.   [13] *M. for M.* 2.2.75ff.

[14] 2 *Henry VI* 4.7.122ff.   [15] *Merch.* 4.1.200.

[16] Calvin, *Inst.* 3.20.45.   [17] *Merch.* 4.1.182ff.

[18] Luther, Serm. on Rom. 12.7-8, Plass anthol., vol. 3, 4107; "To the Christian Nobility," Weimar ed., vol. 6, p. 444; *Lectures on Romans* (12.8), Pauck trans., pp. 339-40.

[19] Zwingli, *op.cit.*, p. 249.   [20] *M. for M.* 2.2.100ff.

[21] Luther, "Against the Robbing and Murdering Hordes of Peasants," Phil. ed., vol. 4, pp. 251f.

[22] *M. for M.* 2.1.297f.   [23] *R. and J.* 3.1.202.

[24] Luther, "Whether Soldiers, too, Can be Saved," Phil. ed., vol. 5, p. 35.

[25] Calvin, *Inst.* 4.20.10.

✦ Moderation

Shakespeare's characters frequently praise moderation or cite its relevance to the conduct of human affairs, and here again we are in an area where classical and Christian ideas overlap. The ethical emphasis on moderation among the Greeks was incorporated into Christian teaching to an extent which has sometimes been overlooked. The place of the mean in the development of Anglican theology does not need to be demonstrated here, as it is so widely recognized, but it will perhaps be useful to point out that much was made of it in the continental Reformation, especially in the works of Calvin.[1] Thus we find Calvin writing that "there is nothing more hard, than to moderate a man's self in such wise as we may keep rule and compass: we see that men cannot make merry except they be over merry," and such intemperance is directly associated with sin in Calvin's view: "we teach that all human desires are evil, and charge them with sin, not in that they are natural, but because they are inordinate."[2] On this basis, Calvin teaches that "it is necessary then to return to the mean, or the middle way, as it is called, for there is where true virtue is found."[3] We can thus see that moderation was emphasized not only in the Greek tradition, and derivatively in the Thomist, but also in the Protestant synthesis of Calvin.

Shakespeare is thus able to set his characters' appeals to moderation against the background of a virtually universal consensus. In A *Midsummer Night's Dream*, Lysander declares that

> a surfeit of the sweetest things
> The deepest loathing to the stomach brings,[4]

while in *The Merchant of Venice* Nerissa says that

> they are as sick that surfeit with too much, as they
> that starve with nothing. It is no mean happiness,
> therefore, to be seated in the mean.[5]

Perhaps the most forceful expression is that of Macduff in *Macbeth*:

> Boundless intemperance
> In nature is a tyranny. It hath been
> Th' untimely emptying of the happy throne
> And fall of many kings.[6]

Other similar references could be cited from the plays, but these are sufficient to illustrate Shakespeare's employment of the commonplace theme. There was no subject on which speakers could appeal to a more universal consensus of classical as well as of Christian opinion in all its major variations.

[1] Ronald Wallace points out that Calvin even speaks as though moderation "was the chief, and indeed the only, Christian virtue." See Wallace, *op.cit.*, p. 179.

[2] Calvin, *Sermons on Job*, *op.cit.*, p. 29a, line 53, and *Inst.* 3.3.12.

[3] Calvin, Serm. on I Tim. 5.23-25, *Opera Omnia* (*Corpus Reformatorum*), Brunsvig: C. A. Schwetschke et Filium, 1895, vol. 53, p. 533.

[4] M.N.D. 2.3.137f.   [5] Merch. 1.2.6ff.   [6] Macb. 4.3.66ff.

✦ Nature

In our study thus far, we have had many occasions to discuss the place of "nature" within various aspects of Christian theology. Major portions of the two chapters devoted to the Reformation background in theology and ethics were devoted to what might be called natural theology, whereas in the present chapter an earlier entry entitled BEASTS sought to analyze the relation of human and animal nature, while under the entry below on SIN we will treat natural depravity. Finally, in the concluding chapter, I will suggest what meaning might best be assigned to the mirror held up to nature, when that phrase is judged in terms of Shakespeare's religious milieu. For a full consideration of the subject, the treatment of nature here must be coordinated with these other analyses.

In sixteenth-century theology, two types of approach to nature are recognized. The first of these is an approach to nature made only in terms of human wisdom, and the second is an approach under the special guidance of Christian understanding. Of these, the first may be related to the words of Duke Senior in *As You Like It*, and the second to Friar Laurence's soliloquy on herbs in *Romeo and Juliet*.

Let us turn first to what Duke Senior says of the school of nature. As we have noted in earlier entries, he speaks eloquently of the distinction between flattery and counsel and of "the uses of adversity," both of which references could as well have been made by a Greek as by a Christian. Such elements of a universal wisdom seem to be the lessons he has learned from the book of nature:

> And this our life, exempt from public haunts,
> Finds tongues in trees, books in the running brooks,
> Sermons in stones, and good in everything.[1]

Hooker writes in terms which are generally the same as the Duke's: "We see then how nature itself teacheth laws and statutes to live by."[2] Calvin not only approves the same principle, but advances it through the use of images not unlike those used by the Duke when he declares that man cannot pretend "that he lacks ears to hear the truth when there are mute creatures with more than melodious voices to declare it," and deplores man's claim "that he cannot see with his eyes what eyeless creatures point out to him," and denies that man can "plead feebleness of mind when even irrational creatures give instruction."[3] Similarly, Hooker teaches that by the light of nature men "learn in many ways what the will of God is."[4]

What man learns from nature alone, however, is no more than the Duke himself seems to have learned, that is, a wiser ordering of his life in the temporal order. Hooker and Calvin both praise the great values which come to man from the contemplation of nature and the use of reason, but when it comes to conversion, Hooker comments that such resources are insufficient for salvation,[5] and Calvin declares that "even if God wills to manifest his fatherly favor to us in many ways, yet we cannot by contemplating the universe infer that he is Father."[6] Man is prevented by the corruption of his own nature from learning more from nature than how to live well in the natural order. To learn "the laws of duties supernatural," in Hooker's phrase, men must look to revelation, but within the limits of this world "nature findeth out such laws of government as serve to direct even nature depraved to a right end."[7] It is to such a use that Duke Senior seems to have put the school of nature.

A different approach may be found in the words of Friar Laurence in *Romeo and Juliet*, who, as is appropriate to his vocation, gives a summary of the traditional theology of the subject.[8] The whole passage is interesting, but we can place it in theological perspective by treating a few of its lines, beginning with a reference to common or general grace:

> O mickle is the powerful grace that lies
> In plants, herbs, stones, and their true qualities.

What Laurence is doing here is to contemplate nature in terms of his theological training. He thus begins with reference to the "true qualities" of uncorrupted nature. "The orthodox faith," Calvin wrote in words which would have been equally acceptable to Thomas Aquinas, "does not admit that any evil nature exists in the whole universe. For the depravity and malice both of man and of the devil, or the sins that arise therefrom, do not spring from nature, but rather from the corruption of nature."[9] What Friar Laurence does is to analyze plants in terms so familiar to Christian doctrine so as to say something about man. Here, then, is a place where Shakespeare clearly employs an analogical approach, and it is significant that he does not do so without telling us in unmistakably explicit terms what he is about. Friar Laurence leaves nothing to the imagination, but translates good and evil uses from the world of plants to the world of man:

> Two such opposed kings encamp them still
> In man as well as herbs—grace and rude will;
> And where the worser is predominant,
> Full soon the canker death eats up that plant.

We are thus given an invitation, without the slightest ambiguity, to treat nature in the light of grace, or in the light of revealed theology, which amounts to the same thing.

Between the two passages which we have quoted, Laurence provides an analysis which is no different in idea from that of Hooker, though the friar speaks in images while Hooker speaks more abstractly: "There is no particular object so good, but it may have the show of some difficulty or unpleasant quality annexed to it. . . ; contrariwise (for so things are blended) there is no particular evil which hath not some appearance of goodness whereby to insinuate itself."[10] When Laurence's words are seen in such perspective, their theological import is unmistakable. The following couplet,

> naught so vile that on the earth doth live
> But to the earth some special good doth give,

states in more incisive form a commonplace to which Luther gives truistic utterance when he says that "no one is so vile that he does not have something good in him."[11] The approach is reversed in the next lines:

> Nor aught so good but, strain'd from that fair use,
> Revolts from true birth, stumbling on abuse.

The point again is a commonplace, and may find a parallel at least in general terms in Calvin's statement that men do good works "not by genuine zeal for good but either by mere ambition or by self-love, or some other perverse motive" so that "by the very impurity of men's hearts these good works have been corrupted as from their source."[12] Finally, where Laurence concludes that "virtue itself turns vice, being misapplied," Calvin holds that "things not evil of their own nature yet . . . become temptations through the devil's devices, when they are so thrust before our eyes that by their appearance we are drawn away or turn aside from God," and where Laurence adds that "vice sometimes by action dignified" Calvin teaches of man that "some vestige [of true honor] remains imprinted in his very vices."[13]

I hope that it is clearly understood that I am not trying to find literary sources for the words which Shakespeare assigns to Laurence. Nor am I trying to dissociate Laurence from Italian Catholicism by comparing his ideas with those of Luther, Calvin, and Hooker, for the attitudes which they express on this subject are, for our immediate purposes, indistinguishable from those of any other orthodox spokesmen of the Christian tradition. Shakespeare has assigned to Friar Laurence an analysis of nature which would have elicited familiar associations in the mind of any thoughtful Christian who heard or read his words. It would, in fact, be difficult to find a more succinct, accurate, and memorable summary of the Christian theology of nature.

[1] A.Y.L. 2.1.15ff.   [2] Hooker, *Eccl. Pol.* 1.10.1.
[3] Calvin, *Inst.* 1.5.15.   [4] Hooker, *Eccl. Pol.* 1.8.3.
[5] *Ibid.*, 1.12.3 and 1.14.1.   [6] Calvin, *Inst.* 2.6.1.
[7] Hooker, *Eccl. Pol.* 1.14.1 and 1.10.1.
[8] R. and J. 2.3.1-30.   [9] Calvin, *Inst.* 1.14.3.
[10] Hooker, *Eccl. Pol.* 1.7.6.
[11] Luther, Serm. on John 3.19, Amer. ed., vol. 22, p. 399.
[12] Calvin, *Inst.* 3.14.3.   [13] *Ibid.*, 3.20.46 and 1.15.6

✦ *Pity*

Mercy, as we have already observed under that entry, is not only a universally human virtue, but was regarded as such by sixteenth-century Christians. As with mercy, so too with pity, we find ourselves in the realm of the common ethics of man.[1] Lear's great speech is to be so understood:

> Take physic, pomp;
> Expose thyself to feel what wretches feel,
> That thou mayst shake the superflux to them
> And show the heavens more just.[2]

"Let your superfluities succor the poor," Tyndale teaches, and Calvin in his commentary on Job directly links the bearing of pain ourselves with the pity for others under affliction: "Then are we warned here to look better upon our neighbors' adversities than we have done, and when God sendeth us any miseries, to pray him to give us the grace to have our eyes better open to consider and mark them well, so as the same may move us to pity, and every-one of us do his endeavor to remedy it as much as they can, and finally to hope that when God hath so laid his hand upon them he will show himself merciful towards them."[3] Calvin's statement about growing through a sense of one's own miseries to a sense of pity for others is made in refer-ence to the Biblical Job, but it could also apply to certain important passages in *King Lear*. Lear himself says that "physic" has been administered to his pomp, while Edgar refers to himself as a man

> Who, by the art of known and feeling sorrows,
> Am pregnant to good pity,

and the chastened Gloucester speaks in a similar vein when he prays:

> Let the superfluous and lust-dieted man,
> That slaves your ordinance, that will not see
> Because he does not feel, feel your pow'r quickly;
> So distribution should undo excess,
> And each man have enough.[4]

[1] See Calvin, *Sermons on Job* (19.17-25), p. 334b, line 30.

[2] *Lear* 3.4.33ff.

[3] Tyndale, *Doctrinal Treatises*, Cambridge: Parker Society, 1848, p. 103, and Calvin, *op.cit.*, p. 335a, line 35.

[4] *Lear* 4.6.225f. and 4.1.70ff.

✧ Prayer

Prayers in Shakespeare cover a wide range of types, from the practice of the soldier who "swears a prayer or two And sleeps again,"[1] through the semi-liturgical forms of Henry V, and the informed but despairing prayer of Claudius, to those earnest struggles of Lear's soul in which the old king seems to pray even when he is not directly addressing the gods.

At the very outset we should note two things about prayer. In the first place, there was strong Christian precedent for affirming the efficacy of pagan as well as Christian prayer. "The prayers of unbelievers are not denied to them," Calvin writes, and he also declares that the door of prayer "is open not to a few but to all mortals."[2] The second point is related to the first. Hooker declares that "Every good and holy desire though it lack the form, hath notwithstanding in itself the substance and with [God] the force of a prayer, who regardeth the very moaning, groans, and sighs of the heart of man," while Calvin again teaches that God "gathereth together those prayers which necessity wringeth no less out of the unbelievers than out of the godly by the very feeling of nature: to which yet he proveth by the effect, that God is favorable."[3] The anguish of soul which we find in Lear may thus be nonetheless effective as prayer though it lacks both the formal pattern of prayer and any acknowledgment of the Christianity which Lear could not have known.

All prayer is in a basic sense ignorant, whether it be Christian or pagan. Menecrates makes the point to Pompey:

> We, ignorant of ourselves,
> Beg often our own harms, which the wise pow'rs

Deny us for our good. So find we profit
By losing of our prayers.[4]

The same observation was made by Plato in a passage which
Calvin treats as follows: "When Plato saw the folly of men
in making requests of God, which being granted, it many
times befell much to their own hurt, he pronounced that
this is the best manner of praying taken out of the old poet:
'King Jupiter give unto us the best things both when we ask
them, and when we do not ask them, but command evil
things to be taken away from us even when we ask them.'
And verily the heathen man is wise in this, that he judgeth
how perilous it is to ask of the Lord that which our own
desire moveth us."[5] God may deny what men ask in their
prayers, or may delay in responding to their petitions. The
proper tone of prayer, then, is not merely to make requests,
but even more importantly it is to subordinate one's own
will to the will of God. Gloucester shows that he has learned
this lesson when he prays:

You ever-gentle gods, take my breath from me;
Let not my worser spirit tempt me again
To die before you please![6]

In response to that prayer, Edgar says "Well pray you,
father." Other virtually impeccable prayers are those of
Henry V; this is what we would expect from Shakespeare's
"mirror of all Christian kings,"[7] and indeed it is as much
through his prayers as through any other single means that
Henry is characterized as an eminently Christian prince.
Especially obvious here is his crediting of victory to God:

O God, thy arm was here!
And not to us, but to thy arm alone,
Ascribe we all![8]

Such expressions are repeated by Henry in varying forms, while the chorus describes him as

> Being free from vainness and self-glorious pride;
> Giving full trophy, signal, and ostent
> Quite from himself to God.[9]

The Christian consensus on this point may be epitomized in Luther's words: "We ought neither to reject this praise and honor as though they were wrong, nor to despise them as though they were nothing, but refuse to accept them as too precious or noble, and ascribe them to Him in heaven, to whom they belong."[10] Henry's prayers of thanksgiving could virtually serve as models.

On the other hand, the plays include prayers which are equally defective in theological terms while in dramatic terms they are equally appropriate to the characters who deliver them. Lady Macbeth's petition to the powers of darkness is essentially a repudiation of humanity in the interests of evil, a fact which is so obvious as not to require further comment.[11] Not so bad perhaps, but still evil enough, are Laertes' words to Hamlet, "The devil take thy soul," to which Hamlet replies, "Thou pray'st not well."[12] Here again the theological comments which we have so frequently found to be part of Hamlet's characterization come to the fore.

One of the most interesting treatments of prayer in the plays is that of the anguished Claudius, in which we find a number of commonplace sixteenth-century attitudes towards prayer. "Pray can I not," Claudius says, and we will note under the entry on REPENTANCE the relation between his refusal to give restitution and the theological positions on the same subject. Another point should also be mentioned in this connection, and this is that Claudius seems never to be quite assured that God will forgive him. Even his closest approaches to affirmation of God's mercy, and of the efficacy of prayer and repentance never quite reach the affirmative, but remain interrogative:

> Whereto serves mercy
> But to confront the visage of offence?[13]

Other and similar questions so punctuate Claudius' soliloquy that we may reasonably doubt that it is possible for Claudius to pray in faith, in any traditional sense of that term. Hooker teaches, however, that without faith there can be no acceptable prayer: "it is of necessity required that they which pray do believe," he writes.[14] Essentially the same view as Hooker's is expressed somewhat more fully by Calvin: "If we would pray fruitfully, we ought therefore to grasp with both hands this assurance of obtaining what we ask, which the Lord enjoins with his own voice, and all the saints teach by their example. For only that prayer is acceptable to God which is born, if I may so express it, out of such presumption of faith, and is grounded in unshakable confidence of hope."[15] As we will see in connection with the entry on REPENTANCE, Claudius' prayer cannot be regarded as truly penitent in sixteenth-century terms, and it may be that it would also have appeared defective in faith, when seen in the same perspective. Every Elizabethan schoolboy had studied Alexander Nowell's *Catechism*, which teaches that "such as pray doubting and uncertain of their speeding, they do without fruit pour out vain and bootless words."[16]

However that may be, Claudius himself certainly declares that his attempt at prayer is a failure:

My words fly up, my thoughts remain below.

Words without thoughts never to heaven go.[17]

In the same terms, Calvin declares that prayer is not only useless but displeasing to God if the words "come only from the tip of the lips and out of the throat," for "the tongue without the mind must be highly displeasing to God."[18] Alexander Nowell's *Catechism* expresses the point more fully: "God doth worthily abhor and detest their prayers that feignedly and unadvisedly utter with their tongue that which they conceive not with their heart and thought; and deal more negligently with immortal God, than they are wont to do with a mortal man. Therefore in prayer the mind is ever needful, but the tongue is not always necessary."[19]

[1] *R. and J.* 1.4.87f.   [2] Calvin, *Inst.* 3.20.15 and 13.

[3] Hooker, *Eccl. Pol.* 5.48.2 and Calvin, *Inst.* 3.20.15, Norton trans.

[4] *A. and C.* 2.1.5ff.   [5] Calvin, *Inst.* 3.20.34, Norton trans.

[6] *Lear* 4.6.221ff.   [7] *Henry V*, prologue to Act Two, line six.

[8] *Ibid.*, 4.8.111ff.

[9] *Ibid.*, prologue to Act Five, beginning with line twenty.

[10] Luther, *Exp. Magnificat*, Amer. ed., vol. 21, p. 330.

[11] *Macb.* 1.5.41-55.   [12] *Ham.* 5.1.281f.

[13] *Ibid.*, 3.3.46.   [14] Hooker, *Eccl. Pol.* 5.48.3.

[15] Calvin, *Inst.* 3.20.12.

[16] Nowell, *A Catechism*, Cambridge: Parker Society, 1853, p. 187.

[17] *Ham.* 3.3.97f.   [18] Calvin, *Inst.* 3.20.31 and 33.

[19] Nowell, *op.cit.*, p. 188.

✦ *Pride* *also use Hotspur +*

Pride has traditionally been placed as the first of the seven deadly sins, and even among sixteenth-century Protestants who regarded the cataloging of everything according to seven's as being somewhat oversimplified and contrived, pride was still castigated as one of the greatest sins and perhaps even as the heart of all sin. Man's basic and originating sin consisted in his attempt to put himself in God's place, and to order all other existence so that every other creature and even the Creator became secondary to the individual man's own personal will and desires. Understood in this particular sense as the will to usurp upon God, pride has certain connotations in the Christian tradition which are not found elsewhere.

Once this observation has been made, however, it is necessary to go on to say that it is not alone the Christian teachers who have objected to pride. The Greek attitude toward hubris comes at once to mind, and though Greek and Christian attitudes differ at points which are of great theological significance, the fact remains that a kind of secular pride was equally repudiated by non-Christian as by Christian writers. "Vainglory or arrogancy," Luther writes, "hath always been a common poison in the world, which the very heathen poets and historiographers have always vehemently reproved."[1]

Instances of overlapping pagan and Christian attitudes may be cited in connection with the treatment of hubris in the Roman plays. It is said of Coriolanus that "he wants nothing of a god but eternity and a heaven to throne in," and that he acts as though he "were a god to punish, not A man of their infirmity," while it is said of Julius Caesar that "this man Is now become a god."[2] Contrast these statements with Calvin's words: "For oftentimes we see that princes reign not to magnify God's name, and to cause him to be honored as he deserveth, but clean contrariwise they would fain make themselves idols, and as it were pluck God out of his seat to sit in it themselves."[3] Now this Christian judgment *can* be applied to Caesar and to Coriolanus, but it is not the judgment implied in the words quoted from the plays themselves. The theologian judges every action in terms of man's chief end "to magnify God's name," whereas the dramatic characters whom we have quoted do not envision the self-deification of Coriolanus and Caesar in contrast to the worship of the true deity himself, but only within the context of the conflicting claims of other men. Thus we see once more that even when Shakespeare places in the mouths of his pagan characters words which are remarkably similar to Christian judgments, he never so violates dramatic propriety as to have imported basic Christian judgments into the Roman and other pre-Christian plays. In *Julius Caesar*, Cassius charges that Caesar wishes to be a god with all men below him, just as Caesar declares of Cassius that he is unwilling to be a man with other men above him:

> Such men as he be never at heart's ease
> Whiles they behold a greater than themselves.[4]

In both instances, the concern is with the secular pride of the other person.

Timon of Athens displays another form of pride. Having fled to the wilderness to live as a misanthropic hermit, he is sought out by Apemantus, who declares that Timon is not castigating his pride but is rather feeding it, in subtler guise, with the affectation of humility:

> If thou didst put this sour cold habit on
> To castigate thy pride, 'twere well; but thou
> Dost it enforcedly. Thou'dst courtier be again,
> Wert thou not beggar.[5]

Luther's remark about Diogenes exemplifies a similar judgment: "Such proud and arrogant wretches develop from these hypocrites that they abuse and defy everybody, even kings and emperors. They do not want honor, yet they seek honor and the worship of all the world because of their 'holiness.' "[6] Timon's peculiar affectation represents much the same form of "holiness" as that which Luther found in Diogenes, and both represent a perverse pride in debasement.

Opposite the pride of humiliation is the pride of heroic achievement. Whether Fortinbras himself is affected by such pride we do not know, but his marching army inspires Hamlet to give it a classic utterance. In Fortinbras, Hamlet visualizes (whether in envy or in irony)

> a delicate and tender prince,
> Whose spirit, with divine ambition puff'd,
> Makes mouths at the invisible event,
> Exposing what is mortal and unsure
> To all that fortune, death, and danger dare,
> Even for an eggshell. Rightly to be great
> Is not to stir without great argument,
> But greatly to find quarrel in a straw
> When honor's at stake.[7]

These lines summarize what Luther would have regarded as princely pride. "The world regards this terrible vice as the highest virtue," he writes. "For all heathen books are poisoned through and through with this striving after praise and honor; in them men are taught by blind reason, that they were not nor could be men of power and worth, who are not moved by praise and honor; but those are counted the best, who disregard body and life, friend and property and everything in the effort to win praise and honor."[8]

Other kinds of pride appear in the plays. Lear's division of his kingdom in return for protestations of love appears prideful as well as foolish. Though Lear finds himself more sinned against than sinning, he is not without serious fault in his attempt to buy his daughter's love. "Even in this world it is true," Luther writes, "that he who does good to another in order to catch him and make him his own does him more harm than good," while Calvin writes that "you may see some who wish to seem very liberal and yet bestow nothing that they do not make reprehensible with a proud countenance or even insolent words."[9]

The ultimate form of pride, according to the sixteenth-century theologians, was pride in one's own righteousness, the pride of man in his own ability to do good works. A man holding to this form of pride, furthermore, would be most likely to judge harshly of others. "No one judges and thinks so harshly of others as do those who are devoted to human exertions and works," Luther declares.[10] This, essentially, is the pride of an Angelo and of a Shylock, to whom Luther's words seem particularly appropriate: "One of the virtues of counterfeit sanctity is that it cannot have pity or mercy for the frail and weak, but insists upon the strictest enforcement and the purest selection; as soon as there is even a minor flow, all mercy is gone, and there is nothing but fuming and fury. St. Gregory also teaches us how to recognize this when he says: 'True justice shows mercy but false justice shows indignation.' True holiness is merciful and sympathetic, but all that false holiness can do is to rage and fume. Yet it does so, as they boast, 'out of zeal for justice'; that is, it is done through love and zeal for righteousness."[11]

[1] Luther, *Commentary on Galatians* (5.25), E. Middleton trans., p. 442.

[2] *Cor.* 5.4.25, 3.1.82, and *J.C.* 1.2.116.

[3] Calvin, *Sermons on Deuteronomy* (5.16), p. 215b.

[4] *J.C.* 1.2.208f.   [5] *T. of A.* 4.3.239ff.

6 Luther, Serm. on Matt. 19.29, Plass anthol., vol. 2, 2081.

7 *Ham.* 4.4.48ff.

8 Luther, "A Treatise on Good Works," Phil. ed., vol. 1, pp. 208f.

9 Luther, Serm. on Luke 18.9-14, Plass anthol., vol. 3, 4071, and Calvin, *Inst.* 3.7.7.

10 Luther, Exp. Isa. 59.5-6, Plass anthol., vol. 3, 4074.

11 Luther, Exp. Matt. 5.7, Amer. ed., vol. 21, p. 29.

✦ *Providence*

What "was wont by the ancient to be called natural destiny," Hooker writes, is among Christians "rightly termed by the name of providence."[1] Though the pagan and Christian meanings would not have seemed simply interchangeable to the theologians, there was sufficient similarity between them so that in the sixteenth century the earlier term is sometimes used as a variant for the later. This seems to be what takes place when Ariel performs Prospero's will in rebuking the shipwrecked nobles in *The Tempest*:

> You are three men of sin, whom destiny—
> That hath to instrument this lower world
> And what is in't—the never-surfeited sea
> Hath caus'd to belch up you, and on this island,
> Where man doth not inhabit—you 'mongst men
> Being most unfit to live.[2]

Hooker continues the treatment of destiny-providence with words which encompass the services of natural phenomena and other agents: "That law, the performance whereof we behold in things natural, is as it were an authentical or an original draught written in the bosom of God himself; whose spirit being to execute the same useth every particular nature, every mere natural agent, only as an instrument created at the beginning, and ever since the beginning used, to work his own will and pleasure withal."[3] Though it must be denied that Ariel's concern is theological in the same sense as Hooker's, Hooker's words do indicate the kind of milieu in which Ariel speaks and the commonplace attitudes which would have reinforced Ariel's references to "the powers delaying (not forgetting)."[4]

What Ariel is, we do not know exactly, and though he may be one of the "ministers of fate," as he declares, he is not human and certainly may not be seen as a Christian, though he serves the essentially Christian plans of the human Prospero. But, as sixteenth-century theology recognizes, Christians do not have exclusive rights on submission to the will of God. Hooker cites heathen precedent to shame Christians for their lack of faith: Are we "to be less advised than that heathen Platonic, uninstructed in the mysteries of our faith? 'In that I understand concerning the works of God,' saith Plotin, 'therein will I praise him: and admire him even in those things which I know no reason of.' "[5] One need not go beyond that spirit to understand such reliance upon the divine will as Posthumus expresses in *Cymbeline*:

> Do your best wills,
> And make me blest to obey![6]

In Hamlet, the situation is quite different, for Hamlet is characterized in the fifth act as relying upon an unmistakably Christian providence. In the development of Hamlet's character, suffering seems to have eventuated in a steady assurance of God's providence. Perhaps there is relevance in Hooker's comment that "affliction is both a medicine if we sin, and a preservative that we sin not."[7] Calvin's words come even closer to describing the perils from which Hamlet has emerged, and though the parallel is not exact it is surely instructive: "If a man light among thieves or wild beasts, if by wind suddenly rising he suffer shipwreck on the sea. . . , if having been tossed with the waves, he attain to the haven, if miraculously he escape but a finger breadth from death, all these chances as well of prosperity as of adversity the reason of the flesh doth ascribe to fortune. But whosoever is taught by the mouth of Christ, that all the hairs of his head are numbered, will seek for a cause further off, and will firmly believe that all chances are governed by the secret counsel of God."[8] Having passed through experiences like those which Calvin hypothesizes, Hamlet has come to sense in what might seem quite inconsequential details that "even in that was heaven ordinant" and to declare

Our indiscretion sometime serves us well
When our deep plots do pall; and that should learn us
There's a divinity that shapes our ends,
Rough-hew them how we will.[9]

Finally, there is his assurance that "there's a special providence in the fall of a sparrow. If it be now, 'tis not to come; if it be not to come, it will be now; if it be not now, yet it will come: the readiness is all. Since no man knows aught of what he leaves, what is 't to leave betimes? Let be."[10] These inescapable tokens of faith form an important part of Shakespeare's presentation of Hamlet, and they would not have been unfamiliar to the Elizabethans, for there was much in the theological milieu to support them. Calvin is by no means unique in emphasizing providence, but expresses a virtually universal Christian consensus when he describes attitudes much like those of Hamlet, though of course not identical with them:

"Yet, when that light of divine providence has once shone upon a godly man, he is then relieved and set free not only from the extreme anxiety and fear that were pressing him before, but from every care. For as he justly dreads fortune, so he fearlessly dares commit himself to God. His solace, I say, is to know that his Heavenly Father so holds all things in his power, so rules by his authority and will, so governs by his wisdom, that nothing can befall except he determine it. Moreover, it comforts him to know that he has been received into God's safekeeping and entrusted to the care of his angels. . . ."[11]

[1] Hooker, *Eccl. Pol.* 1.3.4.   [2] *Temp.* 3.3.53ff.
[3] Hooker, *Eccl. Pol.* 1.3.4.   [4] *Temp.* 3.3.73.
[5] Hooker, Serm. III, Keble ed., vol. 2, p. 370.
[6] *Cymb.* 5.1.16f.   [7] Hooker, *loc.cit.*
[8] Calvin, *Inst.* 1.16.2, Norton trans.   [9] *Ham.* 5.2.48, and 8ff.
[10] *Ibid.*, 5.2.230ff.   [11] Calvin, *Inst.* 1.17.11.

✦ *Reason*

Sixteenth-century non-theological attitudes towards reason have been so thoroughly explored from so many points of view in modern scholarship that little can be added. In this book, too, we have so often needed to cite the theologians' comments that most of our material has already been presented even before we arrive at the entry devoted to reason. In the two chapters on the Reformation background, we have examined numerous encomiums of reason as it may operate within the natural order. The entry on FREEDOM, furthermore, has underscored the doctrinal placing of reason as one of the "means" which God has given man to use freely within secular society. Under the entry on BEASTS, we have seen that reason was regarded as setting man apart from the lower animals, and we have discussed similar matters under the entry on MAN. For a fuller comparison between Shakespeare's references to reason and the treatment given by the theologians, readers should turn to each of these earlier analyses. Here, I shall merely attempt to summarize and to strike a balanced view.

As in so much Christian theology, balance is essential, and as we have so often noticed in our analysis of Shakespearean speeches, it is Hamlet who seems most aware of the full range of Christian doctrine. This is not to say that Hamlet exists as a spokesman or propagandist for Christian doctrine, and we have repeatedly repudiated any such suggestion. What does seem to be true is that Shakespeare has used Christianity in his characterization of Hamlet in the same general way that he used Stoicism in his characterization of Brutus, without attempting to indoctrinate his audience in either. It is simply that he has made his Hamlet a thoughtful Christian prince and his Brutus a thoughtful Stoic senator, and that he has characterized them accordingly.

Hamlet's references to reason are consistent with the major development of his character, so that he emphasizes the limits of reason and also the greatness of reason, depending upon the context within which the subject arises. To the doubting Horatio, he warns that

> There are more things in heaven and earth, Horatio,
> Than are dreamt of in your philosophy.[1]

Here we have the central Christian denial of the validity of reason's operation in supernatural areas. Of God's operation and of the "manner of this divine efficiency, being far above us," Hooker writes, "we are no more able to conceive by our reason than creatures unreasonable by their sense are able to apprehend after what manner we dispose and order the course of our affairs,"[2] while Luther caustically deplores the human tendency to "demand that God should act according to man's idea of right, and do what seems proper to themselves—or else that he should cease to be God."[3]

That is one side of the matter, but it is not the only side. Calvin writes that "when we so condemn human understanding for its perpetual blindness as to leave it no perception of any object whatever, we not only go against God's Word, but also run counter to the experience of common sense."[4] Though we cannot reach an understanding of God by the unaided operation of human wisdom, the fact remains that a denial of reason in the affairs of this life will reduce us to the level of beasts. As we have already treated these matters more extensively elsewhere, we can here restrict ourselves to citing once more a familiar passage from *Hamlet*:

> Sure he that made us with such large discourse,
> Looking before and after, gave us not
> That capability and godlike reason
> To fust in us unus'd.[5]

For Hooker, too, "the law of reason or human nature is that which men by discourse of natural reason have rightly found out themselves to be all forever bound unto in their actions,"[6] while Luther holds, as we have shown at greater length, that "God certainly did not give us our reason and the advice and aid which it supplies in order to have us contemptuously disregard them."[7]

[1] *Ham.* 1.5.166f.   [2] Hooker, *Eccl. Pol.* 1.3.4.
[3] Luther, *The Bondage of the Will*, Packer and Johnston eds., 5.13, p. 232.

4 Calvin, *Inst.* 2.2.12.   5 *Ham.* 4.4.36ff.
6 Hooker, *Eccl. Pol.* 1.8.8.
7 Luther, Exp. Gen. 32.6-8, Plass anthol., vol. 2, 2437.

✦ *Relativism: See Vice and Virtue*

✦ *Repentance* Claudius

In *Measure for Measure*, the Duke in his role as confessor probes the conscience of Juliet, and declares to her

> I'll teach you how you shall arraign your conscience,
> And try your penitence, if it be sound
> Or hollowly put.[1]

He then inquires as to whether she now hates the man who wronged her, and whether she has attempted to shift the major blame from herself to him. Satisfied with her negative response to both of these questions, the Duke proceeds to another crucial matter: whether her penitence is based in repudiation of sin or in fear of punishment:

> lest you do repent
> As that the sin hath brought you to this shame—
> Which sorrow is always toward ourselves, not heaven,
> Showing we would not spare heaven as we love it,
> But as we stand in fear.[2]

Juliet's reply again satisfies the Duke:

> I do repent me as it is an evil,
> And take the shame with joy.[3]

What the Duke is attempting to elicit here involves a very basic distinction, which may be clarified by reference to Luther's words on the subject: "There is a different repentance, not a true but a false one, which Germans call a *Galgenreue* [gallow's repentance], when I repent in such a way that I am not ashamed of offending God but merely regret having injured myself. Such a repentance is very common. I myself have often repented in this way and deplored having done something foolish, stupid, and to my hurt. I was more ashamed of the stupidity and the harm than of the sin, of the guilt, of the offense against God."[4]

Shakespeare makes several references to this distinction between true and false repentance, as when Scroop in *Henry V* responds to the sentence of death upon him by declaring that "I repent my fault more than my death," and when York declares of Aumerle in *Richard II* that "fear, and not love, begets his penitence."[5]

We see, as the Duke pointed out, that all penitence is not equally valid, and it is necessary to distinguish between various types, as Shakespeare carefully does. We will not analyze all the uses of repentance in Shakespeare, but will attempt to treat certain representative instances. We do not need to say much of such obviously perverse repentance as that of Aaron in *Titus Andronicus* and of the Queen in *Cymbeline*, both of whom repent that they have not done more evil,[6] but we should note Lady Macbeth's prayer to the powers of darkness that she be prevented from feeling genuine repentance for her evil actions:

> Make thick my blood;
> Stop up th' access and passage to remorse,
> That no compunctious visitings of nature
> Shake my fell purpose nor keep peace between
> Th' effect and it.[7]

This plea on Lady Macbeth's part represents the unforgivable sin, the sin against the Holy Spirit, which Calvin calls the "apostasy of the whole man," "an impiety deliberately intended," for "pardon is not denied to any individual sins except one, which, arising out of desperate madness, cannot be ascribed to weakness, and clearly demonstrates that a man is possessed by the devil." Lady Macbeth's repudiation of remorse, and the feelings of compunction inherent in a fully humane nature, indicates that she is deliberately placing herself among those who, in Calvin's words, "choke the light of the Spirit with deliberate impiety, and spew out the taste of the heavenly gift."[8] The results of such action, as Shakespeare presents them in the subsequent development of Lady Macbeth's character, accord with what theology had taught Shakespeare's audience to expect, and we have had occasion to treat these matters in another entry.[9]

In Macbeth himself, there is no sign of genuine repentance, though there are signs of chagrin and anger at the equivocation of the fiend. There is also one famous instance of remorse, when Macbeth attempts to avoid fighting Macduff:

> Of all men else I have avoided thee.
> But get thee back! My soul is too much charg'd
> With blood of thine already.[10]

"Certainly even in the reprobate, who seem entirely to have cast off humanity," Calvin writes, "time shows that some residue of it [humanity] remains," for human minds cannot so drug and numb themselves with evil that "a consideration of their own wickedness will not sometimes fill them with remorse."[11] Macbeth's final, brief instance of humanity heightens his dramatic appeal, for it keeps him at least residually humane. Here again we see an instance of Shake-

speare's skillful eliciting of an element of the theological
background for dramatic purposes.

One of the most interesting treatments of repentance in
English literature comes in Claudius' famous soliloquy in
Hamlet.[12] Here Shakespeare has put to dramatic use, in brief
compass, a broad range of theological references—so broad,
in fact, as to cover most of the basic elements in the theology
of repentance. Again, however, the purpose is the development of interesting character and action, and not the provision of doctrinal instruction. The theological material is
thus not presented as an end in itself, but is digested to the
needs of dramatic characterization. Claudius struggles with
his own guilt, with his desire to repent, and also with his
unwillingness to restore the possessions which his sin has
brought him. Almost in despair he asks what repentance
can do "when one cannot repent," and he concludes that
his prayer has been ineffective.[13]

Hooker analyzes the difficulties of reaching true repentance, and writes that some men are "fearful lest the enormity
of their crimes be so unpardonable that no repentance can
do them good, some lest the imperfection of their repentance
make it ineffectual to the taking away of sin."[14] Claudius
considers both of these possibilities, beginning with the first:

> What if this cursed hand
> Were thicker than itself with brother's blood,
> Is there not rain enough in the sweet heavens
> To wash it white as snow?[15]

He immediately concludes, however, that his crimes are not
beyond the possibility of forgiveness:

> Whereto serves mercy
> But to confront the visage of offense?

> And what's in prayer but this twofold force,
> To be forestalled ere we come to fall,
> Or pardon'd being down? Then I'll look up.[16]

Claudius thus considers, and repudiates, the error of those who, in Hooker's terms, fear that their crimes are of such enormity as to be unpardonable.

Having then avoided the first of Hooker's twin errors, he falls into the second, for his repentance is so imperfect as to "make it ineffectual to the taking away of sin," as he himself says:

> Try what repentance can. What can it not?
> Yet what can it when one cannot repent?[17]

"Mere contrition of our sins is not true repentance," Luther writes. "To our contrition there must be joined true faith in the divine promises,"[18] and Hooker writes that "it is of necessity required that they which pray do believe."[19] At no point does Claudius show any vital and viable sign of trust or belief in the active mercy of God toward him. He thus finds himself in the position of those of whom the Scriptures say that when they cry to God, God will not hear them. Calvin comments that such expressions of fruitless prayer "do not designate either true conversion or calling upon God," but are rather marks of the anxiety which, in extremity, destroys the complacency of the wicked.[20]

Claudius' inability to repent is based in two other factors, in addition to those we have already noted: he neither repudiates his earlier sin nor turns from future sin, for he is not only unwilling to restore the profits gained by the murder of his brother, but he is even now plotting the assassination of his nephew. It never occurs to him that his plans for disposing of Hamlet run counter to his attempted repentance,

religious

Mh &o

Major

but he clearly sees that such repentance will be vain apart
from restitution:

> My fault is past. But, O, what form of prayer
> Can serve my turn? 'Forgive me my foul murther'?
> That cannot be; since I am still possess'd
> Of those effects for which I did the murther—
> My crown, mine own ambition, and my queen.
> May one be pardon'd and retain th' offence?[21]

The theological consensus could scarcely be more aptly summarized. Hooker writes that if "a man have wittingly
wronged others to enrich himself; the first thing evermore
in this case required (ability serving) is restitution. For let
no man deceive himself: from such offenses we are not
discharged, neither can be, till recompense and restitution
to man accompany the penitent confession we have made
to Almighty God."[22] Similarly, Calvin warns "guilty parties"
that "without restitution, their confession would be but
illusory," for "hypocrites busy themselves in vain in reconcil-
ing God to themselves, unless they honestly restore what
they have unjustly taken," and "so long as a difference with
our neighbor is kept by our fault, we have no access to
God."[23] Hugh Latimer's comments are to the same effect
as those of Hooker and Calvin, but considerably more lively:
"I had of late occasion to speak of picking and stealing,
where I shewed unto you the danger wherein they be that
steal their neighbors' goods from them; but I hear nothing
yet of restitution. Sirs, I tell you, except restitution be made,
look for no salvation."[24] Or again, Latimer preaches in his
last sermon before the court of Edward VI: "I have now
preached three Lents. The first time I preached restitution.
'Restitution,' quoth some, 'what should he preach of restitu-

tion? Let him preach of contrition,' quoth they, 'and let restitution alone; we can never make restitution.' Then, say I, if thou wilt not make restitution, thou shalt go to the devil for it."[25]

It was for these reasons that Claudius "cannot repent." He seeks to remove the stain of guilt without pulling up its roots, and as Calvin says, "it would be absurd to wish the effect to be removed while the cause remained. We must guard against imitating foolish sick folk, who, concerned solely with the treatment of symptoms, neglect the very root of the disease."[26]

In writing Claudius' soliloquy on guilt and repentance, Shakespeare was not writing either hortatory appeal or theological treatise, as were Latimer, Hooker, and Calvin. His concern was for dramatic characterization and for the heightening of suspense and tension in a particular plot situation. To these ends he successfully employed certain crucial and well-known elements of the Christian understanding of repentance.

At other points, furthermore, Shakespeare poetically summarizes the two major aspects of repentance, technically known as mortification and vivification. Luther gives a practical definition when he writes that "forgiveness of sin demands that sin be both confessed and renounced,"[27] which is essentially synonymous with Hamlet's appeal to Gertrude to "Repent what's past; avoid what is to come."[28] A parallel is found in Ariel's warning to the three men of sin that they can be saved by

> nothing but heart's sorrow
> And a clear life ensuing.[29]

Like Hamlet, Ariel is speaking in well-established theological terms. "Sorrow of heart" or "sorrow of soul" covered what the theologians taught should be man's response to his own evil doing,[30] but repentance was not genuine if it ended there, for as Calvin said "it is impossible for a man to experience a sorrow of this kind, without its giving birth to a new heart."[31] Luther writes that "the proverb is true and better than all the doctrines of contrition which they have taught up till now, which says, 'To sin no more is the highest form of repentance,' and 'A new life is the best repentance.'"[32]

Other attitudes toward repentance appear elsewhere, but always subordinated to immediate dramatic propriety. A case in point is Cleomenes' advice to Leontes in *The Winter's Tale*, assuring him of the sufficiency of his penitence:

> Sir, you have done enough, and have perform'd
> A saintlike sorrow. No fault could you make
> Which you have not redeem'd; indeed, paid down
> More penitence than done trespass.[33]

This remark has sometimes been taken as representing a Catholic attitude, and has been integrated into a Christianizing interpretation of *The Winter's Tale*. Such analysis disregards the fact that Shakespeare deliberately has placed this play in a pre-Christian society. In the opinion of our theologians, moreover, Cleomenes' words are essentially unChristian. Luther teaches that no one should claim "to have sufficient contrition. Such an attitude is presumptuous and fabricated, for no one has sufficient contrition for his sin."[34] According to Luther, such views are essentially heathen.[35] Hooker, speaking in the same terms, declares that "he which giveth unto any good work of ours the force of satisfying the wrath of God for sin . . . pulleth up the doctrine of faith by the roots," and he calls it "a senseless and unreasonable persuasion" that men can not only "make a full and perfect satisfaction" for their sins, but can even perform "a great deal more than is sufficient for themselves."[36] Such an opinion as that of Cleomenes is thus not only un-Christian, when judged by the doctrine of our sixteenth-century theologians, but would appear particularly appropriate to a pagan world in which the major emphasis was placed on man's own initiative and effort.

A contrary instance is found in the sorrow of Henry V for the murder of Richard II. Henry outlines all that he has done to follow the medieval system of penance and satisfaction, but he recognizes, as Cleomenes does not, that his own efforts are not sufficient to "satisfying the wrath of God for sin," as Hooker has it. The "mirror of all Christian kings" speaks very sound doctrine when he declares:

> More will I do!
> Though all that I can do is nothing worth,
> Since that my penitence comes after all,
> Imploring pardon.[37]

Such a statement would have been entirely appropriate for a literate Christian of any age or church, but its explicit repudiation of the satisfying merit of penitential works would have been particularly useful in helping a predominantly Protestant audience to think of Henry as an ideal Christian monarch. Henry thus stands as an exemplary son of the medieval church, and at the same time speaks in accents equally familiar to Elizabethan Protestants: "all that I can do is nothing worth. . . ."

All men need to be forgiven, for all men are sinners. Thus, when we see evidence of the sins of others, we should not concentrate upon the externality of the evil, but should be reminded by another's frailty of our own persistent need for forgiveness. It is not that there should be no recognition of evil in others, for the refusal to recognize the presence of such evil would be the worst form of sentimentality; but where the evil is clearly seen in others, there should also be a concomitant recognition of sin in ourselves. Such was the teaching of the theologians, and we find the balance they sought neatly expressed in the words of the Doctor who has observed Lady Macbeth in her sleepwalking:

> More needs she the divine than the physician.
> God, God forgive us all![38]

The first line represents a clarity and realism of judgment similar to that which Luther showed in connection with another sick patient: "In a word, her illness is not for the apothecaries (as they call them), nor is it to be treated with the salves of Hippocrates, but it requires the powerful plasters of the Scriptures and the Word of God."[39] But upon the objective judgment there at once follows the subjective, as the Doctor cries, "God, God forgive us all!" The theological teachings which lie behind that plea may be summarized in the words of Calvin: "I see that this man is smitten with God's rods. And why? For his sins. And is not God judge of the whole world? Yes. Then doth this matter concern me also: for am I guiltless? Is there nothing in me that God may find fault with? Alas, there is nothing but sinfulness in me, yea and too gross sinfulness. Ye see then how men ought to condemn themselves in other folks' persons as oft as we see that God sendeth punishments upon them; and therewith also God mindeth to inure us to pitifulness and compassion. If we follow this order, we can not do amiss."[40]

[1] *M. for M.* 2.3.21ff.   [2] *Ibid.*, 2.3.30ff.   [3] *Ibid.*, 2.3.35f.

[4] Luther, Lect. on Gen. 27.36, Mueller ed., vol. 2, pp. 116-17.

[5] *Henry V* 2.2.152 and *Rich. II* 5.3.56.

[6] *Titus* 5.3.186ff., and *Cymb.* 5.5.59f.

[7] *Macb.* 1.5.44ff.   [8] Calvin, *Inst.* 3.3.21 and 23.

[9] See the treatment under GUILT.   [10] *Macb.* 5.8.5ff.

[11] Calvin, *Comm. Gen.* (37.25-27), vol. 2, p. 270.

[12] *Ham.* 3.3.36-72 and 97-98.   [13] *Ibid.*, 3.3.66 and 97f.

[14] Hooker, *Eccl. Pol.* 6.6.15.   [15] *Ham.* 3.3.43ff.

[16] *Ibid.*, 3.3.46ff.   [17] *Ibid.*, 3.3.65f.

[18] Luther, Lect. Gen. (42.3-20), Mueller ed., vol. 2, p. 288.

[19] Hooker, *Eccl. Pol.* 5.48.3.   [20] Calvin, *Inst.* 3.3.24.

[21] *Ham.* 3.3.51ff.   [22] Hooker, *Eccl. Pol.* 6.5.7.

[23] Calvin, Exp. Numb. 5.5-7, and Exp. Lev. 6.1-7, *Harmony of the Last Four Books of Moses*, vol. 3, p. 135, and vol. 2, p. 360, and *Comm. Matt.* (5.23), vol. 1, p. 286.

[24] Latimer, *Works*, Cambridge: The Parker Society, 1844-1845, vol. 1, p. 452.

[25] *Ibid.*, p. 262.   [26] Calvin, *Inst.* 3.20.9.

[27] Luther, Serm. on Luke 23.32-43, *Sermons on the Passion of Christ*, trans. E. Smid and J. T. Isensee, Rock Island, Illinois: Augustana Press, 1956, p. 182.

[28] *Ham.* 3.4.150.   [29] *Temp.* 3.3.81f.

[30] Calvin, *Inst.* 3.3.3 and 8, and Comm. II Cor. (7.10), p. 274, and Hooker, *Eccl. Pol.* 6.3.5.

[31] Calvin, *op.cit.*

[32] Luther, *Defense and Explanation of all the Articles . . .* , Amer. ed., vol. 32, p. 38.

[33] *Wint. T.* 5.1.1ff.

[34] Luther, "The Sacrament of Penance," Amer. ed., vol. 35, p. 18.

[35] Luther, "An Exhortation to the Clergy," Phil. ed., vol. 4, pp. 340f.

[36] Hooker, Serm. II, par. 32, and Serm. VI, par. 21, Keble ed., vol. 2, pp. 320f. and 398.

[37] *Henry V* 4.1.319ff.   [38] *Macb.* 5.1.82f.

[39] Luther, "Letter to John Agricola, July, 1527," *Letters of Spiritual Counsel*, trans. T. G. Tappert, Philadelphia: The Westminster Press, 1955, p. 83.

[40] Calvin, Serm. on Job (19.17-25), p. 334c, line 45.

✦ *Reputation: See Honor*

✦ *Revenge: See Vengeance*

✦ *Self-Knowledge*

The requirement of self-knowledge was at least as ancient as Socrates, and was a universal element in classical culture. The presence or absence of self-knowledge is repeatedly cited in connection with Shakespearean characters, as for example with Antony and with Lear, and such references almost always embody the kind of practical human wisdom which would have been equally accessible to Christian and to heathen characters.

There was another form of self-knowledge which was regarded as essentially Christian: the knowledge of one's own sin, and the need for God's grace. To this kind of self-knowledge which served as a prelude to redemption there is not much explicit reference in Shakespeare, though there is some. It is possible that the idealized innocent Orlando in *As You Like It* may be speaking in these terms when he declares, "I will chide no breather in the world but myself, against whom I know most faults."[1] Even if Orlando is speaking of Christian self-knowledge, however, the reference is made in a light tone and is not systematically and seriously developed.

In Hamlet's confrontation of his mother in her chamber, however, the situation is quite different. Hamlet's appeals to Gertrude are so developed that it is difficult if not impossible to interpret them fully apart from the theological emphasis on self-knowledge. "So great is the corruption and blindness of human nature," Luther writes, "that it does not see or sense the greatness of sin," and Calvin observes that men are "so blinded by their wickedness as to lie not only to others but also to themselves."[2] Such is the condition of Gertrude when Hamlet confronts her. What Hooker calls our proneness "to fawn upon ourselves, and to be ignorant as much as may be of our own deformities, without the feeling sense whereof we are most wretched" corresponds to the flattering unctions which the placid Gertrude has thus far been able to lay to her soul.[3] It is not, of course, that Gertrude is exceptionally or actively wicked, as is Lady Macbeth, for example. She is rather the victim of her own spiritual self-ignorance, for as Calvin says many "are so drunk with the sweetness of their vices that they think not upon God's judgment but lie dazed, as it were, in a sort of drowsiness. . . ."[4]

It is against this background that Hamlet declares to his mother:

> You go not till I set you up a glass
> Where you may see the inmost part of you.[5]

The reference to seeing one's inmost self as in a mirror would have been a familiar one to Elizabethans, for the moral law was often referred to in these terms, and it was in terms of that law that Elizabethans were taught to judge themselves. Calvin's words are typical: "The law is like a mirror. In it we contemplate our weakness, then the iniquity arising from this, and finally the curse coming from both— just as a mirror shows us the spots on our face."[6] It is in these terms that Gertrude sees in herself those "black and grained spots" which Hamlet's mirror reveals:

O Hamlet, speak no more!
Thou turn'st mine eyes into my very soul,
And there I see such black and grained spots
As will not leave their tinct.[7]

[1] A.Y.L. 3.2.297f.
[2] Luther, "First Disputation against Antinomians," Plass anthol., vol. 2, 3110, and Calvin, Comm. John (1.47), p. 339.
[3] Hooker, *Eccl. Pol.* 1.12.2.   [4] Calvin, *Inst.* 3.12.8.
[5] *Ham.* 3.4.19-20.   [6] Calvin, *Inst.* 2.7.7.
[7] *Ham.* 3.4.88ff.

✦ *Self-Love*

Parolles in *All's Well that Ends Well* may scarcely be taken as a serious theologian, but when, in his ridicule of virginity, he refers to self-love as "the most inhibited sin in the canon" he employs a valid theological judgment, though to a distorted purpose.[1] Speaking of man's self-love, Luther declares it the essence of all man's faults that he "loves himself above everything else [and] seeks himself in everything."[2] It is in some such terms that we can best understand Shakespeare's allusion in Sonnet Sixty-two:

Sin of self-love possesseth all mine eye
And all my soul and all my every part.

"Self-love is always sinful as long as it stays in itself," Luther writes. "It is not good unless it is out of itself in God."[3] In this sonnet Shakespeare is surely not talking of self-love getting out of itself into God, but rather into the person of the beloved, and yet the sonnet's opening quatrain loses at least some of its force if we do not understand the theological "sin" to which it alludes. Shakespeare continues:

And for this sin there is no remedy,
It is so grounded inward in my heart.

According to Luther, it is not only "hard and very difficult work" to break out of self-love, but even "impossible for nature," just as Shakespeare says that for it "there is no remedy."[4]

Shakespeare's alternative to self-love in the sonnets is the attraction to another person, whereas for the theologians the highest alternative is Christian charity. So far as I can determine, Shakespeare never attempted any full-scale dramatization of Christian charity—or, to put it differently, I know of no play in which he has done so in terms which would have been unmistakably obvious within the frameworks of sixteenth-century theology. Of self-love, on the other hand, there is evidence aplenty.

[1] *All's Well* 1.1.159f.
[2] Luther, *Lect. Rom.* (13.9-10), Pauck trans., p. 266.
[3] Luther, Exp. Gal. 5.14, Plass anthol., vol. 2, 2576.
[4] *Ibid.*

✦ *Sin*

In Shakespeare's plays there are numerous references to the universality of man's sin, as when Henry VI declares that "we are sinners all," or when Isabella says that "all the souls that were were forfeit once," and Hamlet asserts "we are arrant knaves all."[1] As we have seen under the entry on NATURE, such a condition is no part of God's will for man, but results from man's corruption of himself. "Sin," Hooker writes, "is no plant of God's setting. He seeth and findeth it a thing irregular, exorbitant, and altogether out of course,"[2] while Hamlet says of the world that

> 'Tis an unweeded garden
> That grows to seed; things rank and gross in nature
> Possess it merely.[3]

The basic problem is with man himself, as the two lords in *All's Well* recognize when one declares, "As we are ourselves, what things are we!" and the other responds, "Merely our own traitors," while Luther remarks, a "man has no enemy deadlier than himself."[4] Thus, Calvin quotes Augustine to the effect that "if you shall be paid what you deserve, you must be punished," and Hamlet asks, "Use every man after his desert, and who should scape whipping?"[5]

"Through sin our nature hath taken that disease and weakness," says Hooker, "whereby of itself it inclineth only unto evil," and can bring forth nothing acceptable in God's sight, "no, not the blossoms or least buds that tend to the fruit of eternal life."[6] Words of theologians such as Hooker are echoed comically in Falstaff's mood of mock seriousness when he declares, "There is nothing but roguery to be found in villainous man."[7] When Iago refers to human depravity he is no more committed to giving theological instruction than is Falstaff, but he is utterly in earnest, seeking under the pose of conventional honesty which he has assumed to encompass Othello's deception and ruin:

> Who has a breast so pure
> But some uncleanly apprehensions
> Keep leets and law days, and in session sit
> With meditations lawful?[8]

Hooker's remarks are apropos, when he asks, "since the first foundation of the world, what one can say, 'My ways are pure'?"[9]

Again Hooker writes that "the best things we do have

somewhat in them to be pardoned" while Calvin teaches that "nothing proceeds from a man, however perfect he be, that is not defiled by some spot," and Luther maintains that "a righteous man sins in all his good works."[10]

This is not to say that men are totally depraved, at least in terms of the misunderstanding of this phrase which is popular in our time. The major position of sixteenth-century theology in this regard may be summarized in Calvin's words as he cites examples "to warn us against adjudging man's nature wholly corrupted, because some men have by its promptings not only excelled in remarkable deeds, but conducted themselves most honorably throughout life."[11] Nor did the theologians assume that all men were equally sinful, and Lear is on as sound theological ground as he ever reaches when he declares,

> Those wicked creatures yet do look well-favor'd
> When others are more wicked; not being the worst
> Stands in some rank of praise.[12]

Where man gets himself into difficulty is when he concludes that because he himself is not "the worst," he therefore stands "in some rank of praise." Calvin states the problem when he writes that "it frequently happens that, by comparing ourselves with others, the low opinion which we form of them leads us to entertain a high opinion of ourselves. Paul declares that no such comparison ought to be allowed. Let no man, he says, measure himself by the standard of another, or please himself with the thought that others appear to him less worthy of approbation."[13] If judged in these terms, Lear's fault would be obvious when he declares that

> I am a man
> More sinn'd against than sinning.[14]

Luther's comment may also be useful here: "Those who are impatient and complain of the suffering they have to bear while doing the good, thereby show that their doing the good is not from God but that it is, rather, an assumption of human righteousness."[15] All of which will appear very obvious to many, but I outline it here so as to make clear how the theologians treated man's universal depravity. Lear was surely not speaking in Christian terms when he declared himself more sinned against than sinning, but that after all is quite appropriate, for Shakespeare characterizes Lear as a pagan.

Granted that men carry within themselves what we have seen Hooker call "a thing irregular, exorbitant, and altogether out of course," what is the result? As Hooker expresses the theological consensus, there are two directions in which sinners may move. With "God's preventing and helping grace," men are "able to do the works of piety which are acceptable in his [God's] sight." Without God's grace, men will follow their own wills in the doing of evil: "To actuate at any time the possibility of the will in that which is evil, we need no help, the will being that way over-inclinable of itself."[16] Sin exists as a disease in man; the disease may be controlled by the medicine of grace, but if it is not, it will destroy men in one way or another.

Sin then is not a static condition: it metastasizes, proliferates, multiplies, expressing itself in many and varied forms. The process by which an originating condition of sin leads into multiple evil is set forth in words ascribed to Richard II:

> The time will come, that foul sin, gathering head,
> Shall break into corruption.[17]

The reference to sin in terms of infection is a conventional one, as we can see by comparing Richard's metaphor with a simile of Calvin's: "For as the body, so long as it nourishes in itself the cause and matter of disease (even though pain does not yet rage), will not be called healthy, so also will the soul not be considered healthy while it abounds with so many fevers of vice."[18]

Once sin exposes itself in action, the sinner is caught up in a texture of guilt and fear after the fashions we have indicated under those headings. The sinner feels himself threatened both externally and from within himself, and seeks every available means for rendering himself secure. In this sense, security may become man's chiefest goal as well as his chiefest enemy, and Calvin describes how sinners "desire to make themselves secure, and they strengthen themselves with whatever they think can help them." So it is that Macbeth seeks an impregnable assurance, and we are reminded of Calvin's description of the sinner who is always "turning anxiously in all directions, and can have no peace of mind."[19] "Things bad begun make strong themselves by ill," Macbeth says, and again Calvin's words are relevant: "Once a sinner falls, he is immediately forced to go from bad to worse. Thus, those who begin with a mediocre offense thereafter hurl themselves headlong into the most frightful wickedness, which would at first have filled them with horror."[20] Eventually the conscience dies and the sense of horror with it, as with Macbeth.

> I have supp'd full with horrors.
> Direness, familiar to my slaughterous thoughts,
> Cannot once start me.[21]

As we have seen not only here but also under the entries for the DEVIL, FEAR, and GUILT, the patterns of a Christian understanding of sin seem to have contributed in marked ways to the development of Macbeth's characterization. The recognition of these patterns as they are exemplified in our representative theologians should thus help us to appreciate more adequately Shakespeare's dramatic protagonist. I would suggest once again, however, that we must not allow our attention to be diverted from Macbeth on the stage, for that is where we find him. Shakespeare could have placed him in a Dantesque or a Miltonic hell, but he did not do so, and neither should we. In Macbeth, Shakespeare has created one of the most magnificent presentations of the degeneration of the human soul which our culture affords, and he has done so in reference to Christian theology, but his purpose is still to keep the mirror up to nature and to show the course of human life in this world.

[1] 2 *Henry VI* 3.3.30, *M. for M.* 2.2.73, and *Ham.* 3.1.133.

[2] Hooker, "Fragments of an Answer. . . ," Keble ed., vol. 2, p. 46.

[3] *Ham.* 1.2.135ff.

[4] *All's Well* 4.3.23ff, and Luther, "Preface to Lect. Gen. 6," Amer. ed., vol. 2, p. 5.

[5] Calvin, *Inst.* 2.5.2 and *Ham.* 2.2.553f.

[6] Hooker, "Fragments of an Answer. . . ," *op.cit.*, p. 29.

[7] 1 *Henry IV* 2.4.138f.   [8] *Oth.* 3.3.138ff.

[9] Hooker, *Eccl. Pol.* 1.11.5.

[10] Hooker, Serm. II, par. 7, Keble ed., vol. 2, p. 302; Calvin, *Inst.* 3.15.3; and Luther, *Defense and Explanation of all the Articles. . . ,* Amer. ed., vol. 32, p. 83.

[11] Calvin, *Inst.* 2.3.3.   [12] *Lear* 2.4.259ff.

[13] Calvin, Comm. Gal. (6.4), p. 174.

[14] *Lear* 3.2.59f.

[15] Luther, Lect. Rom. (2.7), Pauck trans., p. 43.

[16] Hooker, "Fragments of an Answer. . . ," *op.cit.*, p. 28.

[17] 2 *Henry IV* 3.1.76f. Cf. *Rich. II* 5.1.57ff.

[18] Calvin, *Inst.* 2.3.2.

[19] Calvin, Exp. Hab. 2.4, *Commentaries* (Haroutunian), pp. 225 and 223.

[20] *Macb.* 3.2.55, and Calvin, Exp. Matt. 26.69-75, *op.cit.*, p. 323.

[21] *Macb.* 5.5.13ff.

✦ Vengeance

The Christian teaching on vengeance is so well known that it will not be necessary to give here more than one reference from the theologians and one from Shakespeare. In Calvin's Commentary on Romans we read: "Paul . . . teaches us that it belongs not to us to revenge, except we would assume to ourselves the office of God."[1] From the plays, we may take the remark of Clarence in *Richard III*:

> If God will be avenged for the deed,
> O, know you yet he doth it publicly!
> Take not the quarrel from his pow'rful arm.
> He needs no indirect or lawless course
> To cut off those that have offended him.[2]

[1] Calvin, Comm. Rom. (12.19), p. 475.   [2] *Rich. III* 1.4.220ff.

✦ Vice and Virtue

Close observers of the human condition are not likely to overlook the fact that virtue and vice appear in mixed forms, and not in a pure state. Hooker cites Plato to the effect that "the number of persons notably good or bad is but very small; that the most part of good have some evil, and of evil men some good in them." Hooker then proceeds to cite Mercurius Trismegistus to similar purpose: "So, true our experience doth find those aphorisms of Mercurius Trismegistus, 'to purge goodness quite and clean from all mixture of evil here is a thing impossible.' "[1] Such observations are a part of common wisdom, and of the practical insights which are accessible to men regardless of their religious positions.

This common wisdom is reinforced in Christianity by the doctrines of sin, of grace, and of the image of God in man. We have had abundant opportunity to see these doctrines at work in other contexts, but our purpose here is to see how they contribute to a kind of pragmatic relativism. We recall Hooker's assertion that "the best things we do have somewhat in them to be pardoned" and Luther's statement that "a righteous man sins in all his good works."[2] There we have the relativism of virtue. On the other hand, we are not to despise men for their wickedness, and as Calvin writes "if we do not wish to violate the image of God, we ought to hold our neighbor sacred."[3] That image to some extent inheres in all men, and for it all men must be respected. In addition, some men live under the saving grace of God, which visits the most unlikely and even the most sinful people, so that it is always possible that the worst reprobate will in God's mercy be redeemed. There we have the relativism of vice. It is not that good and evil, virtue and vice, become confused as to essence, or that they appear confused in the eyes of God, for they do not; but in the eyes of man they are inevitably mixed, and from this fact there can be no escape while man lives under the conditions of sin and error.

This much applies to all men, whether they be dedicated primarily to good or to evil, but the uses to which this basic relativism will be put depend upon the primary allegiance of each individual: "Anything that's mended is but patch'd; virtue that transgresses is but patch'd with sin, and sin that amends is but patch'd with virtue."[4] There we have the relativism stated, but serious drama cannot leave it at that, for apart from evaluation, sympathy, and perhaps also identification, the dramatic action would be meaningless and without interest. What counts is what men bring out of the confusion and seeming chaos of choice between mixed goods and evils. The best men may be moulded only out of faults, as Mariana says, for the basic material is faulty, but what counts is the use to which that basic material is put.[5] In *Macbeth*, the Old Man follows one line when he speaks the following benediction upon Ross:

> God's benison go with you, and with those
> That would make good of bad, and friends of foes.[6]

There we have one attitude towards the basic confusion of virtue and vice in this life. The opposite point of view is expressed by Iago:

> So will I turn her virtue into pitch,
> And out of her own goodness make the net
> That shall enmesh them all.[7]

Being sinful creatures, men tend to look for sin, to find it everywhere. Thus Luther writes that "We are so filthy that we only look for what is dirty and stinking, and wallow in it like pigs," so that even goodness seems perverse.[8] It is on the basis of such a broad and general understanding that Albany speaks to Goneril in *Lear*:

> Wisdom and goodness to the vile seem vile;
> Filths savour but themselves.[9]

Not only do predominantly evil people such as Goneril find evil in wisdom and goodness, but all men try to escape from making a moral choice. "The sinner," says Calvin, "tries to evade his innate power to judge between good and evil,"[10] and we see Macbeth's attempt to evade a moral choice by confusing the alternatives:

> This supernatural soliciting
> Cannot be ill; cannot be good.[11]

Banquo is tempted like Macbeth, but he never allows the issues and alternatives to be confused.

Both Goneril and Macbeth attempt either to deprecate virtue or to confuse it with vice, so as to distort the inherent relativism of human judgment to sinful ends. Henry V, on the other hand, attempts to bring good out of evil, turning a worldly relativism to the ends of virtue. Thus he says:

> There is some soul of goodness in things evil,
> Would men observingly distil it out.[12]

And again:

> Thus may we gather honey from the weed,
> And make a moral of the devil himself.[13]

Neither here nor elsewhere is Henry ever profound, but in his ready, manly way he does express thoughts which were regarded as eminently sound and praiseworthy. Henry's position may be seen as a somewhat less sophisticated version of Friar Laurence's soliloquy on herbs, which we analyzed in detail in the entry on NATURE, and what was said there in the way of commentary could also apply here. The central issue may be summarized in Calvin's observation that something "that is neither blessed nor desirable of itself can turn into something good for the devout."[14]

Repeatedly we see the crucial importance of how a man approaches the raw materials of life. He may act on the assumptions of the Old Man, or on those of Iago; he may think like Goneril and Macbeth, or like Banquo and Henry V. His own stance largely determines what he finds and uses in life. Thus, Luther cites a popular proverb, "such as each man's opinion of his condition is, such is his condition," and on another occasion he declares that "nothing is so good and nothing so evil but that it must minister to my welfare if only I believe."[15] Now we surely do not need theological erudition in order to understand Hamlet's "there is nothing either good or bad but thinking makes it so," and yet there is a kind of subterranean connection between similar ideas as they grow out of a particular age. Hamlet is certainly not talking theology to Rosencrantz and Guildenstern, but the theology we have cited forms a part of the background for his expression.

For the theologians, the major significance of relativism of virtues and vices which I have been trying to develop here consists in furnishing a warning against both pride and despair. Luther declares that God comes to the virtuous man and speaks to him through his very sins, so that the very fall from virtue leads the virtuous man to realize that "we are all chips of the same block. No ass need deride another as a beast of burden; for we are all of one flesh."[16] Hooker makes a similar observation: "What is virtue but a medicine, and vice but a wound? Yet we have so often deeply wounded ourselves with medicines, that God hath been fain to make wounds medicinable; to cure by vice where virtue hath stricken; to suffer the just man to fall, that, being raised, he may be taught what power it was which upheld him standing."[17] Luther also declares that "God frequently permits a man to fall into or remain in grievous sin," because the man "could not have kept himself from this great vice of vain honor and fame, if he had remained constant in his great gifts and virtues; . . . and thus one sin becomes the other's medicine."[18] All of which forms the basis for the remark of the lord in *All's Well*: "The web of our life is of a mingled yarn, good and ill together. Our virtues would be proud if our faults whipp'd them not, and our crimes would despair if they were not cherish'd by our virtues."[19]

[1] Hooker, *Eccl. Pol.* 7.24.16.

[2] Hooker, *Serm.* II, par. 7, Keble ed., vol. 2, p. 302, and Luther, *Defense and Explanation of all the Articles. . .* , Amer. ed., vol. 32, p. 83.

[3] Calvin, *Inst.* 2.8.40.   [4] *T.N.* 1.5.53ff.   [5] *M. for M.* 5.1.444.

[6] *Macb.* 2.4.40f.   [7] *Oth.* 2.3.366f.

[8] Luther, *Exp. Matt.* 5.9, Amer. ed., vol. 21, p. 42.

[9] *Lear* 4.2.38f.   [10] Calvin, *Inst.* 2.2.22.   [11] *Macb.* 1.3.130f.

[12] *Henry V* 4.1.4f.   [13] *Ibid.*, 4.1.11f.   [14] Calvin, *Inst.* 3.9.4.

[15] Luther, *Exp. Ps.* 5.11, Lenker ed., vol. 1, p. 258, and *Treatise on Christian Liberty*, Phil. ed., vol. 2, p. 324.

[16] Luther, *Exp. Luke* 15.1-10, Lenker ed., vol. 13, p. 60.

[17] Hooker, *Serm.* III, Keble ed., vol. 2, p. 358.

[18] Luther, *Treatise on Good Works*, Phil. ed., vol. 1, pp. 211f.

[19] *All's Well* 4.3.83ff.

✦ *Worship*

Worship may be taken as the public and communal counterpart of private prayer, though this distinction between the two terms is surely not absolute, and we use it here only for convenience in classification. As we saw under the entry on PRAYER that Shakespeare provides for various characters prayers appropriate to their characterization and historical situation, so we find that he follows the same practice in his references to worship. That, indeed, is his general pattern in the employment of theological references, as should be quite clear by now. Pagan characters are given religious statements appropriate to their religious commitments, and so are devout Christians, nominal Christians, and reprobates, always in terms of Shakespeare's dramatic needs. The references to worship follow the same pattern, with the pre-Christian Britons Belarius, Guiderius, and Arviragus making their simple orisons in *Cymbeline*, while characters in other historical circumstances go to mass and to confession, as is appropriate. (For the interesting and exceptional confession and absolution administered by the Duke in *Measure for Measure*, see below in the Appendix.) The setting of the English history plays in pre-Reformation days and of other plays in Roman Catholic countries or times entails many references to Roman Catholic worship. Shakespeare's knowledge of Roman Catholic practice is what might be expected of a literate Englishman of his time, and was quite sufficient for his dramatic purposes, but there are curious errors in his references at certain points. Richmond Noble has shown how King Henry V's order, "Let there be sung *Non nobis* and *Te Deum*," constitutes a misreading of the words ascribed to the king in Holinshed. This misreading can be accounted for when we recognize that Shakespeare's usage is traceable, not to the Latin service book or to the Vulgate (Noble finds no evidence that Shakespeare's Biblical citations were ever based on the Vulgate), but rather to the Book of Common Prayer, with its particular placing and enumeration of the Psalms.[1] There is another instance in the plays of what appears to be an error relative to Roman Catholic worship when Juliet speaks of coming to "evening mass," though evening mass was condemned and prohibited by the twenty-second session of the Council of Trent and by Pope Pius V in 1566.[2] Despite the prohibitions of Council and Pope, evening mass was celebrated on the Welsh Marches among recusants in 1578,[3] and it is possible that Shakespeare may have been aware of such recusant practice or of more distant Italian breaches of church order.[4] At any rate, Juliet's reference to evening mass is found in Shakespeare's source, and he retained it. Whether he retained it out of indifference to the issue, or out of ignorance as to elementary Roman Catholic custom, or out of so extensive a familiarity with Roman Catholic liturgical customs that he was aware of even the most rare and scattered aberrations must be left to the reader's judgment. Here as elsewhere, however, Shakespeare's references to worship were subsumed to his dramatic need, and fulfilled their theatrical purpose. Even when not precisely correct, Shakespeare's references to worship practices were dramatically appropriate.

1 Noble, *op.cit.*, pp. 8of., and *Henry* V 4.8.128.

2 *R. and J.* 4.1.38; *Canons and Decrees of the Council of Trent*, Twenty-second Session: "Doctrine Concerning the Sacrifice of the Mass," Chapter IX, pp. 150-52; H. Mutschmann and K. Wentersdorf, *Shakespeare and Catholicism*, New York: Sheed and Ward, 1952, pp. 215f.

3 To my knowledge, advocates of the theory that Shakespeare was a Roman Catholic have not yet cited this or any other evidence of the actual practice of evening mass in Elizabeth's kingdom, though they have insisted upon the likelihood of such practices despite official papal prohibition. I have been able to discover reference to only one such occasion, which I cite above for what it is worth. See *The Other Face: Catholic Life under Elizabeth I*, ed. Philip Caraman, London: Longmans, 1960, pp. 51f.

4 Mutschmann, *loc.cit.*, and Thurston, *op.cit.*, p. 749b.

 **CONCLUSION**

It has been the general contention of this book that the mirror of Shakespearean drama was held up to nature, and not to saving grace. With Milton and Bunyan, literary creation was closely geared to theological ideas, and indeed was often structured by those ideas. In their works, both literary character and literary action were explicitly presented in terms of Christian doctrine, and the reader was explicitly informed of the Christian purposes which the authors sought to achieve. Even if there were no overt assertions of theological intent in *Paradise Lost* and in *Pilgrim's Progress*, however, critics would find pervasive and indeed inescapable evidences of such intent throughout both works. The same may be said of the works of Dante, Langland, and Spenser. Nothing of the kind can justifiably be said of Shakespeare.

Generations of competent critics have found an apt description of Shakespeare's dramatic practice in the words of Hamlet that the purpose of playing "both at the first and now, was and is, to hold, as 'twere, the mirror up to nature; to show virtue her own feature, scorn her own image, and the very age and body of the time his form and pressure."[1] It would be a mistake to treat Hamlet's long charge to the players as representing Shakespeare's own detailed view of the theater, for there are too many elements in that charge which perfectly fit Hamlet's character and do not fit Shakespeare's practice. But in the words just quoted we do have a description which most of us would accept as essentially summarizing the scope of Shakespearean drama.

We also know that Renaissance references to art as a mirror had decidedly ethical implications. On this matter, Harry Levin has recently summarized the state of our knowl-

[1] *Ham.* 3.2.22ff.

edge: "The Elizabethan conception of art as the glass of nature was ethical rather than realistic, for it assumed that, by contemplating situations which reflected their own, men and women could mend their ways and act with greater resolution thereafter."[2] Though the view of art as a mirror was in good measure didactic, there is, to my knowledge, no evidence in the critical writings of the Elizabethan age which would lead us to interpret Shakespeare's "mirror up to nature" in terms of saving grace and revealed theology.

We have seen that the sixteenth-century theologians who were most influential and representative in Shakespeare's culture held to views of art as autonomous, as capable of treating the temporal and secular order independent of theological systems, and as competent to form judgments in that sphere apart from an overall appeal to any particularly or exclusively Christian ethic. Luther, Calvin, and Hooker held, in other words, to an understanding of literature which we also find Shakespeare exemplifying in his dramas. Shakespeare's mirror held up to nature represents what Luther expected readers to find in the classics where "they would be able to comprehend, *as in a mirror*, the character, life, counsels, undertakings, successes, and failures, of the whole world from the beginning."[3] Neither for Luther nor for Shakespeare was this the mirror of saving grace: for both it was the mirror of nature.

The purpose of such a mirror, in addition to providing aesthetic delight, was to help a man to know himself and the human situation. Hamlet said that "to know a man well were to know himself," and Calvin wrote that "whenever I see a man I must of necessity behold myself *as in a*

[2] Levin, *op.cit.*, p. 157.
[3] *Luther on Education*, p. 197. Italics mine.

mirror." Implicit in these two statements is the full rationale for self-knowledge gained vicariously through the experience and knowledge of others. This revelation of a man to himself through the mirroring of another man is again a matter of universal human experience, not in the least restricted to Christians,[4] and in Calvin's words it applied even to "a Moor or a barbarian, from the very fact of his being a man."[5] Shakespeare's concerns were in this area, in the temporal order, and with man "from the very fact of his being a man." It was not only aesthetically fortunate that Shakespeare's dramatic concerns were so bounded, but it was theologically proper that they should have been. To argue for a vast theological patterning of Shakespearean drama is at once to miss the point literarily and to ignore certain very important and directly pertinent emphases in the theological milieu of Shakespeare's culture.

If Shakespeare does not invite us to move from the words of his characters into intricate speculations in theology, neither does he invite us to move from speeches carefully devised to suit particular dramatic creations into speculations as to the dramatist's own religious faith. To do so is to misunderstand the nature of drama and to distort evidence, whether the result suggests Shakespeare to have been Christian or non-Christian. Thus when Santayana takes Macbeth's great "Tomorrow and tomorrow" speech[6] as summing up Shakespeare's own view of life, he displays a philosophical rather than a literary reading of the text, assumes the existence of relevant evidence where none exists,

---

[4] Recall the famous Latin line: "Homo sum, humani nihil a me alienum puto."

[5] Calvin, Exp. Matt. 5.43 and Exp. Gal. 6.9-11, quoted by Ronald Wallace, *op.cit.*, pp. 148 and 150. These appear to be Wallace's translations. Italics are mine.

[6] *Macb.* 5.5.19ff.

and misses the dramatic point of the passage in question.[7]

I have earlier commented that most speculation as to Shakespeare's own religious position suggests special pleading of one sort or another, whereby the critic attempts to rationalize the evidence so that Shakespeare will appear to hold views agreeable to the critic himself. Santayana is not guilty on this point, for he dislikes the views which he postulates as Shakespeare's; but though he has not distorted the evidence to fit his own prejudices, he has still misused the texts of dramatic documents, and reads words carefully designed for individual characters in dramatic situations as though they constituted Shakespeare's own dramatic monologue. Shakespeare does not speak for himself in the plays, but for the characters he has created, and we do well to recall Kittredge's dictum that if Shakespeare "lurks somewhere in the heart of Othello, so likewise he lurks somewhere in the brain of Iago; if Hamlet is Shakspere, so also is Claudius, and so are Banquo and Fluellen, Falstaff and Prince Hal, Benedick and Hotspur," and so on.[8] To move from the words of any character to an assumption of Shakespeare's own position is inadmissible both critically and biographically.

We would also do well not to move from the fact that the great tragedies were all produced within the period of a few years to the conclusion that this was a time of near-despair in Shakespeare's life. Neither should the fact that in his last productive years he turned to happy themes lead us to conclude that he had therefore arrived at a triumphant

---

[7] George Santayana, "The Absence of Religion in Shakespeare," *op.cit.*, p. 142. For an analysis of Macbeth's speech in terms of Shakespeare's apt assignment of Biblical and theological allusions to Macbeth at this stage in his life, see my " 'Out, out, brief candle,' and the Jacobean Understanding," *Notes and Queries* (New Series), vol. 2 (1955), pp. 143-45.

[8] G. L. Kittredge, *op.cit.*, p. 47.

and joyous faith of some kind. In neither period do we have valid evidence "of the problems which life set Shakespeare"; the evidence which we do have, on the contrary, is conclusive only as to "the artistic problems which Shakespeare set himself," to quote from C. J. Sisson's brilliant British Academy lecture on this subject.[9] Thus, when Santayana declares that "for Shakespeare, in the matter of religion, the choice lay between Christianity and nothing," he has oversimplified the evidence, and when he concludes that "he chose nothing," he makes a merely assertive statement for which there simply is no evidence.[10]

Though the plays do not furnish us evidence of Shakespeare's religious orientation, they do attest to his theological literacy and to his uncanny ability to adapt his impressive religious knowledge to dramatic purposes. In the topical analysis of theological commonplaces, we have seen abundant evidence of Shakespeare's adaptation of theological subjects to his essentially dramatic purposes. Though Shakespeare could express Christian and other doctrines in memorable and impressive words, he never treats these doctrines as ends in themselves, but always makes them subordinate to his development of character and action.

Our analysis of the theological commonplaces in the plays has sought to clarify the place of theological themes and doctrines in "the artistic problems which Shakespeare set himself," to quote Sisson once more. When those artistic problems concern a character's Christian reflections or

[9] C. J. Sisson, "The Mythical Sorrows of Shakespeare," *Proceedings of the British Academy*, vol. 20 (1934), p. 19.

[10] Santayana, *op.cit.*, p. 140. Though Santayana goes far beyond the evidence in concluding so emphatically as to Shakespeare's repudiation of Christianity, he is essentially correct when he describes Shakespeare's dramatic world as being "only the world of human society." I cannot concur with him, however, when he describes this restriction of scope in Shakespeare as a dramatic "vice." *Ibid.*, p. 141.

relations, Shakespeare admirably employs the appropriate doctrines. In general, however, his theological and ethical references are placed within a context equally accessible to Christians and to the virtuous heathen. The overwhelming concern of his drama is with those areas which are universally human.

The comments assigned to heathen characters, except for a few minor anachronisms, are quite appropriate for non-Christian men, when those comments are judged in the context of sixteenth-century theology. When seen in that context, it is clear that Shakespeare's non-Christian characters are not assigned religious insights which exceed the bounds of pagan wisdom. It is also clear that when Shakespeare wanted a character to express Christian ideas, he communicated those ideas in terms which were readily recognizable by the standards of sixteenth-century theology. Conversely, when he did not write in such unmistakably Christian terms, we should assume that he did not invite a theological interpretation. In each of these regards, our historical analysis indicates that Shakespeare understood theology far better than do those who now try to convert his plays into Christian parables.

The major point throughout is the independence, the integrity, of Shakespeare's literary endeavor. In underscoring such independence and integrity, and in judging literature by universally human standards within the temporal order, Luther, Calvin, Hooker, and the traditions epitomized in them, rendered the greatest contribution to Shakespeare's art which he was ever to receive from theology. It is within the context of such literary freedom that we should understand Shakespeare's dramatically masterful and theologically appropriate use of Christian doctrine.

 APPENDIX, BIBLIOGRAPHY, AND INDEXES

THE ROMAN CATHOLIC CENSORSHIP
OF SHAKESPEARE: 1641-1651

Direct evidence as to attitudes held towards Shakespeare by professional theologians of his own time is exceedingly rare. Beyond mere allusions, the only substantial comment from such a source in Shakespeare's lifetime came from Meres, whose appraisal we have already examined.[1] There is preserved from the mid-seventeenth century, however, a most interesting piece of evidence: the plays of Shakespeare in the second folio censored under the authority of the Inquisition by an English Jesuit.[2] This expurgated volume is now in the collection of the Folger Shakespeare Library, where I have examined it in detail. It is an ordinary copy of the 1632 folio printed in London for

---

[1] See above, pp. 65ff.

[2] This censored folio has not received the attention which, in terms of its significance, it deserves. The major proponents of the theory that Shakespeare was a Roman Catholic have ignored it, and I know of only two other scholars who have examined it and reported on it. Both of their reports leave much to be desired. Sir Sidney Lee wrote an essay on the subject in 1922, but his essay was based on eight-year-old notes dating from a time when he had examined the volume before World War I, and he had not seen it again before publishing his report, as he is careful to point out. The result is that his notes had become "cold," and the article contains a sizable number of errors and misquotations which obviously stemmed from memorial reconstruction of incomplete notes. There are, in addition, other errors, such as ascribing the censorship to Guillén Sanchez and dating it within two decades of Shakespeare's death, which dating is quite out of line with all existing evidence. A second reference to the censored folio was made by Sir Henry Thomas in his Shakespeare Lecture for the British Academy in 1949. Thomas did not mention Lee's essay, and the brief references he makes within the printed lecture to the censored volume perpetuate misinformation gleaned from Spanish secondary sources. In a footnote, however, Thomas corrects the errors made in the main body of his lecture and gives a thumbnail sketch of the censorship itself. See Sir Sidney Lee, "Shakespeare and the Inquisition," in *Elizabethan and Other Essays*, Oxford: Clarendon Press, 1929, pp. 184-95, and Sir Henry Thomas, *Shakespeare in Spain*, London: Geoffrey Cumberlege, n.d., pp. 9 and 21-22.

general sale, which at some time in the decade between 1641 and 1651 was expurgated by the authority of the Holy Office by William Sankey, S.J., and then permitted by the same authority as reading matter for students in the English College at Valladolid, Spain. The evidence provided by this volume is so different in character from that which we have been treating thus far that it could not very well be integrated into the body of this book, and so is being treated in an appendix.

This Valladolid folio is of considerable interest for what it shows of certain Roman Catholic attitudes. That Father Sankey was acting as an official censor is clear from the following words written in ink at the bottom of the title page: "Opus auctoritate Sancti Officii permissum et expurgatum eadum auctoritate per Guilielmum Sanchaeum e Soc^te Jesu." On the dedication page (A2), the ownership of the folio is indicated as follows: "Collegii Sancti Albani Anglorum Vallisoleti." Since Father Sankey arrived in Valladolid in 1641 and became Rector of St. George's College, Madrid, in 1651, we may reasonably assume the censorship to have been carried out between these two dates.[3] It is possible, though by no means certain, that the time of the censorship may be further narrowed to the months of September and October 1649 when, during an interim between an outgoing and an incoming rector of the college, "Father William Sankey was in charge and signed the books."[4] The censorship was customarily exercised with a pen and ink and consisted in the blacking out of particular words, phrases, and lines. The one exception to this method of expurgation is the total removal

[3] See *The English College at Valladolid*, ed. Canon Edwin Henson, London: Catholic Record Society, 1930, p. xxviii, and *The English College at Madrid*, ed. Canon Edwin Henson, London: Catholic Record Society, 1929, p. ix.

[4] Canon Henson in *The English College at Valladolid*, p. xxix. I take it that by "signed the books" Canon Henson referred to the official registers of the college, though he may also have intended to refer to books such as the folio. When Father Sankey was "in charge" of the college, he might have received the folio and read it hurriedly during the press of other duties. There is simply not enough evidence, however, to allow us to say with assurance precisely when he executed this office of censorship.

of *Measure for Measure* from the volume, the pages having been neatly cut out with a sharp instrument.

Aside from the negative testimony of expurgation, the Valladolid folio reveals little in any specific way as to an appreciation of Shakespeare. The extent of the positive comments in the folio is the presence of the single word "good" written on the first page of each of four comedies—*The Merry Wives of Windsor, The Comedy of Errors, Much Ado About Nothing,* and *The Merchant of Venice*—while *Cymbeline* is described in a similar fashion as "rare."[5] No word is devoted to the tragedies. At two points in *Macbeth*, however, lines have been drawn vertically down the margin by words which must have held special poignancy for the exiled priest, as he directs attention to Lenox's reference to "this our suffering country Under a hand accurs'd" and to the more extended comment of the exiled Malcolm contemplating both the present state of his country and the possibility of his own successful return to power:

> I think our country sinks beneath the yoke,
> It weeps, it bleeds, and each new day a gash
> Is added to her wounds. I think withal
> There would be hands uplifted in my right;
> And here from gracious England have I offer
> Of goodly thousands.
>
> (*Macbeth* 3.6.48f., and 4.3.39ff.[6])

[5] "Good" and "rare" are written in a hand which in some ways appears more modern than Sankey's and the pen has a finer point than that which he used in his censorship, though the capital letter G and the open o are much like his. It is possible that these words were not inserted by Sankey at all, but by another hand which appears in the folio. This second hand inscribed a clear signature, Joannes Lucas, with several pen "doodles" below it, in the margin opposite Ben Jonson's poem (p. 2). Lucas appears in the college records for 1691 and 1692 as a student and later as a priest (*The English College at Valladolid*, p. 176). His hand appears elsewhere in scribbles or in a word or two, none of which has any relevance to our concerns (Comedies, p. 101; Histories, p. 117; Tragedies, p. 59).

[6] Here, as elsewhere in this study, my references are to the Kittredge edition cited above. Only where the spelling of the second folio is significant have I reproduced it, in the treatment of "holyday," below. In this Appendix, the references to Shakespeare's plays are either incorporated into my text

Though these marked passages increase our sympathy for Sankey as a person, his expurgations are more revealing theologically.

As a censor, Father Sankey was not very thorough but, as far as he went, he was consistent in his objections. A sufficient amount of material is expunged to show very clear patterns of judgment. These patterns are followed consistently insofar as the censorship progressed, but we may judge the censorship itself not to have been very thoroughly carried out from the fact that within Shakespeare's works there are many more objectionable lines left uncut than are cut, if we judge by Father Sankey's own standards. The point is illustrated where Sankey finds Falstaff's swearing by the mass to be objectionable, and in *I Henry IV* 2.4.400 blots out the word "mass" to leave Falstaff saying "By the ——, lad, thou sayest true," and yet ignores the same oath when it is used elsewhere in Shakespeare.

Father Sankey's sexual delicacy may be seen in his deletion of references to the codpiece in *Love's Labour Lost* 3.1.186, as also in *King Lear* 3.2.27 and 40, though he leaves the word undisturbed in numerous other places where it appears. Similarly, he dislikes and expunges Pandarus' question in *Troilus and Cressida* 4.2.23-24, "How go maidenheads?" He seems especially disapproving of references to sexual intercourse, and deletes the word-play upon "hit it" and "at pricks" from *Love's Labour's Lost* 4.1.120, 123, 125-28, 132-34, 138, and 140. He is offended by the references to a woman bearing the weight of a man or being covered by a man. He expunges such references in *Much Ado about Nothing* 3.4.26ff., 5.2.6-10, and the entire exchange from line 15 through 22, though similar references go unnoticed in other plays. In the same way he objects to Solanio's satiric imitation of Shylock's lament over the loss of Jessica that "She hath the stones upon her" in *Merchant of Venice* 2.8.22, and deletes the words "upon her" so as to render the passage innocuous of the innuendo by which "stones" may be taken as

---

or placed in brackets within it. This variation from the usage followed elsewhere is necessitated by the changed focus here; where the attention is so largely textual, the reader's convenience is better served by placing the references as I do here.

referring to testes. A similar sensitivity comes out when a reference to a woman bearing a sexual burden is obscured by deleting the final half-line of the following passage from *Henry VIII* 2.3.42-44. The omitted words are italicized.

> If your back
> Cannot vouchsafe this burthen, 'tis too weak
> *Ever to get a boy.*

So censored, the lines refer merely to the burden of dignity and title.

In view of Sankey's disapproval of all such talk, it is interesting to see that he not only blots out Margaret's references to the forthcoming consummation of Hero's marriage in *Much Ado*, but even denies Margaret the words with which she defends herself for such references. Hero has jokingly asked Margaret if she is not ashamed of such talk, and Margaret replies as follows, with Sankey's deletions indicated by italics:

> . . . Is there any harm in '*the heavier for a husband*'? None, I
> think, *an it be the right husband and the right wife.*
>
> (*Much Ado,* 3.4.33-36)

Sankey is unwilling, however, to allow even so innocent a defense to stand in the text. In view of so pronounced a sensitivity to the subject of women lying upon their backs, it would appear highly unlikely that Sankey read *Romeo and Juliet* with any care if he read it at all, for with all the Nurse's repetitious bawdry about Juliet upon her back, not a single word is expunged, and neither are any of the other comic passages in this play which openly treats sex in a fashion Sankey found so distasteful elsewhere.

Sometimes Sankey's excisions leave a mutilated but still sensible expression, as when in *Hamlet* 3.2.126 he blocks out the final half line ("to lie between maid's legs") and leaves Hamlet with the innocent words, "That's a fair thought. . . ." On other occasions, the deletions leave a sentence dangling meaninglessly, as when Sankey denies Gonzalo in *The Tempest* 1.1.49ff. any reference to "an unstanched wench," so that the old man's speech is left not only maimed but quite obviously so:

I'll warrant him for drowning, though the
ship were no stronger than a nutshell and as leaky as . . .

Sensitivity of this order would seem to mark Father Sankey
as the first of the Victorians, but I do not wish to make too
much of such prudery. There are numerous other excisions, however, which have unmistakable theological significance. Sankey's
deletion from *Love's Labour's Lost* 4.3.366 and 5.2.87 of the
King's reference to Cupid as a "saint" and of the Princess' line
"Saint Denis to Saint Cupid" indicates a theological disapproval
which could have been found in Anglican and Roman divines
alike, but most of his doctrinaire censorship is clearly based in
explicitly Roman Catholic attitudes. These instances show
Father Sankey's suspicion of English Protestant bias and his
desire to see his own communion represented in a fair and
favorable way.

The first two instances come when profane matters are compared to religious matters in so blatant a fashion as to touch
the censor's official concerns. Thus, when Rosalind in *As You
Like It* 3.4.14-15 declares of Orlando that "his kissing is as full
of sanctity as the touch of holy bread," the entire line is expunged, perhaps because it appeared irreverent in the light of
the doctrine of transubstantiation. Apart from that doctrine,
Rosalind's comparison need not necessarily seem objectionable,
especially if the audience for whom it was intended had been
heavily indoctrinated in views such as those the Swiss reformer
Henry Bullinger expressed when he declared that in married
love couples "please God no less than they do when they go
to church to hear the word of God and to worship the Lord . . .
for by wedlock in faith they shall please the Lord. This our
[Romish] monks could not abide to hear of, although the word
of God doth urge it upon them; they ceased not to magnify
their counterfeit holiness and hypocritical vows."[7] Despite
Bullinger, there is no reason to regard Father Sankey's attitude
as hypocritical, but on the contrary it does appear to represent
a sincere attempt to discharge the office of censorship in faithful
adherence to the theological position of his church.

[7] Bullinger, *op.cit.*, vol. 1, p. 406.

The same honest attempt at expurgation appears elsewhere. In *All's Well that Ends Well* 2.2.28, Father Sankey deletes one phrase from the clown's long catalogue of similes for fitness when he inks out the reference to the fit of "the nun's lip to the friar's mouth." This deletion seems patently dictated by natural resentment for a common Elizabethan disparagement of the chastity of religious orders. Sensitivity of somewhat the same kind is displayed when the word "holyday" in *The Tempest* 2.2.29 is expunged from the hyphenated epithet "holyday-fool," which seems innocent enough to us because we do not so readily sense, as did Father Sankey, the depreciation of saints' days which might have been conveyed by the expression. In *Henry VIII* 2.1.21, Sankey removes the disparagement of a monk by removing the words "confessor to him, with that devil monk."

Father Sankey's attitude toward Shakespeare's portrayal in *Henry VI* of Henry Beaufort, Bishop of Winchester and Cardinal, is quite interesting. As Robert Stevenson has reminded us, Shakespeare makes Beaufort, his most fully drawn cardinal, appear much blacker in the play than he appears in the historical source material.[8] Sankey shows no interest in rehabilitating Winchester's character, but he does alter passages which impugn the dignity of the church. In *I Henry VI* 1.3.35, Gloucester accuses the bishop, among other crimes, of being one "that giv'st whores indulgences to sin." From this catalogue of Beaufort's sins, Sankey strikes out only the single word "indulgences," thus leaving the somewhat ambiguous reference to "giving whores ——————— to sin," but removing what seems to have struck him as a suspicious reference to the misuse of indulgences. Indulgences, after all, were at the root of Luther's first protests, and long continued to draw fire from Protestants, both clerical and lay. The remainder of the altercation between the duke and the bishop is allowed to stand, until the duke declares his intention to trounce the prelate "In spite of pope or dignities of church," and this entire line is expunged at *I Henry VI* 1.3.50.

Sankey is also concerned to obliterate the connection of a priest with witchcraft, and thus deletes words in the opening

[8] Stevenson, *op.cit.*, pp. 15-16.

stage direction of *II Henry VI*, Act one, Scene four, which specify the presence of "the two priests" at the conjuration. He also expunges the name of one priest, John Southwell, from the conjurer Bolingbroke's call to begin the reading of the incantation, and deletes a stage direction which has the priest read (*II Henry VI* 1.4.14 and 25). The altered text leaves Bolingbroke alone in this action, and so eliminates the picture of a priest involved in one of the most fearful acts of witchcraft. At the same point in this play, Sankey is unwilling to allow the conjurer's circle to be called "hallow'd," and deletes that word. Later in the same play, he deletes some twenty lines, so as to avoid the spectacle of the final humiliation of the fraudulent Simpcox and the ridicule of his false claims to have been cured of his blindness at Saint Alban's shrine (*ibid.*, 2.1.142-64). Though the court's jeering cry of "A miracle!" is deleted, Sankey nonetheless leaves the pious king's comment on that cry and on the entire skeptical proceeding: "O God, seest thou this, and bearest so long?" That comment may have come close to expressing Father Sankey's own reaction to the course of religious events in England.

Some of the most interesting theological deletions come in connection with *King John* and *Henry VIII*. In *King John* 3.1.147-207, twenty-two lines or parts of lines are deleted. In these deletions, Father Sankey rendered inaccessible to his students, while inadvertently underscoring for us, the essentially Anglican character of the arguments advanced by John against the papal legate and the papal supremacy. Sixteenth-century Church of England spokesmen, seeking precedents for their own position, often cited King John's resistance to Pope Innocent III as an instance of the pre-Reformation independence of Anglicanism.[9] Bishop John Bale's chronicle play *King Johan* put the theme to vehement and even violent use, and while the later play entitled *The Troublesome Reign of King John* is considerably more restrained, in it too the theme of John's pre-Reforma-

[9] William Tyndale, *Expositions of Scripture*, pp. 19 and 295; Thomas Cranmer, *Works*, Cambridge: The Parker Society, 1846, vol. 2, p. 388; John Jewel, *Works*, Cambridge: The Parker Society, 1850, pp. 687 and 1076.

tion defense of Anglican integrity is of major interest. If Shakespeare's *King John* is compared with these earlier plays, such themes pale into relative insignificance, and we are likely to pass over them without notice. What Father Sankey has done, however, is to point out how Shakespeare's play accords to King John a more noticeably "Anglican" position than most of us have been accustomed to find.

When the papal legate Cardinal Pandulph arrives on stage, his first act is to inquire of King John why he has kept the Archbishop of Canterbury from his see. Now under the practical polity of the Church of England in the sixteenth century, the monarch was able to do as he would with the English primate, as Elizabeth so effectively demonstrated when she sequestered Edmund Grindal, also an Archbishop of Canterbury. It was against the background of Anglican doctrine and practice that Father Sankey read King John's reply to the legate, and Sankey correctly saw in it an accurate statement of Anglican polity, as it was assumed to have been defended under a Plantagenet king and as it was actually practiced under the first Elizabeth. Thus John replied to Pandulph, not as the spiritual subject of the pope, but as one who claimed independence of the pope "and his usurp'd authority." Sankey faithfully deletes the entire caustic reference to the pope: "all reverence set apart To him and his usurp'd authority" (John 3.1.159-160). England's claim of historic independence both in empire and in church is officially made in the Restraint of Appeals Act of 1533. This act was passed again in 1534, was repealed under Mary, and was restored when Elizabeth came to the throne. The pope was thus a "foreign power," as Tudor legislation and propaganda alike never tire of repeating. Closely associated with the claim of English independence was the charge of usurpation leveled against the papacy. This charge was a common Reformation theme, and it became legally enshrined in the Dispensations Act of 1534, which was still the official position when Shakespeare wrote and when Sankey censored.[10]

[10] *Documents of the Christian Church*, ed. Henry Bettenson, New York: Oxford University Press, 1947, pp. 309-21.

Further evidence of Sankey's suspicions may be seen when he expunged the last two lines (italicized) of the following passage, and left the first line to stand as at once innocuous and meaningless:

> Thou canst not, Cardinal, devise a name
> *So slight, unworthy, and ridiculous*
> *To charge me to an answer, as the Pope.*
>
> (*Ibid.*, 3.1.149-51)

These two lines again express a thoroughly Henrician and Elizabethan attitude in repudiating any obligation on the part of an English sovereign to answer to the pope. Even more explicit, however, is John's rationale for England's religious independence, which he, like the Anglican dogmatists, placed in the royal supremacy over the church in England, where "we," he says, "under heaven, are supreme head" (*ibid.*, 3.1.155). The English monarch was recognized as supreme head of the Church of England "as far as the law of Christ allows" by the Convocations of 1531. In 1534, the Supremacy Act was passed by parliament, and the English monarch was legally established as "Supreme Head."[11] As we would expect, Sankey struck out of John's claim the words "are supreme head," for the Roman view that claim was essentially blasphemous, and we may recall that when Mary Tudor restored the Church of Rome in England some century before Sankey's time, one of the first directives to the English clergy prohibited the use in any document of any phrase even implying the royal supremacy.[12] The phrase which John uses is the very one applied to Henry; Elizabeth was content to be known as "supreme governor," but "supreme head" better fit the meter of Shakespeare's line at this point, and there was little practical difference between the two titles.[13]

To the Anglican tone of John's claims, the king of France responds in horror, "Brother of England, you do blaspheme in this," whereupon John launches into a declaration of English

[11] *Ibid.*, pp. 321-22.

[12] Sir Maurice Powicke, *The Reformation in England*, London: Oxford University Press, 1961, p. 121.

[13] For the Elizabethan Supremacy Act of 1559, see Bettenson, *op.cit.*, pp. 332-33.

independence from Rome. In the following passage, italicized
words and lines indicate Father Sankey's excisions. John is reply-
ing to France, and beyond him to all Christendom:

> Though you and all the kings of Christendom
> Are led *so grossly by this meddling priest,*
> *Dreading the curse that money may buy out,*
> And by the merit of vile gold, dross, dust,
> *Purchase corrupted pardon of a man,*
> *Who in that sale sells pardon from himself—*
> Though you, and all the rest *so grossly led,*
> *This juggling witchcraft with revenue cherish,*
> Yet I alone, alone do me oppose
> Against the Pope *and count his friends my foes.*
>
> (*Ibid.,* 3.1.162-71)

A reading of this statement as shortened by Sankey may still
make a bit of sense, but it is very different sense from that of
the original speech. John's words, taken in their entirety, underscore common Church of England positions which to the
Church of Rome seemed not only unfair but exceedingly dangerous and heretical. The references to the "meddling priest,"
"the curse," the sale of "corrupted pardon," and the rest were
thus expunged.

Such expurgation is what we might expect, though it may
serve for some readers (as it has for me) to point up the presence
of more pronounced Anglican doctrine in the speeches of King
John than has often been seen by modern commentators. Father
Sankey's next excision is perhaps less predictable, for it comes
in Pandulph's excommunication of John. Here Sankey stops
the speech half-way through, so as to expunge all of the Cardinal's references to the merit accrued from the subject's murder of
an excommunicated king as well as the promise of elevating the
murderer to sainthood. Such references, again, must have seemed
to Sankey to reflect the Roman position unfavorably, and though
he allowed Pandulph's blessing upon rebels to stand, he eliminated the promise of canonization for murder. Perhaps he displays here a sensitivity to the "king-killer" charge commonly

leveled at the Jesuits. The italicized words are blocked out by Sankey's pen:

> Then by the lawful power that I have
> Thou shalt stand curs'd and excommunicate,
> And blessed shall be he that doth revolt
> From his allegiance *to an heretic,*
> *And meritorious shall that hand be call'd*
> *Canonized, and worshipp'd as a saint,*
> *That takes away by any secret course*
> *Thy hated life.*
>
> (*Ibid.*, 3.1.172-78)

Thus Sankey is careful not only to prevent the spread of Anglican heresy through the words spoken by John, but also to relieve Pandulph of expressions which placed the Church of Rome in an unfavorable light and which might even mislead the Jesuits' students at Valladolid.

The question of a Roman Catholic subject's relation to an heretical and excommunicated sovereign was much mooted in this age, and it is possible to relate Sankey's censorship to a number of well-known attitudes by noting what was and was not excised from Pandulph's speech. No Roman Catholic, of course, denied the church's right of excommunication, and so we would not expect any censor to delete the first two of Pandulph's lines—lines of curse and excommunication. The next two lines are more questionable: "And blessed shall be that doth revolt From his allegiance." That Sankey allows these lines to stand shows him to have been closer than were most English Catholics to the official position of the church (which is what should be expected of a Jesuit), as that position was expressed in the famous *Regnans in Excelsis* bull of Pius V excommunicating Elizabeth and freeing her subjects from allegiance. Even more forceful than the original bull was the *Admonition to the Nobility and People of England* which William Allen, the "Cardinal of England," had prepared for distribution in England at the time of the Armada in 1588. In this document the people of England were urged to rise in revolt against Elizabeth as a "deprived, accursed, excommunicate heretic."[14] Cardinal Allen's conditions and charges are the same as those which Cardinal Pandulph laid down against John. That Father Sankey allows those words to stand is again what we would expect from a member of the Society of Jesus operating under authority of the Holy Office, even though we know that the rank and file of English recusants remained faithful to the crown despite all pressures to the contrary.

Even more interesting are other lines which Sankey cuts from Pandulph's speech—the lines promising that assassination of the excommunicated monarch would be regarded as a meretorious and even saintly act. Many English Protestants believed that Rome took just this attitude towards the assassination of Queen Elizabeth, and there were historical grounds for such a belief. The Roman Catholic scholar E. I. Watkin, in his history of Roman Catholicism in England, provides the following relevant insight: "Nor was [Pope] Gregory XIII averse from political assassination. An English priest approached Sega, the Papal nuncio at Madrid, on behalf of a group of anonymous English noblemen who were plotting to kill Elizabeth but would not make the attempt unless the Pope assured them it was not sinful. Sega transmitted their inquiry to the Cardinal Secretary of State and through him the Pope replied 'that if these English nobles decide to undertake so glorious a work they do not commit sin.' On the contrary: 'whoever sends "the Queen" out of the world with the pious intention of doing God service . . . gains merit.'"[15] Again, Pandulph's words reflect the papal position, though not that of most English Catholics, toward the English monarch. That Sankey was unwilling to allow the students at Valladolid to read these words shows him to have represented the more liberal position among his co-religionists.

Throughout this entire scene in *King John* Sankey is being quite meticulous, as he recognizes that he is treating issues which are of exceptional importance. He thus deletes Constance's hyperbolic cry that unless the legate's curse is connected with

---

[14] E. I. Watkin, *Roman Catholicism in England from the Reformation to 1950*, London: Oxford University Press, 1957, p. 39.

[15] *Ibid.*, p. 37.

the wrong which John has done to her, then no one (including the pope) has the power to curse John aright (*King John*, 3.1.181-83). Sankey then expunges the Bastard's words expressing his desire to "hang a calve's-skin" on the "recreant limbs" of the papal legate, and even Blanch's simple reference to the curse of Rome (*ibid.*, 3.1.199 and 207).

In the final act of *King John* we again find Sankey concerned to expunge references to priestly regicide. Where Hubert reports on John that "The king, I fear, is poison'd by a monk," Sankey blots out the final three words ascribing the deed to the member of a religious order. A few lines later he again blots out the words "A monk" from Hubert's assignment of responsibility for taking John's life (*ibid.*, 5.6.23 and 29).

The expurgations in *King John* are clearly doctrinal in character and are primarily concerned with the government and reputation of the church. The excisions in *King Henry VIII* are dictated by equally cogent doctrinal considerations, but here they represent an attempt to delete references which appear most flattering to those arch-heretics of England, Archbishop Cranmer and Queen Elizabeth. There are also minor deletions such as that of King Henry's reference to "tricks of Rome," but the censor's main purpose in this play seems to be the elimination of the praise heaped on Cranmer and Elizabeth (*Henry VIII*, 2.4.237). How much of this particular section of the play is from the pen of Shakespeare is a matter of some disagreement among scholars. Without attempting to reach a determination on this textual problem, I shall merely report upon the expurgations which Father Sankey has carried out.

It would be difficult to denigrate Cranmer in this play, but Father Sankey can and does eliminate certain flattering adjectives applied to him as when he expunges "virtuous" from before his surname, or when he systematically purges "good" and "honest" from the king's references to him, leaving those references merely as "this —— man" in the king's moving speeches of rebuke to Cranmer's enemies and praise of the Archbishop himself (*Henry VIII*, 4.1.105 and 5.3.130, 138 and 139). When Henry tells the lords to respect Cranmer, he adds that "he's worthy of it," and Sankey expunges these words too (*ibid.*, 5.3.154). It is difficult to think that an intelligent man, such as Father Sankey presumably was, could have expected to make any effective change in the total portrait of Cranmer by such minor deletions, for the total action of the scene is so designed as to create great respect for Cranmer. Without entirely eliminating the major action, all that Sankey can do merely serves to show his own resentment of the fact that so flattering a portrait was painted of a man whom Sankey's church condemned and executed as a relapsed heretic. But feelings ran high in those times, and we will understand Sankey's work better if we try to imagine the satisfaction which an English Jesuit, in exile from his country, might have derived from denying to Cranmer the adjectives "virtuous," "good," and "honest."

What Sankey could not do to Cranmer in this play, he could do to Elizabeth in depriving her of the praise heaped upon her in Cranmer's prophecy. That prophecy runs for forty-nine lines, of which Sankey deletes a total of twenty-five. Sankey is willing to leave the assertions of Elizabeth's material success, and even to allow that she shall be "A pattern to all princes . . . that shall succeed," as a model of practical (and perhaps by implication, Machiavellian) effectiveness (*ibid.*, 5.5.21-24) but he expunges all of what immediately follows in Cranmer's prediction of her "wisdom and fair virtue," "pure soul," "princely graces," "all the virtues that attend the good," "truth," and "Holy and heavenly thoughts" (*ibid.*, 5.5.24-33). Expunged also is the prophecy of true religious reformation, when in Elizabeth's reign

> God shall be truly known, and those about her
> From her shall read the perfect ways of honour.
>
> (*Ibid.*, 5.5.37-38)

And although her successor James I is not stripped of all the virtues which Cranmer foresees for him, he is denied the predicted "starlike rise" "as great in admiration as herself." So the following passage is entirely blacked out:

Her ashes new create another heir
As great in admiration as herself,
So shall she leave her blessedness to one
(When heaven shall call her from this cloud of darkness)
Who from the sacred ashes of her honour
Shall starlike rise, as great in fame as she was,
And so stand fix'd. Peace, plenty, love, truth, terror,
That were the servants to this chosen infant. . . .

(Ibid., 5.5.42-49)

Here the excision abruptly ends, having excluded King James from a small modicum of praise and Elizabeth from heaven's call. In Cranmer's last speech, Sankey also expurgated the assertion of Elizabeth's reign being "to the happiness of England," as well as the parallel assertion that her reign would have "yet no day without a deed to crown it" *(ibid.*, 5.5.57 and 59). The last of Cranmer's prophecy which is allowed to stand as acceptable are the words "But she must die—"and all that follows is deleted:

She must [die], the saints must have her—yet a virgin,
A most unspotted lily, shall she pass
To th' ground, and all the world shall mourn her.

(Ibid., 5.5.61-63)

Just as all references to Elizabeth in heaven are deleted, so too are the expressions by Henry VIII of his joyful confidence in his daughter's future and in his own salvation:

O Lord Archbishop,
Thou hast made me now a man! Never before
This happy child did I get anything.
This oracle of comfort has so pleas'd me
That when I am in heaven I shall desire
To see what this child does, and praise my Maker.

(Ibid., 5.5.64-69)

One final excision occurs in the play: where the Epilogue commends the play to "The merciful construction of good women," the adjective "good" is expunged, so that the commendation of the play under Sankey's revision applies only to "women."

There is one other major deletion in Father Sankey's folio, and this is his total excision of *Measure for Measure*. Where this play once appeared in the Valladolid folio, nothing now remains but the stubs of pages cut back almost to the binding. Why, we may ask, was this play alone completely removed by the censor—this play which has been cited as the most Christian drama in Shakespeare's canon? The first observation which strikes us is that *Measure for Measure* obviously did not seem so very Christian to this Jesuit censor who was expressly operating under the authority of the Holy Office. That much appears quite indisputable, and should at least give pause to those who declare the play to be a Christian parable. Since such claims have been most popular among critics who interpret Shakespeare in terms of a basically "catholic" tradition (whether it be Anglo-Catholic or Roman), Father Sankey's judgment would appear to be particularly relevant.

Sankey, unfortunately, gives no reasons for his aversion to the play, but I would suggest that at least one reason for this aversion may be found in the manner in which the Duke, though a layman, assumes both the dress and the prerogatives of a priest. The Duke's actions would not have appeared so offensive to Elizabethan Protestants who were schooled in the doctrine of the priesthood of all believers. Protestants, after all, were taught that they might turn to laymen as well as ministers for confession and absolution, but at a time when such practices struck Roman Catholics with the unique shock of novelty combined with heresy,[16] a Jesuit censor might well have been ex-

16 An interesting debate over this issue occurs between the Church of England apologist John Jewel and the Roman Catholic Harding, in which Jewel (*op.cit.*, vol. 3, p. 357) defends the Reformed teaching that laymen may both hear confession and absolve, and points out to Harding that such teachings were a part of the pre-Reformation tradition which had seemingly been abandoned by Rome. Calvin (*Inst.* 3.4.12) teaches that though it is better to confess to a minister, confession may be made to a suitable layman, and Luther (Plass anthol., vol. 1, 7 and 974) holds to the same general conception.

pected to object passionately to *Measure for Measure.* Father Sankey's actual objection—whatever its grounds—is recorded in his total expurgation of the play.

Our examination of Father Sankey's censorship for the Holy Office is now complete, and we may in summary make several observations as to his practice. His word-by-word and line-by-line excisions are of two types. The first type concerns matters of distaste, primarily as to sex. The patterns of Father Sankey's objections here are clear and unmistakable, but his censorship of the plays in terms of these patterns was far from thorough: there was a good deal, perhaps even most, of Shakespeare which he gives no evidence of having read at all, and it appears likely that his knowledge of Shakespeare was rather limited.

The second type of line-by-line censorship concerns theological and ecclesiastical matters. In this connection Father Sankey expunged three kinds of material: words and phrases which either did or might reflect unfavorably upon Roman Catholic doctrines or institutions; clear statements of Anglican ecclesiology in *King John*; and the exaltation of Anglican leaders in *Henry VIII.*

In addition to these various line by line deletions, there is the complete elimination of *Measure for Measure.*

Having observed how and what Father Sankey censored, we come now to consider the significance of his censorship. Its significance lies in the fact that we have here the only extended evidence of any official Roman Catholic attitude toward Shakespeare which dates from his own age. The censorship was carried out within fifty years of the height of Shakespeare's career, and between twenty-five and thirty-five years after his death. Attempts by various writers to associate Shakespeare in some direct fashion with Roman Catholicism have consisted largely if not entirely in surmise and speculation, but in the Sankey folio we have the only early document containing an appraisal of Shakespeare from the Roman Catholic viewpoint, and it is an officially authorized expurgation and permission under authority of the Inquisition.

It is not, as we have seen, an exhaustive censorship, but it does show an extensive range of objections. On the basis of what

Sankey did, it would be possible to extrapolate his patterns so as to arrive at a thorough censorship of the Shakespeare corpus. If a thoroughgoing expurgation were to be carried out on the principles which Sankey followed in relation to sex alone, the result would be a radically bowdlerized text of Shakespeare. To extend Sankey's efforts would surely be a work of supererogation, however, for in his censorship he has provided sufficiently extensive evidence of the bearing upon Shakespeare's plays of the position he represents.

Our age will fortunately not regard Father Sankey's pioneering work as a model for the treatment of Shakespeare. What Sankey's expurgation may do is to put us on our guard, from yet another point of view, against the overly eager identification of Shakespeare's plays with Christian teachings in general and with the Catholic tradition in particular.

Aeschylus. *Agamemnon*, trans. Richmond Lattimore, *The Complete Greek Tragedies: Aeschylus*, Chicago: University of Chicago Press, 1959.

Aquinas, Thomas. *Summa Theologica*, 3 vols., trans. Fathers of the English Dominican Province, New York: Benziger Brothers, Inc., 1947-1948.

Bainton, Roland. *Here I Stand*, New York: Abingdon Press, 1950.

Baldwin, T. W. *William Shakspere's Petty School*, Urbana, Illinois: The University of Illinois Press, 1943.

Barker, Peter. *Exposition Upon the Ten Commandments*, London, 1633.

Barnet, Sylvan. "Some Limitations of a Christian Approach to Shakespeare," *ELH*, vol. 22, pp. 81-92.

Battenhouse, Roy W. "*Measure for Measure* and Christian Doctrine of the Atonement," *PMLA*, vol. 61, pp. 1029-59.

Becon, Thomas. *Writings*, Philadelphia: British Reformers Series, n.d.

Bishop, John. *Beautiful Blossoms*, London, 1577.

Borgeaud, Charles. *Histoire de L'Université de Genève: L'Académie de Calvin*, Genève: Georg et Co., Libraires de L'Université, 1900.

Bradley, A. C. *Shakespearean Tragedy*, London: Macmillan and Co., 1937.

Brathwait, Richard. *A Spiritual Spicerie*, London, 1638.

Breen, Quirinus. *John Calvin: A Study in French Humanism*, Grand Rapids: Wm. B. Eerdmans Publishing Company, 1931.

Bryant, J. A., Jr. *Hippolyta's View: Some Christian Aspects of Shakespeare's Plays*, n.p.: University of Kentucky Press, 1961.

Bullinger, Henry. *The Decades*, 4 vols., trans. H. I., Cambridge: The Parker Society, 1849-1852.

Calvin, John. *Against Astrology Judicial*, trans. G. G[ylby], London, 1561.

Calvin, John. *Commentaries*, 45 vols., ed. Calvin Translation

Society, Grand Rapids: Wm. B. Eerdmans Publishing Co., 1948.

Calvin, John. *Commentaries,* trans. Joseph Haroutunian, Philadelphia: The Westminster Press, 1958.

Calvin, John. *Commentary upon St. Paul's Epistles to the Corinthians,* trans. T. Tymme, London, 1577.

Calvin, John. *Institutes of the Christian Religion,* trans. Thomas Norton, London, 1611.

Calvin, John. *Institutes of the Christian Religion,* 2 vols., ed. John T. McNeill and trans. Ford Lewis Battles, Philadelphia: The Westminster Press, 1960.

Calvin, John. A *Little Book Concerning Offenses,* trans. Arthur Golding, London, 1567.

Calvin, John. *Opera Omnia (Corpus Reformatorum),* 59 vols., Brunsvig: C. A. Schwetschke et Filium, 1863-1897.

Calvin, John. *Sermons on Deuteronomy,* trans. Arthur Golding, London, 1583.

Calvin, John. *Sermons on Job,* trans. Arthur Golding, London, 1574.

Calvin, John. *Tracts and Treatises,* 3 vols., ed. Thomas F. Torrance, Grand Rapids: Wm. B. Eerdmans Publishing Co., 1958.

Canons and Decrees of the Council of Trent. Trans. H. J. Schroeder, London: B. Herder Book Co., 1941.

Carpenter, Nathanael. *Achitophel,* London, 1638.

Chambers, E. K. *William Shakespeare: A Study of Facts and Problems,* 2 vols., Oxford: The Clarendon Press, 1930.

Charlton, H. B. *Shakespearian Tragedy,* Cambridge: Cambridge University Press, 1952.

Clarke, M. L. *Classical Education in Britain: 1500-1900,* Cambridge: Cambridge University Press, 1959.

Coghill, Nevill. "The Governing Idea: Essays in Stage-Interpretation of Shakespeare," *Shakespeare Quarterly* (Vienna), vol. 1, pp. 9-17.

Copley, Anthony. A *Fig for Fortune,* Manchester: The Spenser Society, 1883.

Cramner, Thomas. *Works*, 2 vols., Cambridge: The Parker Society, 1844-1846.

Crofts, Robert. *The Lover or Nuptial Love*, London, 1638.

Cunningham, J. V. *Woe or Wonder*, Denver: University of Denver Press, 1951.

Curtis, Mark H. *Oxford and Cambridge in Transition*: 1558-1642, Oxford: Oxford University Press, 1959.

Documents of the Christian Church. Ed. Henry Bettenson, New York: Oxford University Press, 1947.

Donne, John. *Biathanatos*, London, 1644.

Downame, John. *The Christian Warfare*, London, 1634.

Dunkley, E. H. *The Reformation in Denmark*, London: SPCK, 1948.

Edgar, John. *History of Early Scottish Education*, Edinburgh: J. Thin, 1893.

The English College at Madrid. Ed. Canon Edwin Henson, London: Catholic Record Society, 1929.

The English College at Valladolid. Ed. Canon Edwin Henson, London: Catholic Record Society, 1930.

Frye, Roland M. *God, Man, and Satan*, Princeton: Princeton University Press, 1960.

Frye, Roland M. "John Donne, Junior, on 'Biathanatos': A Presentation Letter," *Notes and Queries*, vol. 197, pp. 495-96.

Frye, Roland M. "'Out, out brief candle,' and the Jacobean Understanding," *Notes and Queries*, vol. 2 (New Series), pp. 143-45.

Fulke, William. *A Defense of the Translations of Holy Scriptures*, Cambridge: The Parker Society, 1843.

Gardner, Helen. *The Business of Criticism*, Oxford: The Clarendon Press, 1959.

Gardner, Helen. "The Noble Moor," *Proceedings of the British Academy*, vol. 41, pp. 189-205.

Gerrish, B. A. *Grace and Reason: A Study in the Theology of Luther*, Oxford: The Clarendon Press, 1962.

Gollancz, Sir Israel. *Allegory and Mysticism in Shakespeare*, London: Printed for private circulation by Geo. W. Jones, 1931.

Gouge, William. *Of Domestical Duties*, London, 1634.

Griffith, Matthew. *Bethel*, London, 1634.

Hakewill, George. *King David's Vow*, London, 1621.

Harbison, E. Harris. *The Christian Scholar in the Age of Reformation*, New York: Charles Scribner's Sons, 1956.

Hastings, James. *Encyclopedia of Religion and Ethics*, 13 vols., New York: Charles Scribner's Sons, 1908-26.

Holl, Karl. *The Cultural Significance of the Reformation*, New York: Living Age Books, 1959.

Homilies Appointed to be Read in the Time of Queen Elizabeth. Philadelphia, 1844.

Hooker, Richard. *Works*, 2 vols., ed. John Keble, New York: D. Appleton and Co., 1849.

Hooper, John. *Later Writings*, Cambridge: The Parker Society, 1852.

Hooper, John. *Writings*, Philadelphia: British Reformers Series, n.d.

Jewel, John. *Works*, 4 vols., Cambridge: The Parker Society, 1845-50.

Joseph, Bertram. *Conscience and the King*, London: Chatto and Windus, 1953.

Kittredge, G. L. *Shakspere: An Address*, Cambridge, Mass.: Harvard University Press, 1916.

Knappen, M. M. *Tudor Puritanism*, Chicago: University of Chicago Press, 1939.

Knight, G. Wilson. *Principles of Shakesperian Production*, New York: Macmillan, 1937.

Knight, G. Wilson, *The Wheel of Fire*, London: Methuen and Co., 1949.

Kristeller, Paul Oskar. *Renaissance Thought*, New York: Harper and Brothers, 1961.

Kuyper, Abraham. *Calvinism*, Grand Rapids: Wm. B. Eerdmans Publishing Co., 1943.

Latimer, Hugh. *Works*, 2 vols., Cambridge: The Parker Society, 1844-45.

Lee, Sir Sidney. "Shakespeare and the Inquisition," *Elizabethan and Other Essays*, Oxford: The Clarendon Press, 1929, pp. 184-95.

Leech, Clifford. *Shakespeare's Tragedies and other Studies in Seventeenth-Century Drama*, London: Chatto and Windus, 1950.

Legrand, Jacques. *The Book of Good Manners*, London, 1507.

Levin, Harry. *The Question of Hamlet*, New York: The Viking Press, 1961.

Luther, Martin. *The Bondage of the Will*, ed. J. I. Packer and O. R. Johnston, London: James Clarke and Co., 1957.

Luther, Martin. *Commentary on Galatians*, trans. Erasmus Middleton, London: William Tegg and Co., 1850.

Luther, Martin. *Commentary on Genesis*, 2 vols., trans. J. T. Mueller, Grand Rapids: Zondervan, 1958.

Luther, Martin. *Lectures on Romans*, trans. Wilhelm Pauck, Philadelphia: The Westminster Press, 1961.

Luther, Martin. *The Letters of Martin Luther*, trans. Margaret A. Currie, London: Macmillan and Co., 1908.

Luther, Martin. *Letters of Spiritual Counsel*, trans. T. G. Tappert, Philadelphia: The Westminster Press, 1955.

Luther, Martin. *Luther on Education*, St. Louis: Concordia Publishing Co., n.d.

Luther, Martin. *Luther's Correspondence*, 2 vols., trans. and ed. Preserved Smith and Charles M. Jacobs, Philadelphia: United Lutheran Publishing House, 1918.

Luther, Martin. *Luther's Primary Works: The Greater Catechism*, ed. Henry Wace and C. A. Buchheim, London: Hodder and Stoughton, 1896.

Luther, Martin. *Luther's Works*, 21 vols. *et seq.*, American Edition, St. Louis: Concordia Publishing House; and Philadelphia: Muhlenberg Press, 1955-.

Luther, Martin. *The Precious and Sacred Writings of Martin Luther*, 31 vols., ed. John N. Lenker, Minneapolis: The Luther Press, 1903-1910.

Luther, Martin. *Reformation Writings of Martin Luther*, 2 vols., ed. Bertram Lee Woolf, London: Lutterworth Press, 1956.

Luther, Martin. *Sermons on the Passion of Christ*, trans. E. Smid and J. T. Isensee, Rock Island, Illinois: Augustana Press, 1956.

Luther, Martin. *Table Talk*, trans. William Hazlitt, London: George Bell and Sons, 1902.

Luther, Martin. *Werke*, 57+ vols., Weimar: H. Böhlau, 1883-.

Luther, Martin. *What Luther Says: An Anthology*, 3 vols., ed. Ewald M. Plass, St. Louis: Concordia Publishing House, 1959.

Luther, Martin. *Works*, 6 vols., Philadelphia: Muhlenberg Press, 1915-32.

Manschreck, Clyde L. *Melanchthon: The Quiet Reformer*, New York: Abingdon Press, 1958.

Maritain, Jacques. *Saint Thomas Aquinas*, New York: Meridian, 1958.

McNeill, John T. *The History and Character of Calvinism*, New York: Oxford University Press, 1954.

Milton, John. *Paradise Lost*, ed. Merritt Y. Hughes, New York: Odyssey Press, 1935.

Mueller, William A. *Church and State in Luther and Calvin*, Nashville: Broadman Press, 1954.

Mutschmann, H. and Wentersdorf, K. *Shakespeare and Catholicism*, New York: Sheed and Ward, 1952.

Myrick, K. O. "The Theme of Damnation in Shakespearean Tragedy," *Studies in Philology*, vol. 38, pp. 221-45.

Niesel, Wilhelm. *The Theology of Calvin*, Philadelphia: The Westminster Press, 1956.

Noble, Richmond. *Shakespeare's Biblical Knowledge and Use of the Book of Common Prayer*, London: SPCK, 1935.

Nowell, Alexander. *A Catechism*, Cambridge: The Parker Society, 1853.

Orwell, George. *Shooting an Elephant and other Essays*, New York: Harcourt, Brace and Co., 1950.

The Other Face: Catholic Life under Elizabeth I. Ed. Philip Caraman, London: Longmans, 1960.

Parker, M. D. H. *The Slave of Life: A Study of Shakespeare and the Idea of Justice*, London: Chatto and Windus, 1955.

Peter, Brother Baldwin. "*Hamlet* and *In Paradisum*," *Shakespeare Quarterly*, vol. 3, pp. 279-80.

Phillips, Edward. *New World of English Words*, London, 1658.

Powicke, Sir Maurice. *The Reformation in England*, London: Oxford University Press, 1961.

Quinlan, Maurice J. "Shakespeare and the Catholic Burial Services," *Shakespeare Quarterly*, vol. 5, pp. 303-06.

Quistorp, Heinrich. *Calvin's Doctrine of the Last Things*, Richmond: John Knox Press, 1955.

Ribner, Irving. *Patterns in Shakespearian Tragedy*, New York: Barnes and Noble Inc., 1960.

Rusk, Robert R. *The Doctrines of the Great Educators*, London: Macmillan and Co., 1918.

Santayana, George. *Essays in Literary Criticism*, ed. Irving Singer, New York: Charles Scribner's Sons, 1956.

Seibel, George. *The Religion of Shakespeare*, London: Watts and Co., 1924.

Shakespeare, William. *The Complete Works of Shakespeare*, ed. G. L. Kittredge, New York and Boston: Ginn and Company, 1936.

Shakespeare, William. *Mr. William Shakespeare's Comedies, Histories, & Tragedies*, London, 1632.

Shaw, G. B. *Selected Plays with Prefaces*, 4 vols., New York: Dodd, Mead and Co., 1948-1957.

Siegel, Paul N. *Shakespearean Tragedy and the Elizabethan Compromise*, New York: New York University Press, 1957.

Sisson, C. J. "The Mythical Sorrows of Shakespeare," *Proceedings of the British Academy*, vol. 20, pp. 3-28.

Smith, Henry. *A Preparative to Marriage*, London: T. Orwin for T. Man, 1591.

Spenser, Edmund. *The Works of Edmund Spenser: A Variorum Edition*, 11 vols., ed. Edwin Greenlaw et al., Baltimore: The Johns Hopkins Press, 1932-1957.

Spivack, Bernard. *Shakespeare and the Allegory of Evil*, New York: Columbia University Press, 1958.

Sprott, S. E. *The English Debate on Suicide from Donne to Hume*, La Salle, Indiana: Open Court Publishing Co., 1961.

Stevenson, Robert. *Shakespeare's Religious Frontier*, The Hague: Martinus Nijhoff, 1958.

Strode, George. *The Anatomy of Mortality*, London, 1632.

Thomas, Sir Henry. *Shakespeare in Spain*, London: Geoffrey Cumberlege, n.d.

Thomson, J. A. K. *Shakespeare and the Classics*, London: George Allen and Unwin, Ltd., 1952.

Thurston, Herbert. "The Religion of Shakespeare," *The Catholic Encyclopedia*, vol. 13, New York: Robert Appleton Co., 1912, pp. 748-50.

Torrance, Thomas F. *Calvin's Doctrine of Man*, Grand Rapids: Wm. B. Eerdmans Publishing Co., 1957.

Trinterud, Leonard. "A Reappraisal of William Tyndale's Debt to Martin Luther," *Church History*, vol. 31, pp. 24-45.

Tyndale, William. *Doctrinal Treatises*, Cambridge: The Parker Society, 1848.

Tyndale, William. *Expositions of Scripture*, Cambridge: The Parker Society, 1849.

Vaughan, William. *The Golden Grove*, London, 1600.

Vyvyan, John. *Shakespeare and the Rose of Love*, London: Chatto and Windus, 1960.

Vyvyan, John. *The Shakespearean Ethic*, London: Chatto and Windus, 1959.

Wallace, Ronald S. *Calvin's Doctrine of the Christian Life*, Grand Rapids: Wm. B. Eerdmans Publishing Co., 1959.

Watkin, E. I. *Roman Catholicism in England from the Reformation to 1950*, London: Oxford University Press, 1957.

Weil, Simone. *Intimations of Christianity among the Ancient Greeks*, London: Routledge and Kegan Paul, 1957.

Whitaker, Virgil K. *Shakespeare's Use of Learning*, San Marino, California: The Huntington Library, 1953.

Whitaker, William. *A Disputation on Holy Scripture*, Cambridge: The Parker Society, 1849.

Willet, Andrew. *Harmony Upon I Samuel*, Cambridge, 1614.

Willet, Andrew. *Harmony Upon II Samuel*, Cambridge, 1614.

Wing, John. *The Crown Conjugal*, Middelburgh, 1620.

Woodward, William H. *Studies in Education during the Age of the Renaissance: 1400-1600*, Cambridge: Cambridge University Press, 1906.

Zwingli, Ulrich. *Zwingli and Bullinger*, trans. G. W. Bromiley, Philadelphia: The Westminster Press, 1953.

INDEX TO SHAKESPEAREAN REFERENCES

Note: For references to individual characters, see Index to Names and Subjects.

INDEX TO NAMES AND SUBJECTS

Note: Luther, Calvin, and Hooker are not given index headings because they are cited on the average of several times to the page, and a proper indexing for them would be disproportionately long. Their comments may be found most conveniently by looking under the relevant subject headings in this index.